Michel Tournier and
the Metaphor of Fiction

Michel Tournier and the Metaphor of Fiction

DAVID PLATTEN

University of Leeds

LIVERPOOL UNIVERSITY PRESS

First published 1999 by
LIVERPOOL UNIVERSITY PRESS
Liverpool L69 3BX

© 1999 David Platten

The right of David Platten
to be identified as the author of this work
has been asserted by him in accordance with
the Copyright, Design and Patents Act, 1988

British Library Cataloguing-in-Publication Data
A British Library CIP record is available

ISBN 0–85323–843–X (hardback)
0–85323–853–7 (paperback)

Typeset in 11/13 pt Sabon
by Wilmaset Ltd, Birkenhead, Wirral
Printed by Bell and Bain Ltd, Glasgow

Contents

Acknowledgements

I would like to thank my many colleagues and friends in the profession who, through their helpful comments, suggestions, and general encouragement helped in the preparation of this book. Material from Chapters 3 and 5 appeared in an earlier form as articles in the *Journal of European Studies*, *Romanic Review* and *The French Review*. My thanks go to the editors of these journals. Special recognition is extended to Rufus Wood who inspired my early thinking about metaphor, to my series editor Ed Smyth for his unstinting support during the long gestation period, to Terry Bradford for his detective work, to Andrew Rothwell for hours of stimulating conversation and technical assistance, to David Roe who ensured that no new information on Tournier ever passed me by, and finally to Tracy Platten who was there at the start, is still here at the end, and to whom this book is dedicated.

List of Abbreviations

The abbreviations below denote the following Tournier texts. References are made to the Gallimard Folio edition unless stated otherwise.

Vendredi ou Les limbes du Pacifique: V
Le Roi des aulnes: RA
Les Météores: M
Gaspard, Melchior et Balthazar: GMB
Gilles et Jeanne: GJ
La Goutte d'or: GD
Le Coq de bruyère: CB
Le Médianoche amoureux: MA
Éléazar ou La source et le buisson (Gallimard): E
Le Vent Paraclet (Gallimard): VP
Le Vol du vampire (Mercure de France): VV
Petites Proses (Folio): PP
Le Miroir des idées (Mercure de France): MI

Preface

A guided tour of Michel Tournier's home reaffirms the impression created by the public image of a writer who is often presented as a throwback to the great age of the author-journalist, the modern-day Balzac, Dickens, or even Zola. He lives in an old village presbytery, south of Paris, which has been converted into a functional dwelling. Inside, the décor is not ostentatiously old-fashioned, and there is a large television set in the living room. The staircase positioned in the centre of the house leads to the room at the top. Sheaves of paper, thick like parchment, and a bulbous-shafted antique fountain pen crowd the surface of the single desk, prominently placed half way along the wall opposite the doorway. The room should be expansive; square-shaped, it covers the full surface area of the house. However, the desk and its accoutrements, the writing lamp and the chair, are cocooned in the uniform, dark pine of the floor, walls and ceiling. There is no word processor or computer screen anywhere to be seen. As the humble guest ventures the words, 'Ça fait un peu le genre Proust', the writer, with a characteristically dramatic gesture, and impeccable timing, flings open the shutters by the desk, and the green sweep of the Vallée de Chevreuse, with its pockets of trees and narrow lanes weaving in and out of the meadows like dollar signs, floods the field of vision.

Tournier has operated what Marcus Hester, writing on the nature of metaphorical insight, terms the 'gestalt switch',[1] a device that transforms the world in which the protagonist exists in the absence of any permanent alteration of its sensible features. In this case it is a trick of the light caused by the sudden opening of the shutters. Its effect is one of spectacular *agrandissement*, but it is not a simple *trompe-l'oeil*, for the eye has already been deceived as to the proportions of the writer's den. Over the years Tournier has brought his readers to a multitude of transitional viewpoints such as this. His work has been understood by some as a vehicle for different ideas about society based on the durability of mythical archetypes, deconstructed by others into a myriad of quotations from other texts near and far-gone. The literary deconstructor, in his ceaseless unscrambling, goes backwards to a time before the text has been put together, whereas the literary sociologist picks and chooses some time after, and from a well-established corpus of references. All literary commentators are a blend of these two figures. However, Tournier aims to activate what may be nefariously described as the pleasure of reading; thus he is guided by the illusory ideal of an eternal 'reading' present. His narrative inscribes the flight of the vampire,[2] homing in unerringly on its target, which is the experience of the reader.[3] He sees the relationship with his readers as a form of sacred communion and worries about the baleful influence of profaners (who are likely to be journalists). He wishes for a genuinely reciprocal arrangement. Once someone has accepted Tournier into his or her world, then elements of this reader's world should flow back and somehow infiltrate Tournier's. This has less to do with interpretation and the open text; it is more about the way and context in which literature is read. It talks of the impact of prose narrative, of initial reactions that are often submerged in the ebb and flow of considered critical debate.

Reality, in Tournier's eyes, is an objective, material entity rather than the interaction of conflictual discourses. This metaphysical gamble is most clearly seen in his attitude to language, which recalls Tom Stoppard's metaphor of the cricket bat.[4] Language is an instrument that can be used by the writer to express a diversity of ideas and perceptions, just as the bat is employed by the batsman in a variety of different strokes. Thus, in Tournier's writing there is no sense of a genuinely postmodern insecurity about language and how it signifies meaning. On the contrary, he glories in the range of communicative possibilities afforded by the French language, which he sees as infinitely richer than the televisual or the cinematic image. For example, the pun is eulogised because it brings to the fore two different meanings at the same time and not because it casts doubt on one or both of the meanings expressed or on the integrity of language as a vehicle of communication.[5] The pun is thus seen as a figure which amplifies knowledge rather than fractures meaning. This distinction is an important one, for throughout his work Tournier has constantly endeavoured to overcome negative dialectics which are seen as threats to positive unifying forces.

It has been and still is unfashionable to use words such as 'reality' and 'the real' in a positive sense. However, George Steiner is the most notable of a number of cultural critics formerly associated with the structuralist movement of the 1950s and 1960s who now argue that we must retain the capacity to read as if the text before us 'incarnates a real presence of significant being'.[6] Steiner is worried about the pressures exerted by modish, though philosophically irrefutable, critical practice over our appreciation of great Art. Irritated by the 'autistic echo chambers of deconstruction',[7] he evokes the silent joy of the Talmudic scholar who participates in a 'ceremony of intellect'. The rhetoric is no accident, for his argument culminates in an appeal to Art as a form of communion between the artist and his solitary interlocutor which lies beyond language:

> To be 'indwelt' by music, art, literature, to be made responsible, answerable to such habitation as a host is to a guest ... is to experience the commonplace mystery of a real presence. Not many of us feel compelled to, have the expressive means to, register the mastering quality of this experience—as does Proust when he crystallises the sense of the world and of the word in the little yellow spot which is the real presence of a riverside door in Vermeer's *View of Delft*, or as does Thomas Mann when he enacts in word and metaphor the coming over us, the 'overcoming of us', in Beethoven's Opus 111. No matter. The experience itself is one we are thoroughly *at home* with—an informing idiom—each and every time we live a text, a sonata, a painting.[8]

The notion of a textual reality and the implied existence of a dialogue between author and reader are, though the latter may be more of a Platonic Ideal than a reality, crucial to Tournier's enterprise. Each of his titles designates a scenario, and each scenario solicits a metaphorical statement whereby Tournier articulates a vision of the world which is not literally real, but, to the extent that he consciously engages with what he anticipates to be the deep-seated desires and fears of his readership, may well be metaphorically true. As the series of haunting photographs he assembled for an exhibition of photography at the Musée d'Art Moderne de la Ville de Paris testify,[9] he is interested in the way that artists invest what is already there with something more. Tournier likes to put on a show. Confronted with a bullish reader, he feints like a matador; however, if we are prepared to take him more often at his word, he will lead us to the literary equivalent of the alchemist's laboratory.

CHAPTER ONE

Perspectives on Metaphor and Literary Fiction

Metaphor used to belong to poetry. As a trope or figure, its scope in prose narrative is traditionally limited to an aspect of style. In a recent empirical study Gerard Steen sets out to prove that this commonly-held perception is misguided. In one of the tests devised by Steen a team of language experts were presented with a 25-line extract from Norman Mailer's *Miami and the Siege of Chicago* and asked to identify and isolate examples of metaphor. They agreed on nineteen cases.[1] That there should be such a concentration of metaphors in any small text, let alone one written by a well-known literary star, should no longer be regarded as exceptional, for an increasing number of language specialists are moving towards the view articulated by the two scholars cited in the introduction to Steen's study who speak of metaphor as being situated in the 'deepest and most general processes of human interaction with reality'.[2] Current research driven by the work of Ortony, Lakoff and Johnson, and Dirven and Paprotté aims to investigate what the metaphorical basis of language reveals about the cognitive capacities of the human mind. However, just as interest in the workings of metaphor has extended far beyond the domain of literature, so the literary text has lost its privileged status as the site of metaphorical meaning. Literature is not an habitual mode of expression, therefore literary language is less interesting to researchers absorbed by the question of how we organise the reality around us than recorded speech, or even standard journalists' reports. Thus, in metaphor studies literature has been sidelined. This general obliviousness may explain in part why comparatively few literary commentators have tapped into the rich fund of material resulting from the explosion in 'metaphorology' of the last twenty or so years.[3]

Living at the end of the twentieth century, we are accustomed to contrast literary fiction as genre with documentary fact. This is a relatively recent development predicated on an assumption which is not always reliable. Stein Haugom Olsen cites writers as disparate in style,

1

content and epoch as Richardson, Henry James and Malcolm Brad-
bury, all of whom refute the idea that literature, and in particular the
novel, should be read as fiction.[4] Witness Henry James, insisting in *The
Art of Fiction* that 'the novel is history'. He lambasts Trollope for
conceding to the reader that he and 'this trusting friend' are only
'making believe'. This seems to James a 'terrible crime',[5] and yet the
distinction between history, journalism and biography on the one hand,
and fiction on the other is a basic ingredient in the conceptual diet of
literary critics and reviewers alike. How do we read the work of writers
who are either oblivious to this tension, or happy to absorb it? In many
literatures, the modern American novel for example, the application of
the fact/ fiction dialectic yields precious little insight; writers such as
Saul Bellow, Truman Capote, Don Delillo, John Updike even, seem
unconcerned as to the fictive character of their fiction, to the extent that
those who can tolerate horrendous neologisms have begun to talk of a
new genre called 'literary faction'. However, the conspicuous strain of
self-consciousness in modern European literature, where the reader is
frequently made aware of the fictional identity of the work and of the
distinction between narrator and author, has coincided with a theoretical appropriation of metaphor. In competition with a host of other
interesting concepts and approaches, metaphor seems to have lost the
privileges it once enjoyed when it was venerated by the Romantics, and
upheld subsequently in the thinking of Proust and Valéry. Modern
literary theory has circumscribed metaphor by taking it out of the
speculative domain of thought and identifying it as a figure of speech
associated with a fundamental tenet in modern linguistics. The principle at issue, which has its source in Saussure's exposition of language
as a synchronic phenomenon, states that language is generated from
our ability as human beings to discriminate between various paradigms. This skill derives from a perceptual faculty by which we
differentiate between things or phenomena on the grounds of similarity
and contrast. In the discourse of literary theorists, 'metaphor' is
sometimes used to qualify this process of paradigmatic selection. The
figure of metonymy is correspondingly elevated, to illustrate what
Saussure termed the 'rapports syntagmatiques' of our language.[6]
Metaphor and metonymy are henceforth apposite figures, presiding
over the dual process of selection and combination in which language is
produced. Much of the theory involved in modern poetics resides in this
distinction, between the syntagm and the paradigm, and the alternating
modes, defined as metonymy and metaphor, in which they are 'figured'.

In preparing the ground for a discussion of Tournier's fiction from a metaphorical perspective, my intention has been to create a narrative which is applicable to Tournier's fictional project and may also make a modest contribution to current thinking about the role and value of literature in today's society. In this perspective the restrictions imposed on metaphor by the poststructuralist view of the figure as limited to an analysable feature of language need to be lifted, for my argument is rooted in the presupposition that the study of metaphor helps considerably in the evolution of a theory of the imagination. Once the theory is in place, new avenues are opened on a number of questions which have been highlighted and debated in discussions of Tournier's work, notably the respective roles of author and reader in the literary construction of meaning, the value of thematic studies in a postmodern era, and the possibility that, at this self-same moment when cultural values are seen as relative, aesthetic judgements may still be validated. An introduction to the history of metaphor will be followed by three case studies, the function of which is to ground more securely my readings of Tournier's fiction. These are Paul Ricoeur's theory of metaphor as imagination, developed by Ricoeur as a form of readerly response to the 'phenomenon' of narrative fiction; Jean Ricardou's less systematic, though recurrently illuminating writing on the all-pervasiveness of metaphor in both literary and non-literary discourse; and finally George Lakoff and Mark Johnson's universalist theory of metaphor as the primary organiser, the one and only conceptual agent at work as the human being constantly situates and resituates itself in relation to the world around it.

Lakoff and Johnson advocate the abolition of boundaries between discourses seen in terms of the literal and the metaphorical. This radical departure from the empiricist norm adumbrates much of the discussion on the value of literary fiction to society at large, for if metaphor is seen as not only blurring but conspiring actively to break down literary distinctions between reality, truth and fiction, it will be doing so in the interests of clearing the paths of communication between the novelist and his readership, paths which have become, in the postmodern age, rather overgrown. The discussion is balanced on a knife-edge, between the aesthetic and the sociological dimensions of the literary process. A literature which constantly reaffirms its status as fiction will distance itself from the 'real world' influences which shape the responses of its readers. If literature has become too self-conscious, too abstract, too far removed from the perceptions of its audience, it is axiomatic that literary aesthetics will have followed suit. If we have reached a point where the novel is too often a foil for the illustration of a theoretical concept, there may be a heavy price to pay. In its drift from the democratic to the esoteric, what value does the novel as an art form have to society as a whole?

Tournier has always sought to reach a wide audience. At a time during the late 1960s and early 1970s when advocates and exponents of experimental art and literature were in the ascendancy in France, he was writing novels that flesh out the clear, uncompromising objective to be announced later in *Le Vent Paraclet*, the first and by far the largest of his many autobiographically-tinged essays: 'Mon propos n'est pas d'innover dans la forme, mais de faire passer au contraire dans une forme aussi traditionnelle, préservée et rassurante que possible une matière ne possédant aucune de ces qualités' (VP, 190). For Tournier, provocation presupposes intelligibility. He is a messenger. He is also, first and foremost, a philosopher: 'Mon seul problème littéraire est donc d'ordre pédagogique: comment rendre claires et agréables ces choses subtiles et difficiles que j'ai à dire'.[7] The well-documented switch, prompted by his failing the *agrégation* in 1949, from a career teaching philosophy to an eventual niche in the literary world failed to dampen Tournier's early passion for philosophy. On the contrary he was to see the potential for a far wider dissemination of philosophical ideas and arguments in the form of fictional narratives than could be achieved, even in France, through the more conventional channels of philosophical discourse. This self-image, reflecting hues of Rabelais, La Fontaine, Voltaire and Diderot, is perhaps one reason why Tournier is still described as the most traditional of contemporary French novelists. And in many ways he is. He is also a radical for all times. Few if any writers over the ages have pursued a policy of cultural democratisation through their art as far as Tournier, who has consistently claimed that his novels and short stories should be read as productively by children as by adults. To this end, *Vendredi ou La vie sauvage* was published in 1971 as a 'corrective' to his first novel, *Vendredi ou Les limbes du Pacifique*, and in 1983 *Les Rois Mages*—a rewriting of his fourth, *Gaspard, Melchior, et Balthazar*—appeared. Both these rewritten texts are characterised by the suppression or alteration of key episodes in the original novels, a more direct form of narration, and a simplified rhetorical structure. However, in spite of these 'improvements', the original novels were not withdrawn from circulation. Having analysed the specific character of the self-censorship in *Vendredi ou La vie sauvage*, Gérard Genette concludes that through his rewriting enterprise Tournier has abdicated artistic integrity in favour of personal profit: 'Je suis seul devant ce texte, et pourtant je me sens deux: l'enfant qu'il vise et l'adulte qu'il atteint. D'où j'infère qu'il louche.'[8] *Vendredi ou La vie sauvage* is Tournier's best-selling book. Recently it has topped the three million mark for sales in France alone.

The idea of a child-friendly literary style goes to the heart of Tournier's fictional project. Baffled academics point to the thesaurus of cultural references embedded in his *oeuvre*, a cleverly constructed intertext existing on a scale unmatched in the fiction of any other modern writer which is designed to activate a knowledge and experience that a child reader could scarcely be expected to possess. Until recently little attention has been paid to some of the author's declarations in this respect: that he would have sacrificed his life's work in order to have created Hans Christian Andersen's *The Snow Queen* (VP, 48); that the simple, 'childish' *contes*, 'Amandine ou Les deux jardins' and 'Pierrot ou Les secrets de la nuit', constitute the summit of his literary achievement;[9] that his fifth novel, *La Goutte d'or*, was (with the exception of one or two abstract pages on the art of calligraphy) explicitly written so as to be read as profitably by children of ten as by adults.[10] Tournier aficionados may have recognised in these proclamations his weakness for hyperbole and taste for the melodramatic and chosen quietly to ignore them. However, in the course of a *table ronde* discussion published as part of the proceedings of the 1990 conference on Tournier held at Cérisy-la-Salle, the author took the opportunity to provide a trenchant restatement of his position. Asked about his wish to rewrite his second novel, *Le Roi des aulnes*, so as to make it a more appropriate read for children, he replied in the following terms:

> Ce que je voudrais faire, c'est réécrire *Le Roi des aulnes* dépouillé de tout un fatras qui l'encombre ... tout ce qui n'est pas essentiel à l'action. J'aimerais fournir du roman une épure qui pourrait être illustrée et que les enfants pourraient lire, ce qui ne signifie pas que cette version aurait été écrite pour eux. Ce serait une version améliorée, et tellement améliorée que les enfants y trouveraient leur pâture alors que, dans l'état actuel des choses, je ne pense pas qu'on puisse le lire avant quinze ans.[11]

As his literary career has flourished, Tournier has retained a visible profile in the world of education. He regularly visits French schools, particularly the *collèges* (intermediary or high schools), where he reads his stories before classes of attentive listeners. It would appear that he sees in these children troops of mini Socrates, a most rigorous audience because the need to question and the will to discover are at that time of life, prior to the onset of puberty, at their most acute. 'Angus', one of the short stories in *Le Médianoche amoureux*, is, so Tournier reveals in a postface, a narrative that takes as its starting-point unanswered questions arising from the plot of Victor Hugo's *L'Aigle du casque*, questions which should puzzle any reader who approaches the Hugo text with a child-like inquisitiveness (MA, 256–57).

It is tempting to read Tournier's child-centred narrative policy as a logical refinement of the reasoning behind his original choice to deal in myths. Myths are sacred, eternal stories, often exchanged in non-western societies as part of initiation rites. In the context of western civilisation Tournier revealingly talks of myth as the 'enfance de la littérature'.[12] In *Le Vent Paraclet* he explains their attraction with reference to Plato's 'Allegory of the Cave', which can be read simply as a children's story, 'la description d'un guignol qui serait aussi théâtre d'ombres chinoises' (VP, 188) but can also be elevated to a theory of knowledge, and higher still, to the status of an ethical, ontological treatise, without the original story having changed. Tournier has become ever more adroit in the way that he addresses two audiences 'in one go': the sophisticated adult cognoscenti, and younger minds unencumbered with the chores of the everyday and uncluttered by the cultural junk of intellectuals. Still, the difficulties encountered by Tournier readers, especially problems raised by the rewriting enterprise, are not easily whisked away. In his excellent book Martin Roberts advises a benignly cautious approach to the issue. Roberts accepts that Tournier is constantly rewriting his own and others' material to the extent that artistic creation for this writer is not strictly about inventing plots, characters and scenarios; rather it defines a process of re-invention. Like the thieving magpie he professes to be,[13] Tournier picks up on stories, ideas, themes, and conceits that have been used elsewhere and recycles them in different combinations. Thus, Roberts argues, he is a literary 'bricoleur'. Moreover, as his career has gone on, Tournier's 'bricolage' has been leavened with a fair dose of 'autobricolage'. This latter tendency denotes neither vanity nor paranoia, instead a recognition on the part of the author that he is imbricated in a concomitant process of change and repetition. Tournier's instincts as a *bricoleur* are thus revealed towards the end of Roberts' study as an artistic fascination with the relationship between the model and the copy, and, more precisely, with the potential activated by the copy to change the way in which the model is perceived.[14] In the specific context of the child-oriented rewritings however, the author does what he conspicuously avoids doing in his own literary discourse, which is to supply a clear value judgement in favour of the copy. As Roberts says, it would be nice to be able to judge *Les Rois Mages* as a text 'in its own right', but, given that it has mutated from an earlier, still widely available text, this is precisely 'what we cannot do'.[15] With the publication of works such as *Vendredi ou La vie sauvage* and *Les Rois Mages*, the keen Tournier reader is presented with the literary equivalent of a cleft stick. Tainted forever by his knowledge of the father-text, it is impossible for him to approach the new version with an open mind. The world of Tournier's fiction is quite literally left to the young.

Although initially it skirts the periphery of my argument, the debate about Tournier's children narratives will eventually find its way to the core. As Michael Worton pointed out in the discussion at Cérisy, the child is in itself an unassailable concept—where does childhood end and adulthood begin? However, Tournier's express desire to jettison the 'fatras' raises the less child-specific idea of the search for a more effective form of literary communication. And it is in the conjunction between the writer's world-view and the world-view of his projected reader—and that projection embraces both the sophisticated adult and the child of reasonable reading age—that metaphor plays a vital role.

METAPHOR: TRADITIONS AND MOVEMENTS

Professional metaphor-spotters, the sort of specialist literary critic or psycholinguist who would have participated in Steen's research, may not all have realised quite how far this standard trope has travelled. Metaphor is a key concept in such far-flung scholarly territories as theoretical physics, theology, psychoanalysis and the cognitive sciences, its interdisciplinarity an immediate clue to what a small amount of preliminary research on the subject should reveal: that scholars have very different ideas about what exactly metaphor is. Even within its traditional stamping-grounds of philosophy, linguistics and literary study, metaphor divides opinions sharply. In broad terms our understanding has evolved via two epistemological traditions: the Continental or European tradition, and the Anglo-Saxon/American tradition.

The European tradition reactivates Aristotle's original identification of the concept in the modern context of linguistics and literary theory. Aristotle describes metaphor as 'consisting in giving the thing a name that belongs to something else; the transference being either from genus to species, or from species to genus, or from species to species, or on grounds of analogy' (*Poetics*, 1457b).[16] This would indicate that he understood it primarily as a linguistic operation, a nominalist transgression involving the substitution of what is normally held to be a literal referent with a 'figurative' replacement. The linkage of Aristotle with Saussurian linguistics is not immediately evident, not least because according to Saussure there could be no such thing as a 'figurative replacement'. Fundamental to Saussure's most influential teachings—those sections of the *Cours* which promote an exclusively synchronic linguistics—is his assertion that the linguistic unit contains no semantic value in itself. It may gain semantic value, but only when it becomes a sign, when it is included in the physical manifestation of *langue* as *parole*, in the form of speech or writing. Thus the effect of Saussure has been to distil Aristotle's original definition of metaphor, which is now frequently understood as the transposition of names, or as Lacan surmises with minimalist clarity, 'un mot pour un autre'.[17]

The connection between metaphor and language is explicitly made by the Formalist critic and linguist, Roman Jakobson, who argues that metaphor and metonymy are two fundamental principles guiding the formation of all discourse. Jakobson's thinking on metaphor evolved through a series of papers on the topic of aphasia, or speech malfunction, that derive in part from psycho-linguistic experiments.[18] He conceives of metaphor as one element of a dialectic, of which the other is metonymy. Together they form a polar coupling that governs certain patterns of speech. In these classical figures he observes 'the most condensed expression of the two basic modes of relation: the internal relation of similarity (and contrast) underlies the metaphor; the external relation of contiguity (and remoteness) determines the metonymy'.[19] Jakobson argues, from the evidence of some bread-and-butter tests on the language acquisition of children, that two distinct kinds of aphasia correspond to these metaphorical and metonymic relations. In the one kind a speaker finds it difficult to substitute for a given word others which have similar or contrasted meanings (e.g. 'bubbly' for 'champagne'). He insists instead on substituting words connected through 'contiguity' relations (e.g. 'bottle' or 'hangover'). Hence, says Jakobson, only 'metonymy is used and grasped by him'. With the other kind of aphasia the speaker's difficulty is the reverse: she or he can only substitute words related by similarity or contrast of meaning. Their respective inabilities to produce the figures of either metaphor or metonymy identify these two aspects of aphasia.

In a second, widely acclaimed paper, Jakobson develops his argument, blending his notion of metaphorical and metonymic speech deficiencies into the mainstream of Saussurean linguistics. To reiterate, one of Saussure's most durable claims is that the transition from *langue* to *parole* effected by the utterance of a sentence requires two axes, or modes of arrangement of linguistic items. There must be a *paradigmatic* axis of related words from which the speaker selects for insertion into the sentence. And he must be able to string the words available for selection along a linear or *syntagmatic* axis. Jakobson reasons that the two kinds of aphasic are distinguished by their inability to perform adequately in either one of these two 'modes of arrangement'. Those with a problem of 'paradigmatic selection' are held to be deficient in metaphoric substitution based on similarity or contrast of meaning. Those who have a problem combining terms along the syntagmatic axis are held to be deficient in metonymic association. Profiting from his work on speech disorders, Jakobson then applies the same principles (of similarity and contiguity) to speech construction. He writes:

> The development of a discourse may take place along two different semantic lines: one topic may lead to another either through their similarity or through their contiguity. The metaphoric way would be the most appropriate term for the first case and the metonymic way for the second, since they find their most condensed expression in metaphor and metonymy respectively.[20]

In support of this argument Jakobson describes the most rudimentary of practical situations, in which one person talking about a hut may proceed to talk metaphorically about dens or cottages, while another may go on to talk metonymically about thatching, poverty, or wild animals. Although his ideas were challenged by Stephen Ullmann,[21] and later more robustly by the philosopher David Cooper—who has shown that the dual category system of metaphor and metonymy is far from stable[22]—Jakobson's unequivocal statement on the active roles of metaphor and metonymy in the production of discourse has founded the majority of semantic interpretations of Saussure since the publication of his papers.

The most seductive theory of metaphor as a purely linguistic phenomenon is provided by the famous psychoanalyst, Jacques Lacan. My earlier elision of Lacan's deceptively simple 'one name for another' formula with Aristotle's original definition of metaphor is peremptory;

the fuller version of Lacan's definition integrates Jakobson's meta-phor—metonymy polarity into a psychoanalyical context, entailing some interesting modifications:

> L'étincelle créatrice de la métaphore ne jaillit pas de la mise en présence de deux images, c'est-à-dire de deux signifiants également actualisés. Elle jaillit entre deux signifiants dont l'un s'est substitué à l'autre en prenant sa place dans la chaîne signifiante, le signifiant occulté restant présent de sa connexion (métonymique) au reste de la chaîne.[23]

In this essay Lacan advocates the classification of the mechanisms of the unconscious as 'figures of style', and as tropes. Many people find his lexicon abstruse, and suspiciously mystifying. This is because he attempts to show what others pass over, namely the means by which purely symbolic phenomena—those that dominate dreams or neuroses—come into relation with language. Preempting Kristeva,[24] he identifies Freud's key concepts of *condensation* and *displacement* with the figures of metaphor and metonymy respectively. In both *The Interpretation of Dreams*, and its abridged version 'On Dreams', Freud attempts to describe the specific nature of dream images.[25] He remarks that dreams consist of several strong, spotlighted (and therefore remembered) images, which tend to recur in the subject's other dreams, and occasionally in the dreams of other people. These images appear to have symbolic meaning. Freud termed the coming-together of these symbolic images in the unconscious mind of the sleeping subject *condensation*; the need for interpretation springs from the fact that these symbols have been *displaced* from the context in which they normally feature, which is the conscious mind of the subject. *Condensation* and *displacement* govern one synchronous process, which allows us to dream. Once the essence of Freud's interpretation of dreams is abstracted, we can see how neatly it fits Lacan's linguistic model. In Lacan's definition, metaphor governs the instance when one signifier is substituted for another. This is a conscious deformation of the metonymic chain of signification, recognisable as such because, for an utterance to be understood as metaphorical, the proper mode of discourse (which Lacan claims is fundamentally metonymic) must remain perceptible. Metaphor is therefore the presence in discourse of the normally absent work of selection, the unusual showing or mani-festation in the living language of the paradigmatic function, the workings of which are accentuated in the sub-conscious phenomenon of dream language.

Although Lacan's schema is persuasive, there are good reasons that militate against the useful appropriation of a Lacanian concept of metaphor by the reader of literary narratives. David Macey has emphasised the inconsistencies that become evident when Lacan's formula is read alongside his other 'tropological' utterances. Macey points out that, four years earlier, in 'Fonction et champ de la parole et du langage en psychanalyse', metonymy is classified with metaphor under the heading, 'semantic condensations'.[26] He goes on to expose other discrepancies, on the evidence of which, he argues, the metaphor—condensation and metonymy—displacement equation, generally considered an integral part of Lacanian linguistics, rests upon unstable foundations. Moreover, notwithstanding the far-reaching connotations integral to Lacan's conception of metaphor as the figure of Freudian repression, Macey is sufficiently worried about its denotative aspect. Taking Lacan's habitual example, Victor Hugo's line— *sa gerbe n'était point avare, ni haineuse*—he effectively deconstructs it, in order to demonstrate how Lacanian metaphor works, 'thanks to the suppression of its context and to a very cavalier use of elements of poetics'.[27] Macey's counter-analysis of Hugo's metaphor, which draws on a context derived from both the text in which it features, the poem *Booz endormi*, and the history of that text in terms of its reception and of its place in the Hugo *oeuvre*, and thus ventures outside the world of psychoanalysis, illuminates the conundrum in which the supporter of a Lacanian reading of metaphor will find himself. Although Lacan has brought the activity of rhetoric to the forefront of the system, his figures are destined always to reveal a law of psychoanalysis—the dominant or master trope, the figure of the Father, or in Lacan's case, the 'nom du Père'. The reader will, therefore, always be constrained by this specific set of symbols. Reading Lacan demands that one accepts the truth of psychoanalysis, which is in itself a form of blind assent.

Other structuralist and post-structuralist thinkers such as Tzvetan Todorov and Paul Ricoeur, and latter-day rhetoricians such as Brian Vickers and Chaim Perelman take a different approach to the topic of metaphor. They too claim Aristotle for their own by situating metaphor as part of a general rhetorical praxis. Todorov argues that Aristotle's definition of rhetoric as the 'faculty of observing in any given case the available means of persuasion' (*Rhetoric*, 1355b) has been adopted with a degree of complacency. According to Todorov, Aristotle meant by this much more than the idea that rhetoric targets eloquence or good style; he was referring to the composition of effective speech that makes it possible to act on others. Thus, the rhetoric of the Ancients saw language at its most dynamic:

> La rhétorique ne saisit pas le langage comme forme—elle ne se préoccupe pas de l'énoncé en tant que tel—mais le langage comme action; la forme linguistique devient l'ingrédient d'un acte global de communication (dont la persuasion est l'espèce la plus caractéristique). C'est sur les fonctions de la parole, non sur sa structure, que s'interroge la rhétorique. L'élément constant est l'objectif à atteindre: persuader (ou, comme on dira plus tard, instruire, toucher et plaire); les moyens linguistiques sont pris en considération dans la mesure où ils peuvent servir à atteindre cet objectif.[28]

In classical terms, therefore, rhetoric covers the various forms of functional speech at work in a predominantly oral culture. As Todorov reads Tacitus, rhetoric is situated at the very heart of things, in the formation and practice of government. It is the dynamic principle informing what we now understand as democracy.[29]

Ricoeur attempts to deduce the rationale behind Aristotle's persistent definition of rhetoric in terms of the art of persuasion. Given that rhetoric controls the speaker's means of persuasion, then the language of rhetoric must be its praxis, the public manifestation of the word, a forum engendering the specific use of a language which is, however, removed from the stipulated exactitude of the philosopher's text. Aristotle's genius (to Ricoeur's way of thinking) was to insist that rhetorical praxis be contingent on the philosophical notion of *vraisemblance*, in that the public speaker, seeking to convince his audience of the truth of what he is saying, must appear authentic. Similarly, in the *Poetics* literary language is defined in accordance with its mimetic function, 'sa visée est de composer une représentation essentielle des actions humaines; son mode propre est de dire la vérité par le moyen de la fiction, de la fable, du mythos tragique'.[30] Ricoeur proposes a discursive triad, *rhétorique—preuve—persuasion*, which is clearly distinct from the *poesis—mimesis—catharsis* series exclusive to the functioning of literary language. However, situated at the face of this difference is the unique structure of metaphor, which, unlike other classified tropes and figures, entertains the possibility of the transference of the meaning of words. Hence, Ricoeur argues, metaphor facilitates the interaction of different spheres of discourse. It is unique precisely because it has a dual function, being both rhetorical and poetic. Metaphor essentially conveys *vraisemblance*, whether through oral or literary discourse.

Ricoeur and Todorov emphasise the illocutionary force of the metaphorical act. They stress the importance of persuading an audience to think that the metaphorical substitute for the literal referent of Aristotle's equation is plausible, that it should be taken as some kind of truth or spur to action. They espouse a revival of the rhetorician's art, as a means of restoring a lost vitality to contemporary discourse. This need for an energising rhetoric of persuasion conjures up the anachronistic figure of the orator. It demands the virtuosity of an oral culture, a facility for oral discourse which may seem inappropriate in an intellectual climate dominated by the written word and a general culture seemingly in thrall to the image, or computer graphic. However, scholars like Perelman are unambiguous in their call for a return to the study of rhetoric as a necessary, applicable discipline:

> ... toute argumentation se développe en fonction d'un auditoire et ... le 'vraisemblable' dont il est question dans les raisonnements dialectiques doit être conçu comme l'acceptable, le raisonnable qui ne peut être défini à l'aide de critères impersonnels, indépendants des esprits qui le jugent (...) Les figures de rhétorique ne doivent plus être étudiées isolément, en dehors de leur contexte, en n'examinant que leur structure, mais doivent être envisagées en fonction de leur action sur l'auditoire.[31]

Although both camps—formalists and rhetoricians—tend to pull in different directions, they are united to the extent that they see metaphor principally as a feature of language. They have developed theories which are anchored, initially, by readings of Aristotle and then filtered through or modified by the injunctions of Saussure. Now Saussure's ideas were revolutionary, in that he dispelled the concretist perception of language as nomenclature, as a set of name-tags given to each and every pre-existing object in the natural world. Instead Saussure asks us to think not in terms of what appears to be there, but in terms of how we recognise what is there, and then of how we process this information. Consider this passage from the *Cours*:

> Le signe linguistique unit non une chose et un nom, mais un concept et une image acoustique. Cette dernière n'est pas le son matériel, chose purement physique, mais l'empreinte psychique de ce son, la représentation que nous en donne le témoignage de nos sens.[32]

The emphasis on mental images, on the imaging structure of language, is both attractive and amenable to a theory of metaphor. However, Saussure's conceptual apparatus of *langue* and *parole* appears to limit its usefulness. The process of selection and combination by which *langue* is manifested in *parole* implies that *la langue* can only be conceived as a repository of the individual's pre-existing linguistic knowledge. It is a concept which takes no account of the dynamic principles of language bequeathed by classical rhetoric, nor does it allow for any notion of semantic innovation.[33]

In pragmatic terms the view of metaphor as nominal substition is even more limited. Consider the following examples given by David Cooper. The substitution view *tout court* takes no account of even the simplest of 'active' metaphors, such as 'The ship ploughed the sea', in which metaphorical intent centres on the verb rather than on the noun. The identification of metaphor may also hinge on another grammatical constituent of the phrase, on an adverb or even on a preposition, as in the case of the ludicrous 1960s expression: 'She's into LSD'. As Cooper points out, 'Did anybody ever confess to being "underneath LSD"?'[34] Another prerequisite for the substitution view of metaphor is the presumption that the metaphorical term substitutes for a literal term which is absent from the metaphorical expression, but available to be recaptured at will. Here again the generally accepted view is shown to be thoroughly inadequate. Resorting to Cooper again, we may wonder what Churchill actually meant when he described Mussolini as 'that utensil!'? What would be the literal paraphrase of a metaphor like 'Architecture is frozen music', or Dostoievsky's 'Eternity is a spider in a Russian bath-house'? From these examples alone, it is clear that metaphor follows a different 'symbolic' logic, in so far as it forces us to make comparisons which previously we may not have been able to perceive. Metaphor seeks to change perspectives on things, and therefore it is outward-looking, whereas Saussure holds that we grasp language as a set of internal relations. It also bears repeating that for Saussure language has no symbolic status—the linguistic sign can only refer to other linguistic signs.

There remains the intriguing possibility that Saussure's innovatory work on synchronic linguistics may have been misappropriated. A significant feature of Saussure's *explication* is the attribution of the syntagmatic order to *parole*—it is physically there, available to analysis—and of the paradigmatic order to *langue*. Therefore, Saussure relates the syntagm to a particular feature of a given language, whereas the paradigm has a universal application:

> Le rapport syntagmatique est *in praesentia*; il repose sur deux ou plusieurs termes également présents dans une série effective. Au contraire le rapport associatif unit des termes *in absentia* dans une série mnémonique virtuelle.[35]

He uses the example of a column, which exists in a certain physical relationship with the architrave that it supports. This structure, in which two unities are equally present in space, is the equivalent of a syntagmatic relation; however, if the column is Doric it will contrast with many other variants of column (Ionic, Corinthian, etc.), which are not present in space but which, nonetheless, constitute a paradigmatic or associative relation. In practice, the syntagmatic order describes the nuts and bolts of language, the mechanisms of phonology and grammar which are constantly refined so that any given language continues to function efficiently. However, the syntagmatic order always cedes to, because it is always preceded by, the paradigmatic order, which, on account of the principle of identity and contrast, allows for the creation of language. Questions of meaning therefore revert to the speaker's intention. If meaning is, as Austin initially claimed in *How to do things with words*, always the speaker's utterance meaning, then language meaning, or semantics, belongs exclusively to the realm of the paradigm. One might even venture that Saussure's concept of *la langue* is most easily and accurately apprehended as his perception of the fundamental human faculty by which we differentiate in terms of identity and contrast. Both metaphor and metonymy—if metonymy is a viable means of cognition, which is doubtful—arise initially, therefore, in the build-up to their expression in language, or discourse, in the mind of the individual speaker. Both are, or can be, assimilated to Saussure's paradigmatic order; neither form part of the syntagmatic order. Of course, Saussure bequeathed the intractable problem of quite how the human being is able to string words together syntactically in such accomplished fashion to Noam Chomsky, whose theories have since revolutionised thinking on the nature of syntax.

The prospect emerges that metaphor is not predominantly a fact of language. It is first and foremost a means of cognition, and moreover, a cognitive process which is relayed through the imagination. Our capacity to see Jastrow's diagram (famously borrowed by Wittgenstein) firstly as a duck, then as a rabbit (or vice versa) is a metaphorical function of the imagination.[36] Once metaphor is freed from linguistic shackles and considered as a possible means of cognition, then it may play a more purposeful part in literary theory.

The English literary critic, I. A. Richards, was the first to speculate on the idea that metaphor represents an intrinsic conceptual faculty of the human mind. Richards saw metaphor neither as the substitute of a literal referent, nor as a comparison, but as the interaction of two thought-domains: 'In the simplest formulation, when we use a metaphor we have two thoughts of different things active together and supported by a single word, or phrase, whose meaning is a resultant of their interaction'.[37] Metaphor no longer embraces the innovative combination of two units of language, it now relates to the interaction of two modes of thought. To illustrate his definition, Richards chooses the example, 'The poor are the negroes of Europe'. Applied to this metaphor, the 'substitution view' tells us that something is being indirectly said about the poor of Europe, but we are not exactly sure what. The 'comparison view' claims that the epigram presents some comparison between the poor and the negroes. In opposition to both, Richards says that our 'thoughts' about European poor and American negroes are 'active together' and 'interact' to produce a meaning which is the resultant of that interaction. In the given context the focal word 'negroes' obtains a new meaning, which is not quite its meaning in literal uses, nor quite the meaning which any literal substitute would have. The new context imposes an extension of meaning upon the focal word, but, for the metaphor to work, the reader must remain aware of this extension of meaning; he must attend to both the old and new meanings together.

The most far-reaching consequence of what has since been called the 'interaction' theory of metaphor is the one Richards fails to stress, namely that it posits an account of metaphorical meaning which works essentially on the prior, unstated, and necessarily variable knowledge of the reader, or addressee. For example, the metaphorical intent of the classical example of the figure, 'Man is a wolf', will be lost on a reader who is sufficiently ignorant about wolves. On the other hand, for the metaphor to obtain the reader need not know the standard dictionary definition of 'wolf', or be able to use that word in literal senses; he need only know what Max Black has termed the 'system of associated commonplaces' which, in this case, would be a collection of imaginary statements recording those things or qualities which he holds to be true about wolves. To an expert on wolves the reader's 'system of commonplaces' may include half-truths or complete errors (that the wolf hunts alone); however, the important thing for the metaphor's effectiveness is not that the commonplaces be true, but that they be readily and freely evoked. This is why a metaphor that works in one society may seem preposterous in another. People who take wolves to be reincarnations of dead humans will give a rather different interpretation of the metaphor than that offered by the natural scientist.

The effect, then, of (metaphorically) calling a man a 'wolf' is to evoke the wolf-system of related commonplaces. If the man is a wolf, he preys upon other animals, is fierce, hungry, a scavenger and so on and so forth. Each of these implied assertions has now to be made to fit the principal subject (the man) either in normal or abnormal senses. The reader, or addressee, will be led by the wolf-system of implications to construct a corresponding system of implications about the principal subject. But the corresponding set (the new meaning) will not be those comprised in the commonplaces normally implied by literal uses of 'man'. The new implications must be determined by the pattern of implications associated with literal uses of the word 'wolf'. Any human traits that can without undue strain be talked about in 'wolf-language' will be rendered prominent, and any that cannot will be pushed into the background. The wolf-metaphor suppresses some details and emphasises others. In short, it organises the reader's view of the man.

Two important factors emerge from Richards' analysis. Firstly, the prospect of metaphorical meaning is conditional on the prior, possibly shared knowledge of the addressee. Therefore—and this is the second point—metaphor works through time, as well as through space.

The publication in 1962 of Max Black's *Models and Metaphors* marks a milestone in the study of metaphor. In this book Black sets out to prove that behind the 'stroke of genius' or 'remarkable insight' which, typically, accounts for scientific discoveries or inventions there are conceptual processes at work, one of the most important of which is metaphor. Metaphor equates to what scientists term 'theoretical models'; Black's example is Clerk Maxwell's representation of an electrical field in terms of the properties of an imaginary, incompressible fluid. There is nothing new in scientists' use of theoretical models; however, in this case Black is interested in Maxwell's insistence on the 'imaginary' character of the fluid evoked. It has the status of a model and yet one can neither point at it nor construct it. This imaginary existence of the fluid allowed Maxwell in his discourse on electrical fields to move away from the concept of an imaginary ideal and towards ontological commitment. He no longer regarded Faraday's lines of force as 'purely geometrical conceptions'; they became 'the directions in which the medium is exerting a tension like that of a rope, or rather, like that of our own muscles'.[38] The difference is between thinking of the electrical field *as if* it were filled with a material medium, and thinking of it *as being* such a medium. The first approach, classified by Black as the implementation of the model as 'heuristic fiction', supposes a detached comparison reminiscent of simile; the second requires an identification typical of metaphor. Referring both to

Rutherford's solar system and Bohr's model of the atom, each of which is associated with monumental developments in the history of science, Black argues that this latter, 'existential' use of models is 'characteristic of the practice of the great theorists in physics'.[39]

Having established some sort of historical validity for his theorisations, Black pursues the analogy between the theoretical model in relation to science, and metaphor in relation to literature. He argues that theoretical models, whether treated as real or fictitious, are not literally constructed; rather 'the heart of the method consists of talking in a certain way'.[40] They introduce a new language which, under specific conditions, may produce a better understanding of the original field of investigation. In order to substantiate this claim Black resorts to another example of the use of the theoretical model, taken this time from a published account of investigations in pure mathematics.[41] The problem to be solved, that of finding some method for dissecting any rectangle into a set of unequal squares, serves no practical purpose other than that of interest to those who enjoy playing mathematical games. In the course of the investigation the usual methods of trial-and-error and straightforward computation produced no results. It was only when the mathematicians 'abandoned experiment for theory' that they started to make progress. The last in a series of different kinds of diagrams representing rectangles suddenly 'made' their problem part of the theory of electrical networks. Black elaborates on the mathematicians' introduction of a point-for-point model in their procedure. We learn that geometrical lines in the original figure were replaced by electrical terminals, and squares by connecting wires through which electric currents are imagined to flow. Then, by suitable choices of the resistances in the wires and the strengths of the currents flowing through them, a circuit is described conforming to known electrical principles (in this case Kirchoff's Law). The resources of a well-mastered theory of electrical networks are thus applied to the original geometrical problem.

The lesson imparted by Black is that the theoretical model initiates a novel discourse. In the language of science it is essentially an heuristic instrument that seeks, by means of a fiction, to break down an inadequate interpretation and pave the way for a new, more adequate interpretation. The radical aspect of Black's work concerns this stress on the use of fictions and therefore on the role of the imagination in the pursuit of knowledge in the sciences. However, the value of his contribution to a theory of literary or philosophical metaphor should not be underestimated. He reminds us that, according to the interaction theory, a successful metaphor has the power to bring two separate domains into cognitive and emotional relation by using language directly appropriate to the one as a *lens* for seeing the other. The implications, suggestions and supporting values entwined with the literal use of the metaphorical expression enable a new subject matter to be viewed in a new way. Importantly, the extended meanings that result, the relations between initially disparate realms created, can neither be antecedently predicted nor subsequently paraphrased in prose. Equally, Black insists, the memorable models of science are 'speculative instruments' which bring about a wedding of disparate subjects by a distinctive operation of transfer of the implications of relatively well-organised cognitive fields. Often the use of a particular model may amount to nothing more than a strained and artificial description of a well-mapped domain. But on other occasions it may highlight what has previously been overlooked, or shift the relative emphasis attached to details; in general it may help us to see new connections.

Recent thinkers such as Goodman (working specifically within the framework of pictorial art), Ortony and Kittay have wrestled with the difficulties involved in discriminating between the literal and the metaphorical use of language. Eva Kittay's contribution is especially valuable in that she forwards an account of metaphorical reference which is elegant and relatively simple. If the literal referent is the referent of an expression understood literally, she argues, then the metaphorical referent is the referent of an expression understood metaphorically. This means that the referent of the metaphorical expression—when that expression takes the form of a singular referring term—is the literal referent that would be specified by an appropriate term from what Kittay calls the 'topic domain', that is, the set of connotative options proposed by the metaphor in the first instance. Thus, metaphor is the process by which one of a number of existing connotations is privileged. Metaphorical reference is then whatever this privileged connotative element would normally (literally) refer to in circumstances where it is regarded as denotative, rather than connotative. In simple terms, metaphor refers to a property or quality of the subject which is either undisclosed or not sufficiently highlighted in its ordinary language denotation, but which has nonetheless always existed. Interestingly, Kittay then speculates that if we can speak of metaphors referring, can we also then speak of sentences in which these singular terms occur as metaphorically true or false? She makes the point, with characteristic understatement, that truth and falsity are relative to a conceptual scheme, and that metaphorical truth and falsity therefore need to be understood in the same terms. Relative to a scheme in which cities are thought of as women, 'The Venice of the Renaissance was a noblewoman' would be true, whilst 'The Venice of the Renaissance was a washerwoman' would be false. The all-important distinction is established: while metaphorical reference can be understood by appeal to simple anaphora, metaphorical truth must be understood through the conceptual detour provided by the second-order meaning specific to metaphor.

In order to demonstrate her theory of metaphorical truth, Kittay proposes an audacious metaphor for metaphor: *Metaphor as Rearranging the Furniture of the Mind*.[42] The bare room, as well as the material essence of the furniture, is the world we humans encounter prior to our activity of structuring and creating our environment. The furniture, the relation the pieces bear to one another, and the rules we follow for placing and using the individual items represent our creation and arrangement of the world we inhabit—our immediate environment. The sentences in the language of our room-world would refer to the furniture, in its relation to the room, to other pieces of furniture, and to our needs, desires and anything that might influence future events. Likewise the meaning of a specific piece of furniture has to do with its form and material, and the success or otherwise with which it slots into the general scheme.

Having projected these linguistic rules on to this 'furniture catalogue' image, Kittay narrates a number of discursive situations. To speak correctly, she suggests, is to utilise the furniture according to conventions reflected in its current placement, and it is also to assent to a proper placement of furniture. Therefore, assenting to the proper placement of furniture is to speak the truth. Conversely, to sit down at a table where there is no chair is to cause oneself a nasty injury, and effectively to utter a falsehood. To assent to a misplaced chair would be to assent to a falsehood. To assent to a bureau placed against the bathroom door would be to speak plain nonsense, and to assent to all the furniture being piled up in the middle of the room would be to speak of possible, but improbable worlds (though the speech act may refer to 'moving house'). The point Kittay makes is that truth is 'relative to what is the proper order',[43] although, in view of later implications she introduces, it might be wiser to say that truth is relative to what is the *pre-existing* order. 'Metaphorical placements' occur when there is a meaningful violation of this proper order, as would be the case with the moving of the straight-backed chair for the convenience of a guest who has a bad back. This productive capacity of metaphor is part of a general law of life. When a room is completely refurbished there is initially a great disruption. However, with time we forget that the furniture was ever differently ordered. To the extent that the change is systematic and widespread, it leaves only the slightest trace of its metaphorical origin. The next tenant who takes the room will assume that the dining area has always been by the sunniest window. It is now the literal truth. However, it would be an odd truth if the next tenant was a Japanese student, since she would view furniture placed against walls as a breach of all aesthetic and pragmatic rules for furniture arrangement. An African friend accustomed to living in a long house would find even the configuration of the room odd. He would be amused at the bed (regardless of its placement) and appalled by the lack of hammocks. Kittay maintains that both these visitors would come to see this arrangement as 'serviceable, given the conditions of western living',[44] adding that neither would be likely to see any merit in the sofa on its side.

Kittay's argument suggests that, although metaphorical truth may be accessible, our perception of metaphor is imbricated in our cultural differences. The conventions and rules informing the 'proper order' are culturally determined. Different cultures will inevitably have different rules responding to different criteria and structured by different concepts. Ultimately, the effectiveness of metaphor relies almost entirely on contextual factors. Semantic fields are an inadequate basis for analysis because they do not provide us with the signification of terms. Words have content. In the field of cooking, to know that 'fry', 'grill' and 'roast' all contrast in a particular way; that they are, in the language of semantics, incompatible co-hyponyms, does not help us to know what to do if we are ordered to roast a chicken. Kittay uses a telling example—*The seal dragged himself out of the office*—to show how the elaboration of the total context of a single metaphor will often lead the analyst out of the immediate linguistic vicinity. In this case, three different, equally plausible, interpretive possibilities are suggested. The seal may indeed be a seal, one of the many animal characters in a modern children's fairy-tale. On the other hand, it could refer to the weary executive at the end of a hard working day, during which he has been constantly on display, trotted out before prospective clients in whose company he behaves like a performing seal. Or, the seal could refer to the physical appearance of a stereotypical office worker in the days before health promotion. He would wear a black suit that had, by dint of habitual use, developed a fine sheen not unlike the seal's coat, his black hair would be worn slicked down, and he would walk with a waddling gait which would become more exaggerated as the day wore on. Thus, at 5 o'clock every weekday afternoon...

Kittay's analyses confirm a number of hypotheses about metaphor: that it inhabits a much larger world; that it embraces the text in which it features; that it refers to myths and truths which are indigenous to a particular culture; that it is culturally defined because it presupposes the existence of an accepted system of knowledge. If I have dwelt too long on these big ideas, it is because they, rather than the 'figure among figures' exactitude of traditional exegetes, provide the stimulus to my own understanding of literary metaphor. I now want to discuss three divergent approaches to metaphor, each of which has a more direct bearing on my investigation of Tournier's fictional project.

THREE CASE-STUDIES:
RICOEUR; RICARDOU; LAKOFF AND JOHNSON

It is evident from the conflicting, multi-faceted approaches to the subject, some of which have been outlined above, that metaphor germinates in the imagination, traditionally the poet's though it may spring from that of the reader or conversationalist. Perhaps the need to establish the location of the agent of metaphor, the identity of its executor, has been overplayed. What now seems clear is that any credible model of metaphoric comprehension cannot afford to dispense with at least a working theory of the imagination. However, of all the interested parties only Paul Ricoeur offers a developed account of the role of imagination in metaphorical insight. Ricoeur claims that an adequate semantic theory of metaphor, that is, 'an inquiry into the capacity of metaphor to provide untranslatable information',[45] requires a theory of the imagination that is both psychological and semantic. The significance of his approach lies in the simple fact that he is prepared to give to metaphor a source, the imagination. Now that it has a beginning we are able to conceive of it differently, as something which is produced, like a narrative, rather than as an ever-present faculty of the mind. As Ricoeur observes, this beginning is the mode of

functioning of the imagination, which is 'immanent ... to the predicative process itself'.[46] This work of the imagination provides the basis
for a theory of metaphorical reference which, Ricoeur claims, is
representative of literary fiction generally.

The pre-plan for metaphorical reference comprises three stages.
Initially Ricoeur leans on Kant. Thus, imagination is described in what
Kant called its *productive* mode, in which it underwrites a synthetic
operation of understanding. In metaphor this synthesis occurs by way
of an imaginative leap which allows us to see how two previously
unassociated systems of implications fit together to reveal an underlying unity (whilst still preserving their surface incompatibility). In the
second stage, imagination is recalled to the pictorial dimension, to the
state in which it is normally conceived and where it begins to supply the
images that fill out the sense of the metaphor. However, the vestiges of
the imagination's conceptual functioning are still prevalent. Ricoeur
emphasises that images are not, or need not necessarily be, mental
pictures; rather, they are ways of presenting relations 'in a depicting
mode'. Finally, imagination in metaphor is conditional on a 'negative'
step, in which primary reference to the everyday world is suspended, so
as to make possible a new creative reference, a 'remaking' of reality (to
paraphrase Nelson Goodman's slogan). Ricoeur sums up this three-fold
movement as follows:

> Imagination does not merely *schematize* the predicative assimilation between
> terms by its synthetic insight into similarities nor does it merely *picture* the
> sense thanks to the display of images aroused and controlled by the cognitive
> process. Rather, it contributes concretely to the *épochè* of ordinary reference
> and to the *projection* of new possibilities of redescribing the world.[47]

Ricoeur's conceptualisation of the productive imagination puts
those who believe that metaphor is cognitively irreducible on a much
firmer footing. Now we can see that it is in the movement of the
imagination prior to discourse—in what Ricoeur calls the schematising
process of predicative assimilation—that new meaning and new insight
are born. Imagination releases metaphor as a tool for understanding.[48]
Upon this foundation Ricoeur builds an impressive theory of metaphorical reference. He takes as his starting point Roman Jakobson's
communication model.[49] In an attempt to embrace the totality of
linguistic phenomena within a single schema Jakobson identifies six
crucial factors—the addresser, the addressee, the code, the contact, the
context and the message—which pertain to all forms of verbal
communication. Any one of these factors may be animated, or rendered

prominent in discourse by any one of six corresponding functions: the emotive, the conative, the metalingual or metalinguistic, the phatic, the referential, and the poetic functions respectively. In literary discourse, or verbal art as Jakobson prefers to call it, the poetic function focuses on the message for its own sake. Therefore, Jakobson argues, this function 'by promoting the palpability of signs, deepens the fundamental dichotomy of signs and objects'.[50] This is, in essence, a restatement of the classic formalist/structuralist position. However, Jakobson finds that it is now vulnerable. The semantic equivalence brought about by phonic equivalence in the poetic text brings with it an ambiguity that affects all the functions of communication. The addresser is split (the *I* of the lyrical hero, or of the fictitious narrator), and so too the addressee (the *you* as supposed addressee of dramatic monologues, supplications and epistles). Thus, poetic ambiguity need not necessarily imply the suppression of the referential function:

> The supremacy of poetic function over referential function does not obliterate the reference but makes it ambiguous. The double-sensed message finds correspondence in a split addresser, in a split addressee, and besides in a split reference, as it is cogently expressed in the preambles to fairy tales of various peoples, for instance in the usual exordium of the Majorca storytellers: 'Aixo era y no era' ('It was and it was not').[51]

It is clear to Ricoeur from Jakobson's analysis that the relation of poetics to the more general science of linguistics is immersed in a logic of metaphor. Indeed, according to Ricoeur the metaphorical expression provides the theatre in which all this drama of the doubles takes place: 'C'est dans l'analyse même de l'énoncé métaphorique que doit s'enraciner une conception référentielle du langage poétique qui tienne compte de l'abolition de la référence du langage ordinaire et se règle sur le concept de référence dédoublée.'[52] At this point Ricoeur starts to think of metaphor in terms of fiction generally. Metaphor is a contracted fiction; fiction is an expanded metaphor. This identification of metaphor with literary fiction becomes the fulcrum of his analysis: 'The "it was and it was not" of the Majorcan storytellers rules both the split reference of the metaphorical statement and the contradictory structure of fiction.'[53] Again, Jakobson provides the basis for the analogy. Since the referential function operates in a context, the 'référence dédoublée' sparked by the ambiguity of the poetic sign cannot, therefore, be constrained within the narrow confines of the message as expressed through its poetic function. Just as the poetic ambiguity juxtaposes two senses of a word, two linguistic universals, so the 'référence dédoublée' juxtaposes the two worlds in which these senses feature, the world of the text and the world outside the text. Thus, Ricoeur lauds the poet as not only the maker of fine metaphors but as 'this genius who generates split references *by* creating fictions'. Herein lies the audacity of metaphor; in its brash resolve to alter not only the sense of the utterance in which it features, but the entire context upon which that utterance is dependent.

Let us summarise the different stages in Ricoeur's account of metaphorical reference. Initially, the poetic function of the text brings about the suspension of ordinary descriptive reference so as to clear the space for the imagination to do its work. The result of this work is a fracture along the entire length of the communicative axis. The double-edged poetic sign replays itself in the various actants and functions designated in the process of communication. The most important of these repercussions concerns the manifestation of a split reference affiliated to a context. This context surrounds the metaphorical relation of the work of fiction to the empirical world of ordinary reference, in which the radical claim to 'redescribe reality' is promoted through the split reference of the language of fiction. The most contentious aspect of Ricoeur's argument is precisely this, that the ambiguity of the poetic sign translates into the double reference of poetic language, which, by virtue of its renewed referential function, gains the capacity to provide new cognitive insight on the world outside the text. The re-creation of the world in the poem is maintained in tensive relation with the external world by the radical copula, the *is* of the metaphorical assertion, which stakes its authority to make the suspension of primary reference to the everyday world an act of permanence.

By way of a happy coincidence, Ricoeur's plotting of metaphor provides a ready-made schema appropriate for the dressing of my chosen model, the Tournier *œuvre*. It may seem an odd thing that Tournier's first novel, the one which ought perhaps to have testified to the 'originality' of this new writer, is *Vendredi ou Les limbes du Pacifique*, an initially faithful rewriting of Daniel Defoe's classic adventure story, *Robinson Crusoe*. Tournier may have sensed something which many readers of *Robinson Crusoe*, on account of Defoe's suffocating moralising, probably miss; that the marooning of a solitary man on a desert island puts the greatest possible distance between that man and the referential concerns of his normal, and now past, existence. Defoe's Crusoe spends his time on the island sustaining a metaphysical system that enables connections with this former, empirical world to be re-established. For a while Tournier's Robinson follows the tracks of his literary ancestor. He, too, discovers a footprint in the sand. But gradually the significance of his situation becomes apparent. Robinson's life is not merely a battle against solitude. He is not merely ship-wrecked; he is suspended in limbo, in the world of the *époché*, freed from the clutter of existence to explore the virtualities of the imagination. *Vendredi* plies the reader with successive representations of this virtual existence—the tranquillity of the womb/tomb in the depths of the grotto, Vendredi's 'vie en marge' from which Robinson is 'culturally' excluded, and Robinson's patch of pink moss. It affords glimpses of what Genette calls the 'espace intérieur' of the text, in the orated ecstasies of the biblical 'Song of Songs'. The reader is lured into this world, which is both the Romantic and the Barthesian 'bower of bliss', a place of sensory expectation, of linguistic sense without meaning.

The myth of Robinson Crusoe puts the innate conservatism of metaphor, in which denomination carries with it the seeds of predication, under enormous strain. However, the umbilical cord remains intact and functional, for in *Vendredi ou Les limbes du Pacifique* we are presented with an unimaginable situation which we know to be (just) possible. This is the essence of myth, in its polyvalent relation to metaphor, which is explored in Chapter 2. As he was writing *Vendredi*, Tournier was also working on what was to become his second novel, *Le Roi des aulnes*. The latter is set in France and Germany during the Second World War. In it the narrative of fiction runs parallel to another narrative, constituted through the historical referents spaced out in the text, a second narrative which relays our conventional knowledge of this history. Presented as a narrative entity however, *Le Roi des aulnes* embodies Ricoeur's radical view of the poetic text as 'référence dédoublée'. The fiction affirms its identity as fiction, primarily through the 'real life' characterisation of a mythological, or fantastic figure, but at the same time asserts its right to speak on matters of the utmost philosophical importance. *Le Roi des aulnes* is, therefore, the representation or the dramatic expression of this relationship between denomination and predication, which is unique to metaphor.

Ricoeur's gallant refusal to abandon the notion of a non-textual reality afforded him pariah status in the poststructuralist heyday of the 1960s and 1970s. Yet via one of the most radical experiments in narrative form, carried out by the most enthusiastic proponent of the *nouveau roman* school of writing, the philosophical foundations of Ricoeur's theory of metaphor and its implications for the narrative arts are exposed and scrutinised. The text is *Les lieux-dits*, its author Jean Ricardou.

Les lieux-dits is a novel born of language. It starts out under the auspices of the travel guide—there are faint echoes here of Barthes' essay on *Le Guide Bleu*—but the signifier is straight away liberated from any constraining, bourgeois-led discourse and embarks on a 'literary' adventure, stopping off at eight different place-names. The linear movement of the narrative is disrupted not only by the repetition of sequential chunks—a characteristic feature of the *nouveau roman*—but by semantic detours generated from a small number of core motifs: the symbol of the cross, fire and water, the reading of the painting, and the two species of ant. At an early juncture a metafictional debate—which will mean little to those readers uninitiated into the arcane world classified in university libraries under the rubrique 'Philosophy of Language'—is introduced. Why is the second destination, Beaufort, which is a settlement on a hill, so called? There has never been a castle at Beaufort, the reader is told, 'Aucune ruine, ni vestige symbolique'.[54] Therefore, the name Beaufort cannot be said to render some prior, historical reality. Moreover, another clue, the clipping of roadside hedges in the shape of crenelated walls, suggests that the opposite is true, that the topography of Beaufort has evolved so as to conform to the place-name. The name comes before the thing. Not everybody is prepared to accept this evidence at face value. Opponents of the word fanatics argue that, in spite of the lack of fortifications, other features such as the narrow windows of the houses grouped along the one spiralling road, give it the 'look' of a citadel: 'Ainsi, contrairement aux thèses d'une doctrine fallacieuse, est-il bien l'origine de son nom ce village qui, en sa singulière géométrie, est beau, fort, et haut'.[55] A conflictual, oppositional dynamic is thus established, 'l'étrange querelle qui s'occupe de définir lequel, des mots et des choses est l'élément majeur'.[56] In this case the quest for origins (including, for example, clear references to Benveniste's famous attack on etymologies[57]) precipitates a 'medieval fantasy' in which the citadel is besieged by underground forces, fighting under a semiological standard, who strive to take it and expel the guardians of the nomenclature.

There is a strong sense that this debate about language, which is, properly speaking, a metaphysical dichotomy, subsumes the other battles that are played out in the narrative. The matter is not, as we shall see, resolved conclusively. This poses a problem, for *Les lieux-dits* exhibits not only a desire for order, but a desire for a natural order. Mathematics is held up as a possible model. In Milan Kundera's work seven is a magical figure; in *Les lieux-dits*, as in Robbe-Grillet's *Le Voyeur*—both could be read as circular narratives—the figure eight and its multiples is a primary structural motif. (There is less emphasis in *Les lieux-dits* on the pictorial dimension of the number, though the arrangement of the words on the cover—which is reproduced identically on the title page—has an eightish shape to it.) We can be certain of the fact that there are eight place-names, each composed of eight letters, which head the eight chapters into which the book is divided. The mid-point and the end of chapter four occurs on page 80, and there are 160 pages in all. The number eight is cited often in the text, not quite to the exclusion of all other numbers—two dates (1908 and 1917) are mentioned. The word used most frequently is 'aujourd'hui' (au jour de huit), suggesting not only the timelessness of numbers but the discursive present of synchronic linguistics. 'Aujourd'hui' occurs (sometimes more than once) on eighteen different pages. When the eight place-names are listed to form a crossword-style grid, the left-to-right diagonal spells out (and thus reiterates) Belcroix, the fourth destination in narrative order:

> B A N N I È R E
> B E A U FO R T
> B E L A R B R E
> B E L C R O I X
> C E N D R I E R
> C H A U M O N T
> H A U T B O I S
> M O N T E A U X

This movement of the eye, scanning down and across the grid, is also the recommended method of reading the allegorical painting.[58]

The mathematical order of *Les lieux-dits* is fixed. Conversely, the answers to the more conventional 'literary' questions posed by this text are extremely fluid. There is a narrator, who is closely identified with the chief protagonist, named in the text as 'Olivier Lasius'. The latter is engaged in a quest for meaning. How to interpret the painting? What happened to the painter, Albert Crucis? Was he taken away in an ambulance? Was the ambulance involved in a crash, and was everything, including the body of Crucis, incinerated in a fire which was caused by the crash? Or was Crucis killed by a pyromaniac who had escaped from a mental institution? There are an infinite number of possibilities for narrative resolution. In this case they revolve around a constellation of signifiers emanating from the central 'star' word, 'croix': *croisade, croissant, La Croix Rouge, la croix des chevaliers de Malte, crucial, Crucis*, etc. Another form of linguistic logic is also at work. The place-name Cendrier generates a contiguous chain of ideas which 'justifies' references to amongst other things Pall Mall cigarettes and the British Royal Family. This language world seems governed by a system. The antique-dealer at Beaufort specialises in medieval weapons, though he is unconcerned as to whether they are genuine antiques or forgeries. However, he must respect the municipal regulations which govern the display of his wares, for he is only one of many antique-dealers concentrated in Beaufort, all with different collections: books, engravings, tapestries, etc. These paradigmatic sets are of most interest to other knowledgeable specialists. In order to attract more ordinary tourists, the Beaufort Tourist Office has instructed the dealers to take turns in mounting a composite display based around a particular theme or narrative, using articles borrowed from their fellow traders. Visitors to Beaufort will therefore delight in finding not only a number of homogeneous collections, but also an heterogeneous display where each article derives its function not from its intrinsic properties but from its place in the overall scheme. 'Faut-il aujourd'hui préciser', the narrator asks with rhetorical menace, 'que certains controversistes, utilisant toute circonstance pour faire rebondir leur querelle, se sont plu à lire dans cette double mise en place, une parabole de la linguistique distinction entre le paradigme et le syntagme?'[59]

The reference to Saussure in the first instance, and then to Jakobson's theory that the process by which language becomes meaningful discourse is governed by the laws of metaphor and metonymy, is unmistakable. However, in *Les lieux-dits* words have a life of their own. Coherence is impossible in a narrative which constantly deconstructs itself. This situation is unbearable for the ants, functional insects whose very existence is instinctively attuned to notions of system and order. The ants are the representatives *par excellence* of the construction industry. Significant ant activity in the text of *Les lieux-dits* means that everything is recycled; words, ideas, concepts keep coming back. Hence the semantic slippage of the text—which may take the reader rapidly from Cendrier to Pall Mall cigarettes and on to the British Royal family and thus imparts a dynamic thrust to the narrative—is negated by the constant re-emergence of certain motifs.

Metaphor, or word associations, wins the battle over metonymy, or narrative discourse. Within this deconstructive/reconstructive process there is, however, stability at the level of the morpheme. If the source words were no longer recognisable, chaos would ensue. And once these words are (metaphorically) stabilised, then the possibility emerges that they may accrue a symbolic function, either in the form of anagrams (belatedly recognised by Saussure as, along with onomatopoeia, an alternative means of linguistic motivation) or as words which, horror of horrors, represent non-linguistic phenomena. As the text progresses, therefore, we are constantly referred back to the physical evidence of language, to the visible presence of the signifier. Ironically, this revives the potential for representation; language may indeed have a mimetic function.

We can circumnavigate this linguistic dilemma by taking our first step outside the world of the text and activating some knowledge based on genre. The unmotivated repetition of a particular narrative sequence is a technique pioneered by Alain Robbe-Grillet. In his novel *La Jalousie,* the death of a centipede is described at several junctures in the narrative. In cases such as these the repetition is both lexical and syntactic. Entire sentences, paragraphs, pages even are reproduced apparently at random. The first of two such privileged sequences in *Les lieux-dits* follows an orthodox robbe-grilletian pattern. The second involves a more fragmented, prolonged, and complex operation performed by a first-person narrator who is now participating actively in events and apparently steering the narrative towards its closure. Both scenarios focus intensively on ants.

In the first a boy by the wayside is acting strangely. He is peering at a small gravelly area, but he is not looking through the magnifying glass which he has in his possession. On closer inspection he is manipulating the glass, so that it captures the trajectory of the sun, and directing the beam towards an army of black ants clustered around a fragment of glass-like material. The ants are exterminated one after the other. In the narrative reprise of this incident only the identity of the persecutor has changed. We are given to understand that this is the boy's account of a scene he has witnessed. The ant-killer is now a woman in a red dress whose example the boy has copied. Nevertheless the narrator administers an appropriate punishment in recognition of the boy's misdemeanour. He whips his bare legs with tapered brambles. The boy's discomfort signifies the revenge of the ants, for the irritation to his skin is caused by formic acid, 'l'acide formique', a form of retribution which is prefigured literally by the fact that he is rather stiff. Indeed he has 'des fourmis dans les jambes',[60] pins-and-needles from having been crouched too long in the same position, absorbed by his ant incinerating.

In the second half of the text, the narrator, who is now a more forceful discursive presence, begins to study the behaviour of warring species of ants. He notices how the big red ant acting alone triumphs over batallions of smaller black ants while the conflict rages in sunlight, but also the defeat of a more docile red ant in the shadows, where it is rapidly 'tronçonnée' by its numerous black cousins. He introduces variations, holding his palm out over the battleground, thereby providing unexpected areas of shade, creating other diversions which cause a red ant to dementedly attack other ants of its own species. The narrator's experiments with ants are revealed as preparation for the *dénouement*, when the ant conflict is re-enacted, only this time on a human stage. As the country lane narrows to a path, Atta, the woman in the red dress, and Lasius, the narrator, abandon their car and continue their journey on foot. Lasius forcefully requests that Atta should undress alphabetically, 'slip' before 'soutien-gorge', showing again the triumph of the paradigmatic set over the naturally syntagmatic order of seduction. She acquiesces to his request. Then he pegs her out on the ground in crucifixion posture, whips her legs with a bunch of nettles and explains what will happen next. Her body will be covered with a thin layer of honey so as to attract a seething horde of red ants. A magnifying glass will be positioned on the ground at such an angle that the beam of the midday sun will ignite the tip of one of eight pathways of dry scrub radiating out from the focal point of the supine human form. This configuration suggests the medieval punishment of the *auto-da-fé*, or burning (of witches or heretics) at the stake, albeit on a horizontal plane. Certainly the resulting conflagration should speed the extinction of the red ants, thereby exacting the vengeance of the black. Lasius will make good his escape, leaving the pyromaniac to carry the can. The pyromaniac, he informs Atta, has been a real presence all along and has now been summoned to the neighbourhood in order that he be implicated for such a creative pyromaniacal achievement.

However, the conclusion we are supposed to arrive at has already been spelled out. The two narrative genres—the travel guide and the novel—are seen to represent the ebb and flow of the oppositional forces brought to life in the text. The narrator observes that these two adversaries contain within themselves the seeds of their own destruction:

> Il n'est pas de guide qui ne succombe au désir du langage et, outre les descriptions assurant aux objets une nouvelle allure, ne propose déjà, sous couvert de légende ou d'histoire, mainte étrange aventure. Quant au roman, pour occupé qu'il soit à inventer l'autonomie de son espace, il ne laisse d'utiliser, en revanche, à chaque instant, des éléments du monde: tout paysage fictif s'établit par référence à de quotidiennes contrées.[61]

All generic distinctions are effectively contaminated by the fundamental metaphoricity of language, which involves the reader in a constant coming-and-going within the confines of the specified language, making links between sound patterns, semantic fields and narrative structures, whilst at the same time building bridges between the text and the world outside it. Connotation and denotation are thus the two faces of the same metaphorical coin. As the resuscitated Albert Crucis murmurs wistfully on the last page of the text, 'Tout cela, une fois de plus, aujourd'hui, est une métaphore'.[62] The text thus adopts a narrative *alternance* in which 'fourmi' succeeds 'cigale',[63] and 'nul doute' replaces 'sans (sens) doute' as each aspect of the terrain is mapped by the intrepid narrator. Poetry cedes to realism which cedes to poetry; we travel from connotation to denotation and on to connotation. Still, the overall picture of *Les lieux-dits* falls some distance short of coherence. The Proper Names are symbolic, each seeming to designate the character's function in the narrative: Crucis is a Latin genitive, meaning 'of the cross'; *lasius alienus* is a breed of tiny black ant; Atta's fate is predetermined by her palindromic name, suggesting the refraction of light or heat, as in a crucible, to a centre-point, and thus incineration by means of the magnifying glass. Yet the title of the opus bequeathed by the père La Fourmi, *Le Jardin des Oppositions*, suggests a medieval allegory. An allegory of what? A human tendency to self-destruct? The père La Fourmi dies having swallowed a vial of the insecticide he had been using in an attempt to wipe out the local population of red ants.

Significantly, La Fontaine's grasshopper is marginalised. On the other hand the text teems with ants. Moreover, the narrator's growing interest in ant behaviour necessitates a change of mode, as the distant third person is superseded by a more involved first-person voice. More importantly, with the repeated narrations of the incineration scene, the narrative eventually transcends connotative symbolism and reaches the brink of a full, metaphorical transition, as the ants are replaced by human actants. Lasius' final plan is the literal enactment of an allegorical potential which has already been the subject of some discussion, namely that the repeated patterns of ant conflict merely reproduce human behaviour:

> Nul doute que l'histoire des humains avec ses quêtes de l'amour, de la richesse, de la liberté fugace ou de la creuse émeraude du Graal, avec ses guerres, ses esthétiques, ses révolutions, ses croisades, ne soit la réplique de la lutte impitoyable que se livrent, depuis des millénaires, les peuples des fourmis. S'il s'interroge sur la nature de telle correspondance, le voyageur ne manquera pas d'être troublé, sans doute, par la simple idée que les activités humaines puissent être une métaphore des conflits qui divisent les populations microscopiques.[64]

The very notion of allegory, the possibility of allegorical meaning, is then immediately quashed by a flurry of rhetorical questions aimed at each of the categories—war, aesthetics, revolutions, etc.—listed in the quotation above. The precarious, physical existence of the narrative is reiterated as the narrator self-consciously cuts to the next scene— '...j'interromps ici cette ligne, aujourd'hui'[65]—which will conclude with a different, contradictory meditation on the figurative sense of the red ant, 'les lignes des fourmis rouges et bleues, avec leurs pattes dépassant de chaque côté de l'axe des mots, n'étaient, selon la formule de Crucis, qu'une métaphore du texte, puisque l'auteur avait commencé à produire son écriture selon telles couleurs alternées'.[66] Nevertheless Ricardou has, perhaps fatally, permitted an anthropomorphic incision of the sort which Robbe-Grillet fought so tenaciously in the halcyon days of the *nouveau roman*.[67] Once aired, the parallelism between ant and human can never be properly despatched, for it signals recognition—though this may be a sub-conscious recognition on the part of the reader—of the fact that all literature, indeed all metaphor is anthropomorphic. Our apprehension of the world can never be 'objective', for it will always be impregnated with the essence of human history. The narrator's pseudo-scientific observation of ant behaviour thus emphasises that so-called 'natural' history is, in fact, 'cultural' history, an anthropomorphic perspective on nature.

According to the crude allegorical schema, ant conflict reifies two oppositional ways of organising human society, in which the rugged individualism of the red ant is pitted against the cooperative, communal black ant. At the same time both species, indeed all species of earthbound ants, are programmed to construct. Ants are instinctive builders, the most functional of functional insects. Of course, *Les lieux-dits* is not about ants, it is about literature. What is it? How does it work? An appropriate response would be that this book, whatever it is, is a 'hell of a job to read', 'c'est la croix et la bannière'. The reader of *Les lieux-dits* risks the fate of a dysfunctional red ant. We are the woman in red, forced to undress alphabetically, and in the end martyred for our cause. In this perspective *Les lieux-dits* may be read as a warning treatise on modern literature. It tells not about the pre-eminence of poetry over realism, of connotation over denotation, for these are essential qualities of the literary text, but of the danger of becoming entombed in a purely linguistic world. Literature records the triumph of metaphor. It is not about the way that texts deconstruct themselves. Instead it speaks of our fundamental desire to make connections, create categorical sets and design the world in the way that Ricardou says metaphor does.

Ricardou's conclusion that all is metaphor,[68] and my reading of his experimental novel, that the ants show the unstoppable, perhaps ultimately futile instinct of humans constantly to organise and reorder their environment, funnels into the re-evaluation of metaphor in a non-literary context conducted with a rare panache by American linguists George Lakoff and Mark Johnson. Lakoff and Johnson's belief, supported by *bona fide* linguistic evidence, is that our ordinary conceptual system, in terms of which we both think and act, is fundamentally metaphorical in nature. Two examples illustrate their approach, the one proviso being that the 'we' in question inhabit an advanced, industrial democracy.[69]

The metaphor ARGUMENT IS WAR is dominant in this culture. Though we may not be aware of it, the metaphor is reflected in our everyday language by a variety of expressions: 'Your claims are indefensible', 'He attacked every weak point in my argument', 'If you use that strategy, he'll wipe you out', and so on and so forth. Lakoff and Johnson insist that we don't just talk about arguments in terms of war; we can actually win or lose arguments, we see the person we are arguing with as an opponent, we attack his positions and we defend our own, we plan and use strategies. Naturally, arguments and wars are different kinds of things—verbal discourse and armed conflict—and the actions performed different kinds of actions. But, Lakoff and Johnson say, 'ARGUMENT is partially structured, understood, performed, and talked about in terms of WAR'.[70] Another example, which has slipped into proverbial usage, is the metaphor TIME IS MONEY. Common expressions deriving from this metaphor are: 'You're wasting my time', 'Is that worth your while?', 'He's living on borrowed time', 'Thank you for your time', and a host of others. Because of the way that the concept of work has developed in modern western culture, where work is typically associated with the time it takes and time is precisely quantified, it has become customary to pay people by the hour, week, or month. In our culture TIME IS MONEY in many ways: hourly wages, hotel room rates, interest on loans, and paying your debt to society by serving time. These practices are relatively new in the history of the human race and by no means exist in all cultures. In fact TIME IS MONEY specifically organises our lives. It is the sign of the Occident, the most entrenched metaphor for western society. We understand and experience time as the kind of thing that can be spent, wasted, budgeted, invested wisely or foolishly, saved or squandered.

On the basis of examples such as these, Lakoff and Johnson define the essence of metaphor as 'understanding and experiencing one kind of thing in terms of another'.[71] Critics might object that an expression like TIME IS MONEY is a classic example of 'dead' metaphor, that is to say, a purely diachronic phenomenon of language. As societies and cultures develop, new and more complex relations evolve and are reflected through semantic innovation. Linguists are agreed that one of the ways in which any given language keeps pace with the changing face of the environment in which it is spoken is through metaphor. However, Lakoff and Johnson reveal, in the most active sense of the word, what in our daily speech is already there and yet not perceived to be there. They note that even our most 'literal' expressions may involve unnoticed 'conventional' metaphors, and, in a series of analyses, they demonstrate that the very ligatures and sinews of our linguistic skeleton are often metaphorical. Most impressively, they classify a set of 'orientational' metaphors based on common spatial delimitations like UP/DOWN, IN/OUT, NEAR/FAR, ON/OFF, and so on. Thus we hear 'You're in high spirits', 'I'm depressed' (HAPPY IS UP; SAD IS DOWN), 'Wake up', 'He dropped off to sleep' (CONSCIOUS IS UP; UNCONSCIOUS IS DOWN), 'She has high standards', 'I wouldn't stoop to your level' (VIRTUE IS UP; DEPRAVITY IS DOWN), and many more. Orientational metaphors tend to have a physical basis; a metaphor such as MORE IS UP; LESS IS DOWN ('My income rose last year', 'He is under-age') proceeds from the simple observation that if you add more of a substance to an existing pile, the level goes up. However, once established, these metaphors combine with each other. Therefore, MORE IS BETTER is coherent with MORE IS UP and GOOD IS UP. LESS IS BETTER is not coherent with them.

A seam of metaphor, encrusted in the foundations of our knowledge of the world, has been tapped. Lakoff and Johnson's mining of language, albeit (some would argue) in the form of a particular idiom, frames a radical philosophy. Their work fleshes out, in a form which is more amenable to the western reader, the notion gleaned from the work of structural anthropologist Claude Lévi-Strauss that Culture (viewed either as a specific entity or as a generality) is born from Nature through metaphor. However, it should not be misconstrued. When Lakoff and Johnson say that 'The most fundamental values in a culture will be coherent with the metaphorical structure of the most fundamental concepts in the culture',[72] they are not trying to change anything. Their work is radical, not revolutionary. What they attempt to prove is that the system of ethics prevalent in any given society does not originate in the teachings of that society's theological orthodoxy. Our sense of Good and Evil is determined naturalistically. The savage mind is 'concrète', Lévi-Strauss wrote in *La Pensée sauvage*, echoing first the concerns of Rousseau, and then of Malinowski and the anthropologists who succeeded him.

When we use the word 'metaphor', we presuppose that there is something which is not metaphor. The obvious objection to Lakoff and Johnson is that they see metaphor in everything, and that consequently their discussion reduces to incoherence. Certainly, those 'orientational' metaphors which are too clearly grounded in the direct physical relation of Man to the earth (the erect posture of the average sensory human being who stands perpendicular to the earth's surface) appear to transgress the category. However, Lakoff and Johnson are primarily interested in the sophisticated language games of an advanced society, and it is in this context that the 'orientational' metaphors serve paradoxically to draw a distinction between the metaphorical and the literal. Language which is literal, they say, speaks of how 'we understand our experience directly when we see it as being structured directly from interaction with and in our environment'. Conversely, 'we understand experience metaphorically when we use a gestalt from one domain of experience to structure experience in another domain'.[73] This definition is only possible, and therefore only relevant, as an overview, a conclusion to the progressive unfolding of truths and myths that has preceded it. Their starting-point is with popular misconceptions about language, according to which any form of rhetoric is held to be incompatible with the truth. Herein lies the philosophical imperative of their work. Lakoff and Johnson set out to demonstrate how the myth wrought by empirical philosophy, which says that literal assertion (untainted by figuration) is somehow the pristine model of perspicuous communication, hides the pervasiveness of 'conventional' metaphors in the way we think, experience, talk, and act in our everyday world. An important reference here is to Heidegger's postulation that the 'original meaning' of the Greek term for truth—*aletheia*—is 'unconcealment'.[74] Lakoff and Johnson's mission is to *disclose* the fundamentally metaphorical nature of our talk. Once we see that unquestionably 'cognitive' and 'true' statements involve many 'conventional' metaphors, then, they insist, we shall lose our prejudice against metaphors as bearers of truth values, because the dichotomy it presupposes will have broken down.

The test of any cognitive theory of metaphor depends on the capacity of any given metaphor to generate fresh insight. Lakoff and Johnson's work is primarily geared towards the revelation of language *as it is*. We discovered, reading Cooper, that it is easy both to talk up and to talk down metaphor in hindsight. The only way to properly test the 'unquestionably cognitive' status of metaphor would be for us to promulgate new insight ourselves, by inventing a metaphor. Lakoff and Johnson do not disappoint. In reply to the pop musician's eternal lament, 'What is love?', they chime 'LOVE IS A COLLABORATIVE WORK OF ART'. It is something lovers must 'work on', as a 'team', and 'treasure the experience of'. The metaphor provides a new, fairly recent concept of love strikingly different from earlier ones 'structured' by talking of it in terms of a chemical reaction or of a journey through life together. And it is precisely because 'the metaphor gives love a new meaning', they write, that (it) 'can acquire the status of truth'.[75] New metaphors highlight changes in the way we perceive reality. In an age when love was metaphorised in other terms, say of combustion, it would have been false to say that love requires effort. Once two people need to make an effort, one can hear Byron and Goethe insisting, it is no longer *love* which is between them. Even now the very word 'love' covers a huge diversity of experience. Lakoff and Johnson investigate what it is that makes this diversity of experience cohere in a mere metaphor. Each metaphor has entailments. LOVE IS A COLLABORATIVE WORK OF ART tells us that love is valuable in itself, that it is creative and involves beauty. It also says that it demands sacrifice, may lead to frustration and brings joy and pain. Love is an act of communication and yet it cannot be achieved by formula. Therefore, a new metaphor may entail both other metaphors and literal statements. It is this final adjustment, by which new metaphors are seen to authorise literal statements, that is the most philosophically audacious.

Consider the sentence 'Love really needs to be worked at'. What makes this metaphorically true is that it leads us to some important literal truths about love, such as that the sustaining of a love relationship typically requires effort and compromise on the part of the two lovers. Our customary perception of metaphor has been reversed. The truth of metaphor, far from deriving in all cases from literal truth, will help determine what the literal truth is. Sometimes metaphors can be 'self-verifying'.

In the ongoing debate over the philosophical status of metaphor, Lakoff and Johnson hold two trump cards, which give them a distinct advantage over the other players. Firstly, their analysis does not contradict the one viable definition of truth, proposed by Kittay, that it must be relative to an accepted system of concepts and beliefs which reflects a given set of relations a language community has to the world it occupies. Lakoff and Johnson presume only to comment on their own, specific culture, in a mode of discourse synonymous with it. Metaphor often highlights the peculiar inwardness of any cultural block. They cite President Carter, who, faced with the energy crisis of the mid- to late 1970s, declared 'the moral equivalent of war'. Policy change and political and economic action were initiated by a mere verbal locution. At the same time, this turn of phrase generated a number of entailments, in which less palatable truths about American society became evident. Following Carter's speech, cartoonists pictured the energy crisis as an external, foreign enemy complete with 'Arab' headdress. Metaphor is not always at the service of ideology; at times it reflects those aspects of cultural difference—xenophobia at a time of crisis, or widespread, institutionalised racial bigotry—that western societies prefer to keep under wraps.

Secondly, Lakoff and Johnson represent a view of language which is unprejudiced by our centuries-long fixation with the written word. Indeed, their use of an upper case typeface to highlight each given metaphor (with entailments), which I have mimicked, is ironic, because it draws attention to and symbolises the word on the page, when Lakoff and Johnson are chiefly concerned with the dynamics of language, as a socially and politically interactive, and, above all, oral phenomenon. They work with a language community in which speaking and hearing meaning comes naturally and the tension between word and object is not obvious, if it is there at all. *Metaphors we live by* cannot be parcelled off and categorised in the library as a linguistic analysis of ordinary language forms, because the entire argument put forward in this text creates a momentum that resists such arbitrary classifications. The carefully chosen title indicates the extent to which we, inhabitants of a highly technological society, still function in a 'verbomotor' culture,[76] in which language is proactive; it performs the event, or at least the event is tangential to its performance in language. This notion, of the language-event, might appear somewhat strange to the high-street shopper, but it is a commonplace in many other societies. Purchasing something at a Middle East souk or bazaar is not a simple economic transaction, as it would be at Marks and Spencers. Rather it is a series of verbal (and somatic) manoeuvres, a polite duel, a contest of wits. Business is not business; it is fundamentally rhetoric. The Hebrew term *dabar* means both 'word' and 'event'. Tournier's literary destination, I shall argue, is located precisely in this desire for a more fluid communication, in the need to achieve the sort of linguistic performativity which underpins the conceptual unity of ancient oral cultures.

CHAPTER TWO

Suspended Animation: *Vendredi ou Les limbes du Pacifique*

TEXT, MYTH, AND IDEOLOGY

There are perhaps too many texts in Tournier's first published novel, *Vendredi ou Les limbes du Pacifique*: the presence of Daniel Defoe's *Robinson Crusoe* as a powerful precursor-text remains a constant preoccupation throughout the narrative; the prelapsarian Tarot card preface provides a forestructure to the narrative proper and as such constitutes a predictive sequence, albeit in symbolic form; the Bible is an important resource for Robinson; the narration of his adventures on the island is animated by a series of transformations and renewals on varying scales forming a verbal edifice that seems to take its inspiration from Claude Lévi-Strauss's structural analyses of myth; finally, the exploration of Robinson's consciousness during his time on the island is recorded in his log-book. The interspersed sections of the log-book give some indication of the complexity of textual interplay which runs through the novel, in that the log-book institutes and perpetuates three distinct discourses: between Robinson and himself, in which the self is viewed temporally in terms of past and future states; between Robinson and the island; and between the first-person voice of the log-book and the third-person narrator of Robinson's adventures. Moreover the theme of language, which is viewed in *Vendredi* as a tool with the potential to open up new areas of cognitive experience, permeates all aspects of the novel. Although *Vendredi* is, as many have surmised, a novel about philosophy, it is specifically a novel which investigates the possibilities inherent in a philosophy of language. Moreover, absorbed in its own other-worldly self-consciousness, it is a novel in which are staked out the initial parameters of Tournier's figurative discourse, the gateway to his imagination.

The Life and Strange, Surprizing Adventures of Robinson Crusoe, by Daniel Defoe, was first published in Great Britain in 1719. Since then there have been numerous borrowings, rewritings,[1] and, interestingly,

41

adaptations in the form of childrens' books of Crusoe's story, to the extent that the character of Robinson has passed into western mythology. *Vendredi* draws on a number of more or less famous *robinsonades*, many of which are freely acknowledged by the author.[2] Tournier even describes how he consulted documents which chronicle the true life story of Alexander Selkirk, the original Robinson Crusoe and real-life inspiration to Defoe.[3] Selkirk was said to have inhabited a Pacific island off the coast of Chile, as does Tournier's Robinson; the nearest mainland to Defoe's Crusoe is the Venezuelan coast. He is also said to have wrestled with a goat on a cliff-top, narrowly avoiding death as the goat's body cushioned his fall. Substituting the colonialist white man for Vendredi, Tournier endows this story with symbolic significance; it is absent from Defoe's novel. Robinson's log-book in *Vendredi* complements Crusoe's journal but is closer in style and register to Valéry's *Extraits du Log-book de Monsieur Testes*; Valéry maintained a keen interest in the Crusoe myth. Already a pattern is beginning to emerge. Though Tournier may frequently draw upon other satellite texts having some bearing on the Crusoe myth in order to underline differences between his own and Defoe's founding narrative, the father-, or precursor-text remains a constant point of intersection. As we shall see, in relation to Defoe's *Robinson Crusoe* the narrative of *Vendredi* orchestrates a play of similarities and differences which is so dense and complex as to render incidental even Tournier's rehabilitation of Selkirk.

The myth of the desert island is also a symbol of the Other, or rather the unknown, everything which is not western life, culture and society and which moreover, like the photographs of the Seychelles and the Bahamas adorning the front pages of travel brochures, constitutes an apparition that, for many people, will never translate into reality. As we can see from the following passage, this idea of the desert island as a symbol of raw existence figured strongly in Tournier's conception of the novel:

> Ce n'était pas le mariage de deux civilisations à un stade donné de leur évolution qui m'intéressait, mais la destruction de toute trace de civilisation chez un homme soumis à l'oeuvre décapante d'une solitude inhumaine, la mise à nu des fondements de l'être et de la vie, puis sur cette table rase la création d'un monde nouveau sous forme d'essais, de coups de sonde, de découvertes, d'évidences et d'extases. (VP, 229)

Interestingly, the myth of the desert island also informs the definition of metaphor given by the *nouveau roman* theorist, Jean Ricardou.

Ricardou describes metaphor as 'toujours en quelque sorte un exotisme, assemblant un ici (le comparé) à un ailleurs (le comparant)'. The suggestiveness of Ricardou's schema for the reading of any Robinson Crusoe narrative derives from the forceful presence of his notion of the *ailleurs*. 'L'ailleurs', he writes, 'n'est plus ce fantôme léger, translucide, qui voltigeait un instant autour de l'ici pour le définir avec élégance'; it is neither a temporary escape into a world of dreams nor the rhetorical froth decorating the rock of language; 'il (l'ailleurs) se propose immédiatement, lui-même comme un autre ici'; it is both physical relocation and nominal displacement, 'l'expression le cède au voyage'.[4] What interests Tournier is the fact that this myth has a historically precise origin, and that it is generated by a work of literature. He has no desire overtly to modernise the eighteenth-century text, for what he admires in Defoe—Tournier refers unstintingly to 'le génie de Daniel Defoe' (VP, 208)—is his ability to reach what Ricardou refers to as 'le fantastique de l'écriture' in spite of, and through, the Puritan ethos of his time and, therefore, of his novel. It is this mythical aspect to Defoe's imagination that both inspires and delimits the narrative of *Vendredi*. Tournier is interested in flesh and blood; in *Vendredi* he attempts to resuscitate Crusoe.

Gérard Genette has proposed a useful theoretical framework to cover the sort of rewriting enterprise exemplified by *Vendredi*. Genette qualifies 'rewriting texts' like *Vendredi* as *hypertexte* and the object of the rewriting as *hypotexte*; he then baptises this specific form of intertextuality, which is the relationship between *hypo-* and *hypertexte*, *hypertextualité*.[5] Before the reading commences, Tournier's choice of title suggests that it should instigate a 'retournement idéologique'.[6] The name of the slave displaces that of the master and offers itself as a focalising point of the narration. We are thrown forward to the point in the text where Vendredi unwittingly triggers the explosion in the cave and the narrative diverges radically from that of Defoe. Henceforth Robinson literally casts aside the trappings of the old (his) civilisation and tries to participate in Vendredi's world. The explosion in the cave appears to function retrospectively as a structural *charnière*, operating the switch from the old to the new. However, this symbolic rebirth of Robinson in the solar kingdom of Speranza is also the final scene of a conflict which has already been played out in the narrative discourse, where differences between the *hypo-* and *hypertexte* have maintained a tension between the old and the new which is refigured in other tensions and conflicts existing at various levels within the text—

between Robinson and solitude, the white and the black rats, the earth and the ether, seriousness and laughter.

In answer to a reader's question as to why he did not dedicate his novel in homage to Daniel Defoe, Tournier stresses the intimacy of the relationship between the two texts: 'J'avoue que je n'y ai même pas songé tant la référence constante de chaque page de ce livre à son modèle anglais me paraissait évidente' (VP, 229). Indeed, the narrative of *Vendredi* draws its reader into a form of textual interlocution which functions at two distinct levels of narration. There is a progressive parity between the two texts in terms of the conventional narrative or plot. Both Robinsons are shipwrecked on a desert island, and recover fortuitously some tools and other accoutrements from the wreck with which they can reconstruct the essence of their former existence in alien surroundings.[7] Moreover, from an initial state of regression both Robinsons follow specific stages in a Rousseauesque History of Man which takes them from the domestication and breeding of animals through to the cultivation of the land. And, of course, they are both provided with a companion to stave off the madness of solitude in the shape of Vendredi, *le bon sauvage*, who is incorporated into the administration of the island and governed according to the dictates of eighteenth-century political thought, which, due to his blackness, make of him a slave. The respective plots diverge dramatically with the explosion that occurs in *Vendredi*, only to converge once more with the promise of possible salvation when the would-be rescue ship drops anchor in the bay. Famous Crusoe experiences and incidents, such as his boat-building efforts and the footprint in the sand, are also recounted in the text of *Vendredi*.

Analysing the salvage operations of both Robinsons, Salkin Sbiroli demonstrates how, at apparently strategic points in each narrative, the two texts enjoy not only a close semantic relationship but, astonishingly, share a common syntax.[8] It is worth reproducing her comparisons, retaining the French translation of Defoe's text in order to emphasise the almost plagiaristic extent to which Tournier's narrative seems to depend on its literary forerunner:

> Comparison 1
>
> 'Là j'éprouvai un renouvellement de douleur; car je vis clairement que si nous fussions demeurés à bord nous eussions tous été sauvés.' (RC, 49)
>
> 'si l'équipage, faisant confiance à cette brave Virginie était demeuré dans l'entrepont au lieu de s'exposer sur le pont balayé par les lames, tout le monde aurait eu peut-être la vie sauvé.' (V, 23)

Comparison 2

'Parvenu au bâtiment, la grande difficulté était de savoir comment monter à
bord ... J'en fis deux fois le tour à la nage, et, la seconde fois, j'aperçus un
petit bout de cordage ... A l'aide de cette corde je me hissai sur le gaillard
d'avant.' (RC, 49)

'Parvenu à l'ombre monumentale de l'épave, il amarra son radeau sur le fond
et entreprit de faire à la nage le tour du bâtiment pour tenter de trouver un
moyen d'accès ... En se hissant à l'aide d'un filin qui pendait d'un écubier...'
(V, 23–24)

Here Tournier's Robinson seems to follow the same itinerary as his
predecessor, demarcated by the same mental procedures. However,
Martin Roberts has indicated that we should proceed cautiously with
such comparative exercises.[9] Just as Tournier latches on to the story
of the goat recounted in the legend of Alexander Selkirk, so incidental
details in Defoe's novel are seized upon and re-used to much greater
purpose in *Vendredi*. Roberts traces the interconnections between each
Robinson's stores of tobacco and gunpowder. In contrast to the
plentiful supplies of tobacco which Defoe's Robinson finds on the
island, Tournier's has precious little. The shortage becomes an issue in
the text. Vendredi is forbidden to smoke it, will inevitably do so
behind his master's back, and ignites the gunpowder. The explosion
is, of course, waiting to happen, because Robinson has recovered an
improbable forty barrels of gunpowder from the wreck which he
stashes in one place at the back of the cave. In contrast, Defoe's
Robinson breaks down his three barrels into smaller packets which he
then stores separately, fearing that his powder may be struck by
lightning. It would seem that the mirror which Tournier holds to
Defoe's novel reflects a distorted, at times grotesque image of the
original.

One of the most significant examples of textual comparison
concerns Robinson's agricultural production. For Salkin Sbiroli it is at
this point in the respective narratives, after the symbolic manufacturing
of the first loaf of bread, that 'la progression des deux itinéraires se
renverse'.[10] Defoe's Robinson recognises the futility and the sinfulness
of a surplus in production:

I found that the forty Bushels of Barley and Rice was much more than I could
consume in a Year; so I resolv'd to sow just the same Quantity every Year,
that I sow'd the last, in Hopes that such a Quantity would fully provide me
with Bread ... I might have rais'd Ship Loadings of Corn; but I had no use for
it; so I let as little grow as I thought enough for my Occasion.[11]

On the other hand, Tournier's Robinson derives a form of sublime consolation from his quantifiably successful harvests. He sees the chafing of the wheat as a purifying process:

> Son âme s'élevait vers Dieu et le suppliait de faire voltiger au loin les pensées frivoles dont il était plein pour ne laisser en lui que les lourdes semences de la parole de sagesse. A la fin il constata avec fierté que sa récolte se montait à trente gallons de blé et vingt gallons d'orge. (V, 60)

Naturally, Robinson becomes fully synonymous with the over-production of the industrial west. He encounters a major problem with the maintenance of his grain silos:

> Les silos de grain qui se multipliait d'année en année posèrent bientôt de graves problèmes de protection contre les rats ... Mais puisqu'il entendait ne pas cesser d'entasser récolte sur récolte aussi longtemps qu'il en aurait la force, il fallait sévir contre les parasites. (V, 85)

There is no possibility of a halt in production, for this Robinson finds value in the rhythm of his labour which helps combat what we are encouraged to perceive as his spiritual and mental deterioration. His less industrious predecessor thrives on the comfort and solace gained from reading the Bible, reassurances that are conspicuously and comically denied to the former. Their difference has an economic root, to which Genette does not hesitate to add a series of ethical and political oppositions.[12] The honest Christianity of Defoe's protagonist gives way to the neurotic figure in Tournier's novel who insists on carving into the rock of Speranza the proto-capitalist maxims he can remember from the almanacs of Benjamin Franklin, just in case any savages happen to pass by: 'Il avait donc entrepris de les inscrire dans la pierre, la terre, le bois, bref dans la chair même de Speranza pour tâcher de donner à ce grand corps un esprit qui lui convienne' (V, 140). However, the physical presence of Franklin's law indicates something other than a mere spiritual accessory to Robinson's existence. For Genette the identification of Tournier's Robinson with Benjamin Franklin frames the ideological difference between the two texts, and, moreover, imputes a critical aspect to Tournier's rewriting of Defoe's novel. This new association of the Crusoe character is seen to be an extension of a bodypolitik latent in the first narrative which contrasts with the notions of colonialism and assimilation present on the surface. In this context the writing of the maxims in *Vendredi* is a crucial event: 'Cette énonciation dégradante vaut évidemment pour une critique du modèle, qui ne percevait ni la détermination historique (accumulation

capitaliste déguisée en morale puritaine) ni la vanité de ses motiva-
tions'.[13]

Genette's formulation is, here, a reductive one within the conceptual
framework of *hypertextualité*, particularly since the grand hyperbole of
Robinson's administration of the island prior to the explosion develops
in proportion to a growing consciousness on his part of the existence of
the 'autre île'. Thus the significance of Franklin's almanac is quickly
attenuated as Robinson perceives the link between the two states of the
island: 'L'île administrée perdait son âme au profit de l'autre île et
devenait semblable à une énorme machine tournant à vide' (V, 140).
The image of Robinson's island as a huge, self-generating machine,
revolving uselessly in space, is telling. It is complemented by the
understated, semi-comical characterisation of the cohort of vultures,
who, from his first days on the island, haunt his every move. Robinson
immediately associates them with death; 'serviteurs de la mort', they
feast on the goat which Robinson has killed in his first act on regaining
consciousness after the shipwreck (V, 19), hover expectantly over the
weakened Robinson, and reappear mysteriously as he makes his final
ascent to the cave (V, 251). In such close attendance they are portrayed
as imitative. Always grouped together, they form a 'conseil d'administration', parodying Robinson's own grotesque attempts to govern
the island. By way of a clever parable Tournier takes the analogy one
step further. Robinson observes one day how a group of vultures gang
up on a small, though bloated, one of their number. They prod and
buffet it with beak and wings until it regurgitates a semi-digested meal
to provide a dish for the community, which is all the more palatable for
having been 'pre-cooked'. The incident is merely described: the absence
of a commentary from either narrator, Robinson, or some *occulté*, lets
the image echo with thoughts of the endless processes of refinement
involved in the production of the foodstuffs we consume.

What we see as the narrative progresses is a stretching of boundaries. The differences between the island as Robinson tries to mould it
(in the image of his culture) and the intangible 'other island' multiply
and begin to destabilise the relationship of *hypertextualité*. The frame
of the metaphorical equation in which the island manifests itself to
Robinson—as something 'other' which lies beyond his powers of
cognition and something which he has conquered and brought within
his albeit narrow conceptual horizon—widens. Yet, as we have seen,
the narrative of the *hypertexte* is constructed almost formalistically in
relation to its model. Robinson's failure to follow adequately the course

of events may be explained by the fact that they follow an alien logic, as the *hypertextualité* model is progressively overwritten by a narrative which functions in a mythic mode.

Tournier has publicly acknowledged that the year he spent studying under Claude Lévi-Strauss at the Musée de l'Homme played an important part in his subsequent thinking and proved especially fruitful when it came to the composition of *Vendredi*:

> Il ne me fallut pas moins de quinze ans pour exprimer à ma manière la leçon des sociétés dites 'primitives' et des bons sauvages qui les composent. Mais, lorsque j'eus publié *Vendredi ou Les limbes du Pacifique*, j'hésitai à envoyer ce petit roman lyrique à mon ancien maître. Pourtant la filiation ne devait pas demeurer secrète. Un critique américain écrivit aussitôt du roman: 'C'est Robinson Crusoé récrit par Freud, Walt Disney et Claude Lévi-Strauss.'[14]

Developed shortly after the end of the war, Lévi-Strauss's structural anthropology gave a renewed impetus to the science of ethnology. It was, and indeed still is, radical, because in identifying myth as a key, organising principle in other, non-western societies, Lévi-Strauss was the first to demonstrate that these so-called primitive societies had evolved in ways that were no less sophisticated than those of any other form of societal organisation, and that therefore the claim to superiority of western civilisation, based as it is on the rationalist ideals of the Enlightenment, was totally without foundation.[15] Comparing a vast array of myths predominating in various tribes of South American Indians, Lévi-Strauss discovered the synchronous presence of irreconcilable opposites: autochthony and biological birth, change and permanence, life and death, agriculture and hunting, peace and war. These oppositions are not always self-evident because at times the original terms have been replaced by others. In Lévi-Strauss's system this permutation of one term by another has as its object the finding of mediating terms between the opposites, which will permit the opposition to be dissolved or transcended. In this way mythical thinking does not operate differently from rationalist logic; it differs in its use of symbols, because in the place of propositions, axioms and abstract signs it makes use of heroes, gods, animals and other elements of the natural and cultural world. A simple example of this fluid structure is found in the customs of the Pueblo Indians, for whom change implies death. However, through the intervention of the mediator, agriculture, the equation is transformed into one resulting in vital growth. Likewise war, another synonym of death, is transformed into life by another mediation: hunting. The slightly contentious issue of Robinson's sexuality is a perfect example of how the binary structure of the Robinson Crusoe *hypertextualité* fuses into the mythic mode of Tournier's narration.

Robinson's sex life is absent from the pages of Defoe's novel. Therefore, it is reasonable to assume that the treatise on sexuality in *Vendredi* constitutes a major opposition between *hypo-* and *hypertexte*. The narrative of Robinson's log-book in *Vendredi* posits sexual desire as a socially constructed phenomenon obeying the unwritten laws and dictates of a specific, historical society. Robinson meditates on the subject at length:

> Ainsi le désir. C'est un torrent que la nature et la société ont emprisonné dans un bief, dans un moulin, dans une machine ... J'ai perdu mon bief, mon moulin, ma machine. En même temps que toute la construction sociale, tombée en ruine en moi d'année en année, a disparu l'échafaudage d'institutions et de mythes qui permet au désir de *prendre corps*. (V, 118)

The expression of Robinson's sexuality is conditional on his contact with the myths underpinning modes of sexual behaviour in his own culture, and, of course, this contact has now been severed. Therefore, in spite of Robinson's later admiration of Vendredi ('Soleil, rends-moi semblable à Vendredi', 216) and the alluring focalisation of the narrative on his physical attributes (see the extraordinarily detailed description of Vendredi's eye, 181), Vendredi and Robinson can never enter into sexual relations with each other, as the duality of their respective cultural histories requires a third-term mediator. Robinson confronts the issue directly in the final, retrospective entries in the log. Begging the question as to the absence of homosexual inclinations on his part towards Vendredi, he verbalises the protean form of his own myth: 'Il ne s'agissait pas de me faire régresser vers des amours humaines, mais sans sortir de l'élémentaire de me faire *changer d'élément*' (V, 229). The new element is Speranza. The physical form of the island itself mediates the conscious desire of first Robinson and then Vendredi: hence the description of Robinson copulating improbably with the 'combe rose', preceded by his 'adolescent' experimentation with the 'voie végétale' and followed by his discovery of the 'mandragore zébrée', and the ensuing comedy of the jealous suitors rivalling for the affections of the island. Like all mediators, Speranza is ambiguous. Robinson's analysis of his love affair immediately contradicts itself. He writes: 'Mes amours avec Speranza s'inspiraient encore fortement des modèles humaines. En somme, je fécondais cette terre comme j'aurais fait une épouse' (V, 229). From the moment when he receives a painful spider bite on the penis (V, 122), our suspicion is that the narration of Robinson's sexual encounters will turn out to be profoundly ironic.

Lévi-Strauss's method draws heavily on linguistic schemas since popularised by semiologists. In particular he reinscribes in his descriptions of the language of myth the fundamental processes of selection and combination which give rise to the linguistic expression, or speech act. Here, of course, he follows Roman Jakobson's delineation and polarisation of linguistic production along the axes of the paradigmatic and syntagmatic series, thus privileging the roles of metaphor and metonymy. For Lévi-Strauss the structure of myth, which is one of transformation and renewal, is governed according to the laws of metonymy. His method involves *in nuce* the transposition of Jakobson's poetic analyses into an anthropological context.[16] However, at the cut-off point between Man and the animal kingdom, at the inception of language, the possibility of metaphor emerges. 'Qui dit homme, dit langage, et qui dit langage dit société', affirms Lévi-Strauss, citing Rousseau in *Tristes tropiques*.[17] Now, the master-metaphor he chooses to represent the opposition in transition of Nature to Culture is that of the raw and the cooked. Or perhaps, remembering Tournier's evocation of the harrassing vulture harrassed, the metaphor chooses itself. In either event the review of 187 myths depicting the relations between the Bororo and Ge tribes of South America in the first volume of the *Mythologiques* is his most ambitious and far-reaching project. The narrative presents a series of contradictory symbols which follow on from each other with a dizzy intensity: the continuous and the discontinuous, the brevity of life and immortality, water and funeral ornaments, the fresh and the decayed, earth and sky, the open and the closed—the orifices of the human body turned into a symbolic system of ingestion and expulsion—the rock and the rotted log, cannibalism and vegetarianism, incest and parricide, hunting and agriculture, smoke and thunder ... Consequently the five senses are transformed into logical categories and upon this code to sensibility is superimposed an astronomy which is transformed into another code composed of the opposition of noise and silence, speech and song. All these myths are culinary metaphors, but in its turn, cooking is itself a myth, a metaphor of culture.

Many of these oppositions are familiar to the reader of *Vendredi*, to the extent that the very fabric of Tournier's novel can be said to reify Lévi-Strauss's myth of Culture. Death and water are both associated with enclosure. Robinson's final resting-place will be the deepest recess of the grotto, given that he has escaped the watery grave of his ship-mates and in particular the hull of the ship where Van Deyssel's corpse gulps grotesquely (V, 24). The inertia of the rocks upon which Robinson engraves the words of Benjamin Franklin is in contrast to the illusory log which turns into a goat (V, 99), and the vibrantly creative quality of the wood from which Vendredi makes his arrows, and to the non-utilitarian character of other Vendredi activities, notably his upside-down ('baroque') replanting of the shrubs (V, 163) and his performance as the 'homme-plante' (V, 164). Robinson witnesses a cannibalistic ritual (V, 76); after the explosion in the cave, he and Vendredi dine on fresh pineapple (V, 187). Also, when Vendredi exhales from Robinson's pipe, the smoke signals accrue writerly signification (V, 183), prefiguring the thunderous explosion; the noise of the explosion contrasts with the passing of the still, silent hours, as the immobile Vendredi contemplates the horizon (V, 180).

The temptation then is to read the novel through a mythological grid, in which Vendredi and Robinson would be seen as emblematic incarnations of Nature and Culture. To do so would be to misread the character of Vendredi, whose function is primarily creative. Vendredi mediates between Robinson and Nature. His mediation is exemplified in the opposition between the earth and the ether. Robinson is generally rooted to the ground, whereas Vendredi is fascinated by 'des choses aériennes', objects which harmonise with the ether—his arrows, the kite and the aeolian harp. And yet it is also through Vendredi that Robinson is finally liberated from the contingencies of his 'règne tell-urique' and accedes to the 'royaume solaire'. Vendredi—*venusté*—is myth itself. Having come from the sea, he departs by way of it, carried away on the 'grand voilier ... l'aboutissement triomphal et comme l'apothéose de cette conquête de l'éther' (V, 242). Water then becomes the third term, and mediates the earth/ether opposition, since, by virtue of its atomic density, it always occupies the central position in the simple chemical formula, solid–liquid–gas.

At the moment of their first dramatic meeting the camera pans out to encompass the perspectival fields of the two protagonists, and for a split second the reader is presented with the image of Robinson viewed by the Other, 'un homme blanc et barbu, hérissé d'armes, vêtu de peaux de biques, la tête couverte d'un bonnet de fourrure et farcie par trois millénaires de civilisation occidentale' (V, 144). Is the Other Vendredi? The employment of this narrative technique is disingenuous on the part of Tournier, for at no other point in the novel do we see events from Vendredi's perspective. Robinson is fascinated by Vendredi and eventually converted to his way of life, but it is the fate of the colonialist with which the book is concerned. Vendredi arrives, then leaves. His origins and destination are unimportant. As Genette reminds us, Robinson is 'le *maître* du récit, et d'un récit qui raconte son histoire, non celle de Vendredi'.[18] In this context, Tournier's assertion that *Vendredi* is dedicated to 'tous ces Vendredi dépêchés vers nous par le tiers monde' (VP, 230) is naïve, and exposes a central weakness in the novel. If Tournier wanted to show glimmerings of what life might have been like had mankind opted for a different evolutionary path—and this, I think, is the likely explanation for his desire to import Lévi-Strauss in such significant measure into the text—then in *Robinson Crusoe* his choice of myth is suspect, for Defoe's novel is shot through with the empirico-colonialist ideology of the eighteenth century. Therefore, in spite of its non-western, 'mythological' structure, Tournier's novel, in its fascination with the historical and literary origins of his chosen myth, is haunted by myth in its socio-political dimension. This is the residue of Lévi-Strauss's anthropological schema, the ways of discussing, preserving, distorting cultural activity that, as Roland Barthes and Umberto Eco have shown, are encrypted in the very fabric of western society. We need look no further than the example Barthes chooses to exemplify his theory of myth as second-order signification, the photograph of the black soldier on the cover of *Paris-Match* saluting the tricolour. This contemporaneous, propagandist image even—Barthes' anecdote relates approximately to a time when the seeds of the Algerian War were germinating—purports to show the Republican ideal of assimilation in an optimistic light, when in every detail it recalls the colonialist practice on which the policy of assimilation was founded and therefore the surviving colonialist attitudes of the French political establishment and the wider populace. As we shall see later, Tournier's characterisation of Vendredi is initially no more than a projection of Robinson's own fears and anxieties. Later, when Vendredi assumes independent status, his activities are subordinated to an abstract, philosophical discourse. Everything he does is motivated by the concerns of a narrator who speaks in no more neutral tones than those of his subject, Robinson.[19]

TEXTUAL METAPHORS: THE TAROT AND THE BIBLE

Readers of *Vendredi* are constantly brought back to issues of language and signification. The question of how we make sense through language and other associated sign systems infiltrates Robinson's story so thoroughly that before even the arrival on the island of Vendredi, the quest for a philosophy of meaning has become the principal point at issue. Two textual metaphors play an important part in this narrative, and these are the Tarot card prologue and Robinson's Bible.

In contrast to the rewriting enterprise, the Tarot prologue suggests innovation. As the tempest rages prior to the foundering of the *Virginie*, a Tarot card reading performed by the demonic figure of the captain, Van Deyssel, is addressed to Robinson. This episode is arranged as a preface to the narrative of Robinson's adventures on the island, and in classical fashion the preface proposes its own interpretive code to the novel. Van Deyssel's marginally retrospective commentary on the divination underlines the narratological importance of the event:

> Le petit discours que je vous ai tenu … est en quelque sorte chiffré, et la grille se trouve être votre avenir lui-même. Chaque événement futur de votre vie vous révélera en se produisant la vérité de telle ou telle de mes prédictions. Cette sorte de prophétie n'est point aussi illusoire qu'il peut paraître tout d'abord. (V, 13)

The Egyptian Tarot is the metaphor for myth *par excellence*. The individual cards depict the gods, heroes, the colour of myth, each card a riddle in isolation, 'un inintelligible galimatias', Van Deyssel warns Robinson, to be solved via its representation in contiguity which is mediated through the person of the divinator. Laid out in predictive sequence the cards assume a totality, a text in effect, anticipating future events in the narrative, etching out a forward movement to counter the desire for a return to source that is always present in myth. The Tarot also dramatises the interpretive process.[20] Each card is a signifier with an iconic aspect, denotative only in its relation to the others but infinitely connotative in itself. In *Vendredi* the Tarot appears as a threshold text in the sense that it invents a chronology to frame each future stage of narration. Van Deyssel literally timetables the next 28 years, 2 months and 19 days of Robinson's life. This corroboration of narrative time proves irresistible to the reader, who is drawn into a game whereby he becomes accustomed to search for the answers to questions posed by the mysteries of Robinson's life on the island in the prophetic mythology of the Tarot. Robinson himself is eventually tempted to review the transformation that has taken place in his life in the light of what remains stored in his memory of Van Deyssel's peroration (V, 228–29).

The Tarot is then a microcosm of the text that it inhabits. Indeed, the network of semantic features linking it to the main body of the text is so carefully constructed that Lynn Salkin Sbiroli, from the premise of a close reading of the main text combined with her personal knowledge of the arcana, is able to identify the missing card in the sequence, the one which Van Deyssel alludes to but refrains from naming.[21] In structural terms, the Tarot acts as a sort of text-generating metaphor, although it is already a text in itself. Salkin Sbiroli maintains that *Vendredi* is based on the rewriting of two named texts, Defoe's original novel and the Tarot reading prologue, each conspiring to launch a narrative that exists consequently under a mode of dual control, in a state of constant *alternance* between the 'répétition syntagmatique', or dependence on the Father text, and the plunge into an 'initiation ésotérique', prompted by the Tarot cards.[22] Salkin Sbiroli's reader is therefore embroiled in a series of cross-checking manoeuvres, necessarily interrupting the temporal flux that is the essence of narrative discourse. By dint of its temporal anachrony, the Tarot weaves an 'intrigue de prédestination', to use Todorov's expression,[23] into the fabric of the narration. However, it is not until the aftermath of the explosion in the cave that the narrative signals its recognition of this structure of prefiguration, when the narrator finally discloses the information: 'Vendredi avait imperturbablement—et inconsciemment—préparé puis provoqué le cataclysme qui préluderait à l'avènement d'une ère nouvelle' (V, 188). Now, with hindsight, Robinson's sexually-charged descent into the cave reads as an initiation to the relationship he subsequently enjoys with Speranza. Likewise, the rush of euphoria he experiences, having realised for the first time that he is no longer subject to the time-clock of his former working life (V, 29), prefigures the morning when he wakes to find that the clepsydra has stopped (V, 93).

If the Tarot prophecy merely cloaks the narrative of *Vendredi* with a sense of the inevitable, it is difficult to see how this new incarnation of Defoe's Providence has significantly altered things. The difference is that in the modern narrative the function of the figure is formalised. The Tarot is a form of prefiguration, which, by virtue of its specific temporal character, is in radical disjunction with the narratological function of another text featured in the narrative of *Vendredi*, namely

Robinson's log-book. We recall that the adventures of the hero in *Robinson Crusoe* are recounted retrospectively. In picaresque fashion the narrative originates in Robinson's journal, but this conceit cannot disguise, however hard it tries, the temporal lapse between event and narration. In *Vendredi*, however, the lacuna is all but erased, as the writing subject is incorporated into the fiction. Robinson's entries in his log-book portray the illusion of a realist actuality, in which the difference in story and narrative time is contracted so as to give the impression of temporal achrony.[24] Robinson's 'live' narrative countermands the overtly anachronistic concept of narrative imparted to the text by the Tarot cards. The disjunction is doubly ironic. The insertion of the first-person narrative into a framework of heterodiegetic narration functions as a technique for conveying realism, and yet in his writing of the self-same narrative Robinson consciously challenges assumptions underlying the realist conception of narrative as representation. Similarly, the Tarot reading that purports to represent the narrative of fiction animates (but only briefly) the ghost of Providence which saw the first Robinson safely through his time on the island.

It is the stability of the figure, preserved in the form of a preface from attrition by a tide of narrative, which poses the central question concerning the Tarot sequence in *Vendredi*. Since it claims to speak not only the truth but future truths, the Tarot aspires to metaphorical status. However, the positioning of the figure outside the body of the text provides flimsy protection, for the truth value of the divination crumbles, before even the start of Chapter 1. Van Deyssel distinguishes between the allusive mode of the Tarot and the impossibility of a clear vision of the future. 'Imaginez-vous les désordres qu'engendrerait une prévision lucide de l'avenir?' (V, 13) is his rhetorical question, spoken moments before the ship is smashed on the rocks. Robinson, the sole human survivor, will ultimately fail to bring order to the chaos of Speranza. The profane version of the Calvinist belief in predestination that framed the life of his literary predecessor has little bearing on his own experience as a castaway. Rather the sum of these experiences leads Robinson to make an existential choice, to remain permanently on the island. On the other hand, the Tarot provides the ultimate illusion of a coherent world in which meaning can be fixed, the foolish certainty of the framed sign, which, as the narrative unfolds, collapses into irony. Whilst scouring the wreck of the ship for provisions, Robinson encounters Van Deyssel, the divinator whom he had credited with supernatural powers, once again. As if by magic the corpse comes to life. The body quivers, the mouth opens, and, having shinned up the dead man's gullet, a rat exits (V, 24).

If the revelatory potential of the Tarot is largely unfulfilled in *Vendredi*, in the sense that it closes down rather than opens up vistas, the function of the Bible in the text, traditionally a restraining influence in people's lives, is liberating. The Holy Bible is the only literature available to Robinson Crusoe. In *Vendredi* he reads it often; in *Robinson Crusoe* less so. Defoe's intrepid pioneer is so sure in his Christian faith that he need only read odd lines of the scriptures and all doubt is banished from his mind (RC, 96–97). His impulse is to pray rather than to read. On the contrary, his twentieth-century ancestor exalts the Text, exclaiming on several occasions during the narrative, 'O Livre des livres' (V, 26, 167, 178, 179). It is not that the Bible is necessarily Robinson's favourite book. Rather, the references to his reading in *Vendredi* suggest an idea which is conceptually absent from Defoe's text; they draw attention to the power which western society invests in the written word. Moreover, Robinson's little epithet allows us a brief glimpse at the *architexte* upon which this power is based.

The term *architexte* is used by Michel Foucault to hypostasise the history of mankind as it is produced, through the development of language and its subsequent appropriation in discourse. Foucault sees the origin of the representative function of language, which we so often take for granted, in the Hebrew alphabet. 'L'hébreu porte donc, comme des débris, les marques de la nomination première',[25] he affirms. Each instance of discourse, each new form of language, is, Foucault argues, an attempt to do what is impossible, to rejoin a primary, edenic state of representation, when nature came into being through discourse. These discourses are the various means at our disposal for interpreting the world around us. The reality of discourse is also the desire to return. Foucault defines both as *l'interprétation*:

> Le langage se donne pour tâche de restituer un discours absolument premier, mais il ne peut l'énoncer qu'en l'approchant, en essayant de dire à son propos des choses semblables à lui, et en faisant naître ainsi à l'infini les fidélités voisines et similaires de l'interprétation. Le commentaire ressemble indéfiniment à ce qu'il commente et qu'il ne peut jamais énoncer; la tâche infini du commentaire se rassure par la promesse d'un texte effectivement écrit que l'interprétation un jour révélera en son entier.[26]

Foucault's writing betrays a desire to allegorise, and yet his theory is only partly allegorical because the other term, the 'texte primitif', is not known. Maureen Quilligan discerns two distinct traditions of allegorical writing: secular allegory (chief practitioners of which would include Swift, Melville and Pynchon) and biblical allegory (of which Spenser's poetry and Kierkegaard's philosophy provide notable examples). The former mode is characterised by a celebration of language and textuality, manifest at the level of the text in a proliferation of puns and alliteration. In the latter, however, allegory figures a quest for truth which is the pre-text for discourse. In the Judaeo-Christian tradition, the pre-text for literature is nominally the Old and New Testaments.[27]

The character of Robinson Crusoe was born of the powerful unison established between the Word of God and the truth claims of empirical science that was to dominate philosophical thinking in eighteenth-century England and thereafter. The language of paradox, or indeed any form of ambiguous thinking, is notionally absent from such an absolutist world, and so it is with the fiction of *Robinson Crusoe*. Although Defoe's narrative is obviously not a biblical allegory, it does have a strong affinity with the genre. All biblical allegory is predicated upon the radical reversal of the descriptive order activated in the first verses of the Gospel According to John, in which it is stated that God's Word preceded the creation of the World. Shipwrecked on a desert island, Crusoe's task is to create a new world in the image of the Word. He draws up an itinerary under the joint headings of Evil and Good (RC, 66). Each aspect of his existence which is categorised as evil has its correlate in the Good section, which therefore defines the path that he must follow. On one occasion during a period of depression Robinson falters, crying out in desperation at his plight, 'Why has God done this to me? What have I done to be thus us'd?' (RC, 92). He is forcefully reproached for such weakness by the Voice of his Conscience, reminding him that he is lucky to be alive.

Robinson's actions are governed by an intentional structure in which life is seen as the mirror of a Pascalian duality. Having worked out a binary system of values, he can then live his life in accordance with those included in the positive set with little need for recourse to biblical intervention. Only on two further occasions does the journal summon up the words of the Sacred Text, firstly in order to extol the virtues of work, and then later as a means to educate Friday. The struggle is a more desperate one for Tournier's Robinson in *Vendredi*. The Bible he has salvaged from the wreck, his 'seul viatique spirituel', mitigates against sensual temptation in the form of the *souille*, the mud-bath in which he likes to wallow from time to time, and which he sees as the symbol of his 'démission en face du monde extérieur' (V, 39).

However, the repetition of the Pascalian schema has a precarious hold on reality this time. When this Robinson asks for a sign to show that God has not forsaken him, he is feted, absurdly, with a divine revelation, 'Plus qu'un arc-en-ciel, c'était comme une auréole presque parfaite' (V, 31). Later he recognises that a second vision, of a ship combing the littoral with the silhouette of his long-dead sister at the prow, was only a mirage.

One of the primary factors which differentiates Tournier's Robinson from his predecessor is his desire to interpret the vicissitudes of his life through the language of the Bible. He is not familiar with the style on account of his Quaker background. Quakers believe that there should be no intercession in the communication that takes place between God and Man, and therefore for them the Bible plays a relatively minor part in what is a highly personal form of worship. Although Robinson may regard the Bible as the one form of spiritual sustenance at his disposal, he has not received the sort of education which transmits the lessons of life through the parables, and therefore his reading of the Text has not been desensitised during childhood. From his initial reading activity on the island, Robinson wonders at the fire and brimstone of the Old Testament (V, 45), and the shadow of Defoe's text soon recedes. Replacing it, a consistent pattern is established whereby each reproduction of biblical text (which is usually read aloud by Robinson) in the narrative is modulated by the emotional state of the protagonist. In each case he turns to the text in need of spiritual support only to embark on a journey of interpretation during which codified religious truths are broken down to reveal new possibilities of meaning. An entire narrative tradition of biblical allegory comes under threat in *Vendredi*, as Robinson begins to read the scriptures as an allegory of his own extraordinary experience.

The first significant reference occurs after his libidinal exploration of the grotto. Due to the drought afflicting the island his two fresh water springs have dried up, so Robinson pushes deeper into the forest in search of a new source. The one he finds is in the shape of 'un mamelon de terre', upon which he joyously clamps his lips to suck in the 'liquide vital'. Into this narrative of Freudian symbiosis (the coalescence of need and desire in the oral-genitory drive) are intercalated the words of Moses, '*Enfants d'Israël, je vous ferai entrer dans une terre ruisselante de lait et de miel*' (V, 113). Moses' invocation to the children of Israel, preceding the parting of the Red Sea, is a favourite refrain from Robinson's past. The literal associations of the

Prophet's words offer a new, less compromising interpretation of his experience in the underground cavern, where, on the brink of sexual satisfaction, Robinson had suddenly confronted the image of his mother. This moment of calm in the days of mental turbulence following his descent into the grotto is the prelude to a triumphal confirmation of his love for Speranza conveyed through oral readings from the Book of Isaiah (V, 134). A few pages on, and he discovers the lovers' discourse in The Song of Songs. The metaphorical nature of this biblical paen to sexuality, in which the sensual pleasure of the lovers becomes part of a terrestrial communion with animals and plants, complements Robinson's relation to his island so perfectly that he and Speranza enact the roles of the eulogising lovers in their own performance of the song (V, 135).[28]

These lengthy citations of biblical verse serve a double purpose in the narrative design of Tournier's novel. Firstly, Robinson's biblical perorations appearing on the pages of the novel as the printed presence of the Bible as text provide a sense of ethical justification for Robinson's conduct that encodes the theologically difficult issue of sexuality. Secondly, and more importantly, the view of language (and especially biblical language) as the pure refraction of the world that it describes (or brings into being) is rebuffed in this demonstration of the fundamentally poetic character of the text. Already the theory has been ventured that Robinson's desire is innately and unconsciously poetic, that it recreates his own historical passage phonetically, from the 'lombes' (which belonged presumably to his mother) through to the 'limbes' of the Pacific to end in the spillage of his sperm over the 'combe rose'. With the reproduction of these archetypal verses in which meaning is primarily dispensed through figurative language, the veil is lifted on the rhetoricity of the Bible. The celebration of Robinson's love affair is also the celebration of the 'imaging' power of language: 'La Bible débordante d'images qui identifient la terre à une femme ou l'épouse à un jardin accompagnait ses amours du plus vénérable des épithalames' (V, 136).

References to the Scriptures in *Vendredi* further awaken a desire on behalf of the reader to interpret texts poetically. Biblical scholars have long maintained that any reading of the Bible in translation is an impoverished one.[29] To appreciate fully the text it is necessary to read Hebrew, though the very nature of the passages quoted in *Vendredi* tends to dispute the idea that semantic richness is dramatically reduced when the original text is filtered through successive translations.

Robinson takes refuge in a modified form of textuality, in which the text is seen to hold the key to human understanding. He describes it with gusto, 'Lire la Bible, c'est monter au sommet d'une montagne d'où l'on embrasse du même regard toute l'île et l'immensité océane qui la cerne' (V, 167). Mortified at the discovery of the striped mandrakes, he charges through his Bible in search of the essential passage that will condemn without equivocation Vendredi's misdemeanour. Initially he hunts out verses he knows to be suitable for the occasion. However, Ecclesiastics Chapter 4 appears reproachful of Robinson's attitude, and the wrath of Yahweh in Isaiah 30 is directed at nobody in particular. Once again Robinson resorts to random selections from the text, which he reads aloud, but this time catharsis gives way to confusion. Hosea 11:4, corroborated by the Book of Jeremiah, castigates the adulteress alone, and Genesis 39 tells the tale of some men who were wrongfully imprisoned for adulteries they had not committed. Robinson is forced to conclude that Vendredi's involvement in the affair is accidental (V, 179).

The materialisation of biblical text in the narrative of *Vendredi* creates the conditions for an allegorical relationship. In allegory the narrative action is reflected on the surface of the letter; it is not, as is assumed by traditionalists, visible through a kind of linguistic disguise. Quilligan demonstrates how allegory provokes an interesting inversion of people's reading habits:

> When a reader is reading the 'literal level' (in traditional parlance), he is actually reading the 'metaphorical' level—that is, he watches the imaginary action in his mind's eye: the landscape flies by, the pilgrimage goes on with its bustle. The only way to return a reader from imagining such a distracting 'level' of action to thoughts about the significance this action ought to hold for him is to deny him the colorful journey.[30]

In order to alert the reader to the coded meanings of its figurative narrative, the allegorical text implements various rhetorical strategies, including an extensive and generally overlooked use of puns. Through what is essentially its self-reflexive mode, allegory thus produces its own commentary. The result, according to Northrop Frye, is the enslavement of the reader, who is led by the nose in quest of a predetermined meaning which the text eventually may, or may not, choose to reveal. Quilligan sees the allegorist as a more benevolent tyrant. She maintains that, through this mode of repressive textuality unique to allegory, the genre sets itself up as a metaphor encapsulating not only the reading process but the entire structure through which art communicates, from inception to reception. The reader of poems, plays, concerts and paintings is traditionally passive and therefore resistant to analysis; the reader of allegory on the other hand is forced into the equation, often quite dramatically. This is what happens to Robinson. Initially happy to use the Text as a foil to his own imagination, his reading is progressively consumed by his desire to interpret, and he is drawn inexorably towards the artefact of the text itself until eventually he is completely captivated, mesmerised by the letters on the page, 'La parole du Prophète se tord en signes noirs sur la page blanche' (V, 177). However, what the reader loses in freedom he makes up in significance, and Robinson enjoys special privileges. Quilligan affirms that in those allegories where the reader is construed as a voyeur looking into the action of a conventional, realist narrative, there is often a shift in each direction along the axis of communication. The reader becomes 'the central character', in an allegory, 'the narrative may be said to "read" him.'[31] From the moment when Robinson is symbolically reborn on to Speranza (as he re-emerges from the cave), his experiences are structured for a considerable period of narrative time (approximately 40 pages) through the text of the Bible. What first appeared in the narrative as *defamiliarisation* (Robinson's copulation with the 'combe rose') is consequently 'understood' when it is read through the poetry of the Bible. Henceforth Robinson's participation in the fiction equates to the active role played by the reader of allegory, one of gradual self-discovery which continues, in his case, after the allegory has been abruptly curtailed.

The effect of allegory in *Vendredi* is one of displacement. Robinson's faith in God is replaced by an equally absolute faith in the Word. More importantly, as Robinson steps into the shoes of the reader of allegory, we, as readers of the book in which this allegorical reading takes place, are distanced from the allegorical functioning of the text. It is not long before the implicit irony attendant at the pressure-point of the allegorical reading, at that moment when the desire to know turns to frustration, erupts. Having rummaged frantically through the text in search of the correct reading of his cuckoldry, Robinson gives up: 'Le Livre des livres s'est prononcé, et il condamne Speranza! Ce n'est pas ce que cherchait Robinson' (V, 177). The sovereign authority of the Bible as firstly the Word of God, and secondly the first poem, is laid to rest.

LANGUAGE AND THE COSMOS

Tournier has always defended the rewriting of *Vendredi* on the grounds
that the metaphysical speculation contained in the first novel detracts
from its aesthetic or narrative qualities. However, notwithstanding the
attendant issues of self-censorship and children's literature (which are
discussed in Chapter 5), few commentators agree that *Vendredi ou La
vie sauvage* constitutes an improvement.[32] This may be because the
most intriguing facet of Tournier's first novel is precisely the philosophical debate which evolves in the course of the narrative and breaks
the skin of the literary discourse at those junctures where the intrepid
protagonist embarks on investigations into the purpose of language and
writing, where he asks what language can and cannot tell us about the
individual and his relation to the world around him. These are the
points at which the novel is at its most exciting, and they are to be
found chiefly in the solipsistic narrative of Robinson's log-book.

In *Robinson Crusoe* the testimony of the hero is never questioned.
His time on the island is viewed retrospectively through the unifocal
lens of a first person narrator who assumes the same identity as the
fictional character. Crusoe, we are told, began to keep a diary, the
carefully-dated extracts of which are reproduced in the body of the text
labelled 'Journal', as if to authenticate the phenomenon of his survival.
But the style of this journal is too full, its author too confident. He is
never fearful of what might happen on the next day, because he already
knows. Crusoe's journal is not, and can never be, a contemporaneous
recording of events; it is an annotated, reflected-upon narrative of
things past. The memoir is normally judgemental in tone. However,
Defoe gathers his narrative under the heading of 'JOURNAL', so that
Robinson's story appears to be historically validated. This scrap of
evidence, amounting maybe to little more than a slip of the pen, entails
that Defoe's teleology is rounded off with a question mark. The legend
of Robinson Crusoe signifies in its widest sense the inevitable appropriation of virgin territory by western culture. What is naturally lacking
in Defoe's novel is the realisation that Robinson Crusoe is only a
metaphor for a historical process set in motion by western imperialism,
and that this history is finite. The expansion of the west has of course
been fuelled by scientific discovery. However, it is only in the last
twenty-five years that philosophers have taken up Hegel's legacy and
begun to expound on the innate contradiction in the idea of Progress;
namely that Man's betterment through technology is in inverse

proportion to the finitude of the Earth's resources. The quicker we progress, the nearer comes the dawn of extinction. And yet the myth of Robinson Crusoe, which is ultimately the myth of Progress, is perpetuated, even as we totter on the edge of a new world in which the bond forged by Descartes between human logic and the function of language, visibly consolidated by, and ratified in, writing, buckles under the strain of technology.

In 1965 Michel Foucault queried the arrogance of our logos, comprising the entire tradition of western metaphysics, in its unquestionable presumption to reflect, describe and order human life:

> Qu'est-ce que le langage? Qu'est-ce qu'un signe? Ce qui est muet dans le monde, dans nos gestes, dans tout le blason énigmatique de nos conduites, dans nos rêves et nos maladies—tout cela parle-t-il, et quel langage tient-il, selon quel grammaire? Tout est-il signifiant, ou quoi, et pour qui et selon quelles règles? Quel rapport y a-t-il entre le langage et l'être, et est-ce bien à l'être que toujours s'adresse le langage, celui, du moins, qui parle vraiment? Qu'est-ce donc que ce langage, qui ne dit rien, ne se tait jamais et s'appelle 'littérature'?[33]

Today, the primacy of the written language with its strategies of grammar and codes of rhetoric, is rapidly being eroded. In societies across the globe the typology of the text has given way to the touch screen and the disk, the voice-activated device and the storage chip. Yet there is little awareness of the possible consequences of this decline. Jacques Derrida maintains that a grammatology, or science of writing, permeates the history of the west at all levels. He draws up an impressive list of the developments in human culture said to be associated with, motivated by, or constructed through the letter:

> ... que tous les clergés, exerçant ou non un pouvoir politique, se soient constitués en même temps que l'écriture et par la disposition de la puissance graphique; que la stratégie, la balistique, la diplomatie, l'agriculture, la fiscalité, le droit pénal soient liés dans leur histoire et leur structure à la constitution de l'écriture; que la possibilité de la capitalisation et de l'organisation politico-administrative soit toujours passé par la main des scribes qui firent l'enjeu de nombreuses guerres et dont la fonction a toujours été irréductible, quel que fût le défilé des délégations dans lesquelles on a pu la voir à l'oeuvre; ... que le sens même du pouvoir et de l'efficacité en général, qui n'a pu apparaître en tant que tel, en tant que sens et maîtrise ... ait toujours été lié à la disposition de l'écriture.[34]

Derrida's extravagant subjunctive clause is intended to demonstrate, with obvious irony in the way that he manipulates the grammatical construction, the absolute arbitrariness of this *écriture* to which we habitually assign such enormous value. These stratifications of meaning are the result of what he terms 'la violence de la lettre'; subsequently, his reading of Rousseau's *Essai sur l'origine des langues* becomes a search for a rhetoric of writing which will allow him to go beyond this epistemology of presence. A derridean perspective will always stress the invidious, ideological character of what we think of as 'writing'. However, Derrida's assertion that *écriture* is like a biological species— its ultimate fate is extinction—allied to the bewildering speed of current technological change begs a number of questions. How we are going to function in a society when the conventions of the language by which that society is organised no longer apply? And what kind of society will it be? We are indeed entering into the age of Nietzsche's Superman, and Robinson Crusoe is once again a significant model.

In *Vendredi* Robinson is only too aware of his need to function within a framework of language. Article II of his Charter for the Island of Speranza reads: 'Perdre la faculté de la parole par défaut d'usage est l'une des plus humiliantes calamités qui me menacent...' (V, 72). In order to exist as a human being he must express himself through language. For his existence to be meaningful, it must connect to his personal history in the form of tangible, unforgettable expression. In Chapter Three he is provided with the means to realise these as yet unstated objectives in the shape of the blanched pages of books he has recovered from the wreck. Significantly, the narrative details the processes involved in the drying out of the paper and the making of the quill and ink substitute. For Robinson the importance of the act of writing cannot be exaggerated: 'Il lui semblait soudain s'être à demi arraché de l'abîme de bestialité où il avait sombré et faire sa rentrée dans le monde de l'esprit en accomplissant cet acte sacré: écrire' (V, 44). However, in contrast to the material problems that need to be solved if he is to embark on his writing project, the narrative reminds us subtly of the ephemerality of the letter, exemplified by the missing text of the ship's books, washed by the sea into oblivion.[35]

Through the medium of his log-book, Robinson conducts an exhaustive philosophical inquiry. At stake is the Cartesian principle, ironically compromised by the lack of that which is excluded from the cogito, namely, the voice of the Other. Robinson wishes to found his existence, his administration of the island, along the lines of classical Rationalism, so that Speranza would become subject to the laws of mathematics, apportioned and classified into different areas of a corporate knowledge. 'Je veux, j'exige que tout autour de moi soit dorénavant mesuré, prouvé, certifié, mathématique, rationnel...' (V,

67), he contests in the log-book, but the tone is almost hysterical. Robinson soon realises that he must embark on a search for a different philosophy if he is to protect his mind from the attacks of insanity induced by solitude, the effects of which are crushing, 'Et ma solitude n'attaque pas que l'intelligibilité des choses. Elle mine jusqu'au fondement même de leur existence' (V, 54). His primary defence mechanism stems from the mere fact of being able to write. Writing the log-book enables him to verbalise his worst fears and leads him indirectly to analyse for the first time the form of linguistic expression, rather than its content, as philosophy. Robinson sees his own command of language as the external indicator of his mental state. The log-book makes this link explicit one day when he is depressed and gripped by lethargy: 'Il est inutile de se le dissimuler; tout mon édifice cérébral chancelle. Et le délabrement du langage est l'effet le plus évident de cette érosion' (V, 68). His solution to this difficulty in thinking is to reduce the scope of his own language. The decision-making process is recorded in a momentous passage taken from the narrative of the log-book:

> Il me vient des doutes sur le sens des mots qui ne désignent pas des choses concrètes. Je ne puis plus parler qu'à la lettre. La métaphore, la litote et l'hyperbole me demandent un effort d'attention démesuré dont l'effet inattendu est de faire ressortir tout ce qu'il y a d'absurde et de convenu dans ces figures de rhétorique. (V, 68)

Robinson laments the prospect of a philosophy that is not founded on the secure basis of a language confident of its referential capacity. Alone on the island, it is this certainty of the functioning of the representational faculties of his thought which is in doubt, 'Des points fixes sur lesquels la pensée prend appui pour progresser—comme on marche sur les pierres émergeant du lit d'un torrent—s'effritent, s'enfoncent' (V, 68). The narrative of the log-book, that grants to Robinson the privilege of his own, private, philosophical discourse, is invaded from all sides by metaphor. In the example cited above, thought is a series of stepping-stones which are crumbling and caving in on each other. Not content with this construction of a geological topos to convey the sense of a language losing its proper, original, intended meaning, Robinson abdicates his role as rhetorician with a phraseological tour de force on a grand scale: 'Je conçois que ce processus dont je suis le théâtre serait pain béni pour un grammairien ou un philologue vivant en société: pour moi, c'est un luxe à la fois inutile et meurtrier' (V, 68). It is an apt description of his cultural estrangement; from the arts ('le théâtre'), religion ('pain béni'), language ('un grammairien ou un philologue') and economic life ('un luxe').

Robinson's self-conscious declaration spotlights a unifying theme, that of the historical distinction between proper and figurative language, which is entirely consonant with Tournier's rewriting project. The narrative of *Robinson Crusoe* exemplifies a philosophical tradition, established by the contributions of Locke and Hobbes and consolidated through Berkeley and Hume, which sees the manifestation of any rhetorical form as a *deviation* from the proper use of language and, therefore, from their concern with the truth. However, we have seen how, starting with the rewriting of the precursor text itself, the narrative of *Vendredi* has erected a panoply of rhetorical devices and effects that confuses this discrimination between the figurative and the proper modes of language, to the extent that such a distinction appears quite arbitrary. For example, early in the novel we learn of the special, symbolic status that Robinson accords to the loaf of bread, 'il attachait un prix infini au pain, symbole de vie, unique nourriture citée dans le *Pater*' (V, 46). However, the manufacture of the bread is primarily a sensual experience, which, in the narrative of the log-book, launches a sexual fantasy about a baker's boy.[36] Here Robinson is possibly recalling a hitherto suppressed incident from his own past; the panification has implications, we are told, 'tout individuelles ... cachées, intimes, enfouies parmi les secrets honteux de sa petite enfance' (V, 80). The truth is immaterial; what matters is the revelation of this 'symbol of life' in its plenitude. Obscured by the hurly-burly of everyday existence, the symbol is consciously remotivated through the act of writing, 'En pétrissant ma pâte ... j'ai fait renaître en moi les images oblitérées par le tumulte de la vie' (V, 80).

If the attention to rhetorical forms in the narrative of *Vendredi* is as pervasive as I have implied, then it is not surprising that, contrary to the express desire of the author, the narrative of his log-book should set off on the trail of a philosophy of language, more in the radical tradition of Aristotle than Plato. Immediately following the first overt reference to the question of language and meaning, the analysis begins. Robinson takes the conceptual schema invoked by the binary opposition in the terms *surface* and *depth* and shows that the values we habitually ascribe to these notions—a person who is described as deep is usually strong of character, intelligent and out of the ordinary, a person described as superficial would therefore be weak, fickle, stupid and mundane—are significant only in their form as linguistic constructs (V,

69). Then he applies the same principles to the relation of his own person to Speranza, only to arrive at the devastating negativity of a version of reality reduced to Saussurean linguistics: 'Je sais bien, moi ... que je ne suis qu'un trou noir au milieu de Speranza, un point de vue sur Speranza—un point, c'est-à-dire rien' (V, 70). The only solution to the dilemma is for Robinson to transcend somehow the spatial and temporal configurations that govern the production of language, those metaphors pertaining to the inner and the outer, surface and depth, to the finite and the infinite, through which we conceive of the world. His endeavour is intimately bound up with the act of writing, the log-book and the logos.

Colin Davis charts the progress of the philosophical speculations in the log-book from a doctrine at the outset of pure Cartesianism through to a radical contestation of Sartrian phenomenology.[37] There is no doubt that Sartre's illustration of 'la structure Autrui' in *L'Etre et le Néant* prefigured the development of a full-blooded structuralism in the French academy. However, Sartre was ultimately unable to jettison a conceptual system of knowledge, in which modes of perception and understanding battle back like salmon against the flow to the fixed abodes of subject and object. Robinson has no such inhibitions. He dispenses entirely with the bulwark of rationalist epistemology: 'Or le sujet et l'objet ne peuvent coexister, puisqu'ils sont la même chose' (V, 100). Gilles Deleuze maintains that Sartre's inability to go beyond subject/object formulations is due to his insistence on defining structure through active perception. Tournier's Robinson accedes to a completely different order of being, one that is governed by metaphor, through what might be called an imaging mode of perception. Deleuze's corrective to Sartre's logic is informative in this case. Rather than existing contemporaneously with the moment of perception, he argues that 'la structure Autrui' precedes it. The look defines that instance when somebody appears in the frame, 'le regard ne fait qu'effectuer, actualiser une structure qui doit être définie indépendamment'.[38]

In philosophical terms, Speranza equates to a state of intemporality, located in the 'limbes du Pacifique', before the boundaries between subject and object are staked out in language. As such it is a metaphor for a primary state of consciousness to which Robinson is now admitted, a natural world existing prior to its coming-into-being through a language where objects signify intuitively. These objects exist in pure sense; the model of the candle illuminating the contents of a darkened room is replaced with the revitalising vision of a display of phosphorescent objects bathing in the light of their own existence. More than anything else, Tournier's desert island is the land of myth and metaphor of Rousseau's *Discours sur l'origine et les fondements de l'inégalité parmi les hommes* that precipitates the fall of Man. By invoking this primordial state of natural communion, Robinson is able to redefine the relation of the island to himself:

> Alors Robinson est Speranza. Il n'a conscience de lui-même qu'à travers les frondaisons des myrtes où le soleil darde une poignée de flèches, il ne se connaît que dans l'écume de la vague glissant sur le sable blond. (V, 98)

This reinscription of the self in metaphor is consistent with Robinson's earlier investigations into the form and meaning of language. Etymologists, philosophers, and scientists have long pondered the possibility that the origins of language are rooted in metaphor. The most famous articulation of the fundamental metaphoricity of language belongs to Rousseau:

> Comme les premiers motifs qui firent parler l'homme furent des passions, ses premières expressions furent des Tropes. Le langage figuré fut le premier à naître, le sens propre fut trouvé le dernier. On n'appela les choses de leur vrai nom que quand on les vit sous leur véritable forme. D'abord on ne parla qu'en poésie; on ne s'avisa de raisonner que longtemps après.[39]

Lévi-Strauss quotes this exact reference in the concluding chapter of his analysis of totemism where it plays a crucial role, underlining the massive influence of Rousseau over many aspects of modernist thinking.[40] For Lévi-Strauss, the *Discours sur l'origine et les fondements de l'inégalité parmi les hommes* is the first anthropological treatise in French literature, because in it the eighteenth-century philosopher poses the central problem of anthropology, which is, namely, the passage of Man from nature to culture. However, this prelude to the development of language is coeval with the total apprehension of man and animals as sentient beings, Rousseau's ideal of the mythological era when men lived fully with nature, which has since been, to a certain extent, borne out in Lévi-Strauss's structural analyses of myths and totemic relationships. The reference in the log-book to this primordial state of existence before and beyond the imposition of linguistic structures, in which objects signify intrinsically, also gives more than a cursory nod towards the aesthetic value placed on the virtuality of the symbol by the German Romantics.

In a ghosted article, published as *Uber die Gegenstände der bildenden Kunst* by Heinrich Meyer, Goethe makes a telling distinction between two key terms: allegory and symbol.[41] Allegory, he says, is transitive, whereas symbols are intransitive but in such a way that they do not cease to signify. Therefore, the symbol speaks to perception along with 'intellection'; the allegory in effect speaks to intellection alone. In the symbol, it is the signified itself that has become a signifier; the two faces of the sign have merged. In allegory, on the other hand, the two faces are quite distinct. The Romantics' insistence that the intransitivity of the symbol is the source of all art—see for example Novalis' *Monologue*—echoes Foucault's allusion to the 'intransitivité radicale'[42] of what we call literature. In *Vendredi* this aesthetic is personified through the character of Vendredi whose influence over the novel permits the exposition of a Romantic ideology (discussed below). However, for the moment Goethe's observation, that the symbol connects primarily with perception, grounds the radical shift in the position of the subject relative to his world that is detailed in the pages of the log-book.

The birth of culture, first described by Rousseau and then re-enacted in the writings of Lévi-Strauss, is also the start of time, the inception of a system, language, that introduced the notion of order into space. Losing patience with Rousseau's imaginings of a pre-cultural life, Derrida stresses this fundamental difference which has allowed for the progress of the species:

> On s'aperçoit alors que la seule différence entre ce que Rousseau voudrait considérer comme la fixité du langage animal et le progrès des langues humaines ne tient à aucun organe, à aucun sens, n'est à chercher ni dans l'ordre du visible ni dans l'ordre de l'audible. C'est une fois de plus le pouvoir de substituer un organe à l'autre, d'articuler l'espace et le temps, la vue et la voix, la main et l'esprit, c'est cette faculté de supplémentarité qui est la véritable *origine*,—ou non-origine—des langues.[43]

Tournier's cleverness in *Vendredi* is to perform novelistically the inversion of this history. In the first instance, Robinson is the product of language, a text, a novel written by Daniel Defoe. Before the ship-wreck he is read by a text, the Tarot, and afterwards he reads a text, the Bible, each purporting in their own ways to order his life, to page his existence. Robinson subscribes to language; he functions in an interpretive mode. It is only when he writes that he starts to question this pecking-order of language that always makes of him the inter-preter. By accident the clepsydra stops, to reveal that time, human time, is a purely arbitrary structure. When the narrative of the log-book eventually enunciates Robinson's long-held desire to be literally at one with Speranza—'Alors Robinson est Speranza'—the transition made from an interpretive to an imaginative mode of thought, from one system of cognition to another, coalesces in the discovery of metaphor.

The presence of metaphor in Robinson's writing does not signify merely the evidence of a schism in the semantic code of his language but rather the possibility of a transference in perspectival fields, which, in philosophical language, would be explained by Wittgenstein's theory of *seeing as*.[44] The ability to see a given visual array first as one thing, then as another (e.g., seeing the duck–rabbit figure first as a duck, then as a rabbit) involves an imaginative activity partially subject to the will and not identical with an act of mere perception. I perceive the formal configuration on the page, but I imaginatively notice one aspect (the duck) or another (the rabbit). Robinson emphasises the *déclic*, the comparative mechanism that enables him to see the goat as a tree stump (V, 99). Thus it appears that metaphorical insight springs from a difference in the perception of symbols.

In his account of how metaphors work, Paul Henle draws on American linguist C. S. Peirce's distinction between a *symbol*, i.e., a sign that signifies by convention, and an *icon*, which signifies by virtue of similarity with the thing signified.[45] The icon is never actually present in the metaphorical expression; rather it represents the under-lying rule which, in a given situation, allows one symbol to replace another. This non-verbal splitting of the symbol, which would not have been countenanced by the Romantics, forms the decisive, original aspect to Henle's theory, for it allows him to argue that not only are metaphors based on similarities, but they may also *induce* similarities. It is through this combination of modern linguistic concepts with the Romantic aesthetic of symbolic perception that we can ascertain the unique qualities that Aristotle first accredited to the trope, when he wrote that it is from metaphor that we 'best get hold of something fresh'.[46] This is the implicit conclusion reached by Robinson in his log-book before he abandons the project, eager to 'fouler le sol ferme de Speranza'. Colin Davis claims that, at this juncture, 'Tournier's philosophical novel has now turned against philosophy'.[47] Davis' judgement is evidence of a consistent underestimation of the serious-ness of the investigation into philosophy conducted through the narration of the log-book. Robinson finds himself in a situation where rationalist forms of knowledge no longer have meaning. Hence his writing becomes an attempt to answer the question most often posed in the work of modern philosophers such as Derrida, Lyotard and Rorty, which asks, 'What is the reason for Reason?' Robinson reaches the decidedly Nietzschean conclusion that Reason, or philosophy, is just one among many metaphors that has gained special status through being enshrined in language. Therefore, in a move that is entirely consistent with the method of his inquiry, he dispenses with the text. In so doing he does not recoil from the staggering implications of his thesis; he pursues them. His search for the metaphor that embraces all knowledge, the metaphor for metaphorisation, takes on the concrete dimension of the journey up/down the birth canal of Speranza, and beyond. It is a narrative which undermines the logos to the extent that it takes metaphor out of the text of philosophy, whilst putting philosophy in the context of metaphor.

There are only two possible controlling figures, two metaphors for metaphor: God and the Sun. Having rejected the former, Robinson has no choice other than to explore the possibility of the latter. Thus, when he resumes his writing under the aegis of Vendredi's *disponibilité*, it is with a flurry of metaphors gravitating towards the source of all light and sensibility:

> Soleil, es-tu content de moi? Regarde-moi. Ma métamorphose va-t-elle assez dans le sens de ta flamme? . . . Je suis une flèche dardée vers ton foyer, une pendule dont le profil perpendiculaire définit ta souveraineté sur la terre . . . Je suis ton témoin debout sur cette terre, comme une épée trempée dans ta flamme. (V, 218)

These final pages from the log are the most philosophical in the entire novel. In his extraordinary essay on metaphor in the text of philosophy, Jacques Derrida shows that the central role of God, which is defined metaphysically by the assumption that there is an absolute referent, is replaced in the philosophies of both Aristotle and Plato by the figure of the Sun. In the *Poetics* the flame-throwing sun as presence becomes the first mover of metaphor; as Derrida says, 'Tout tourne autour de lui, tout se tourne vers lui'.[48] In Plato's *Republic* the sun also appears, only to disappear. We cannot look directly upon it, on pain of blindness. The nearest we get is the rare sighting of an eclipse. In one of those moments that seems to invite intentionally the deconstruction of his own narrative, Derrida qualifies the eclipse (ellipsis) of the sun as 'l'essence—être et paraître—de ce qui est'.[49] We are privy here to the paradox of the figure caught in the dialectical process of thought and cordoned off, separated by the text of philosophy from the sensible sun, the source of life, visibility, seed and light. *Vendredi* ends with the transfiguration of Robinson, his coronation in the kingdom of the sun. We are left, it seems, with the image of Robinson as the incarnation of

Hegel's western man, surveying the twilight of History from his privileged perch. The great dichotomies that plagued the minds of the classical thinkers, encapsulated in the resistance of the philosopher's circle to the unforgiving narrative of History, are finally rolled out and into Hegel's synthesis of mind and matter:

> ... by the close of the day man has erected a building constructed from his own inner Sun; and when in the evening he contemplates this, he esteems it more highly than the original external Sun. For now he stands in a *conscious relation* to his Spirit, and therefore a *free* relation. If we hold this image fast in mind, we shall find it symbolising the course of History, the great Day's work of Spirit.[50]

The sensible sun, which rises in the east, is interiorised, in the evening of its journey, in the eye and the heart of western man. But Crusoe's return to the *limbes du Pacifique* is Tournier writing philosophically against the grain. There he discovers that truth is the obverse of the figure. Having spent the day glorifying in the sunlight of Reason, the insomniacal Robinson turns his eyes towards the 'ciel désastré par son rayonnement, le Grand Luminaire Halluciné' (V, 230). There in the 'jeu d'arabesques' he sees the stellar image of his own writing, the true reflection of his own knowledge present in perfect form, and emptied of intelligibility (V, 231). The Holy Grail turns out to be the continuation of the quest, what Derrida terms the 'surdéterminabilité sans fond'[51] of metaphor; for, once it is admitted that in an analogical relation all the terms are already individually set in a metaphorical relation, the whole begins to function, no longer as a sun but as a star, 'la source ponctuelle de vérité ou de propriété restant invisible ou nocturne'.[52] Metaphor shares with the whirlpool that point of suffocation where the centripetal force which has sucked the object in from the outside generates the centrifuge to expel it. Robinson is now once more on the outside, ready to resume his role of interpreter: 'Vénus, le Cygne, Léda, les Dioscures ... je tâtonne à la recherche de moi-même dans une forêt d'allégories' (V, 232).

THE MEANING OF THE ALLEGORY

The main objective of the philosophical enterprise undertaken in the log-book is to make sense of the Other, or rather the 'autre île'. Robinson's appropriation of the island and its resources has taught him that if he is to make further headway in his understanding of this other, alternative existence and thus conquer his own fears and unhappiness, then he must forgo the referential framework, the memory of a past civilisation, which, in material terms, has helped him to survive. In this pursuit of sense, of the need to make sense of the relation between Robinson and the island, one important vestige of the civilised world, the act of writing, is privileged. But writing is not enough. Ultimately, Robinson is unable to make sense of his existence on the island without the active intervention of the Other, which he may potentially achieve through an interperspectival alliance with Vendredi. Vendredi, however, personifies the philosophical figure of the Other, the absolute otherness of the stars in the night sky, dazzling figurations that lie beyond Robinson's intellectual capacity.

For Robinson the problem is that he has no means of representing Vendredi other than on his own redundant terms. Initially Vendredi plays a structural role in the narrative, like that of the *comédien* who deliberately lets his mask slip from time to time in order to reveal a priori the next stage in the plot. Robinson eventually comprehends that his 'vie en marge de l'ordre' (V, 163) is one possible manifestation of the psychic structures that he, Robinson, had initially attributed to Speranza. The outward signs of Vendredi's existence—wooden masks, blow-pipe, hammock, reptile skins etc.—form part of an exclusive semiological system. Likewise other behavioural traits (Robinson is, of course, always in the position of the analyst), such as his habit of silently meditating without moving from a squatting position, and, above all, his derisory outbursts of ironic laughter, are, or seem to be, in apposition to the culture that Robinson has brought to the island. However, Vendredi's transgressive behaviour is, can only be, an external manifestation of Robinson's inner fears, anxieties and subli- mated desire. Robinson's own a priori preoccupations with contin- gency, need and time are carried over; they receive their confirmation in the apparently alien existence of Vendredi. Thus, Vendredi's battle with the monster goat may be read as a kind of 'post-figuration' of Robinson's libidinal exploration of the cave. Robinson's decision to descend the pot-hole beyond the gunpowder storage area involves taking a serious risk for no utilitarian purpose. The main problem is one of visibility. He considers various engineering strategies to provide lighting and ventilation for the expedition but is forced to reject them, and relies on tactile perception alone. This venture into the cavern is no less dangerous than Vendredi's later encounter with Andoar. It indi- cates that Vendredi's non-utilitarian sense of adventure is already in place in Robinson's psyche. Moreover, it is consonant with the 'intrigue de prédestination' which predetermines the sequence of events in the narrative.

What Robinson does not perceive is that Vendredi functions in a purely creative mode, in which there is no conception of either means or end. Thus when he enforces a Sisyphean style punishment, making him repeatedly dig a hole in order to fill it in, he is stupefied at the cheerfulness with which the Araucanian goes about his task (V, 156). Vendredi appears to represent some sort of pure aesthetic consciousness. He is totally imbricated in what amounts to a form of creative play. His art is surreal in the sense that it transgresses recognised boundaries, as when he uses Robinson's possessions to decorate the immediate environment around their living quarters (V, 159). It is revolutionary in the most literal sense of the word; see, for example, Robinson's discovery of the uprooted, inverted, replanted and still thriving trees (V, 163). And it communicates through different media; most strikingly by means of the *corporage* of the 'homme-plante' surging out of the bushes in front of the incredulous Robinson (V, 164). However, this 'inspiration baroque', as it is qualified in the narrative, is manipulated so as to conform to a general schematism in which Vendredi embodies a kind of Romantic ideology. The sequence, instigated by Vendredi's stated intention to 'faire voler et chanter le grand bouc' (V, 200), traces an interesting history. It ensues from the aftermath of a gladiatorial combat in which Vendredi triumphs somewhat fortuitously over the force of Evil, represented by the monster goat Andoar. In typically self-obsessed vein, Robinson later interprets the slaying of the goat as the symbolic death of the old order, equating the hoary king of the herd with his former self. However, in Christian mythology the goat's head (which generally appears luminous in modern horror films) is also the traditional emblem of Satanism. It is equally possible that Vendredi's deed represents the victory of Man, and therefore the victory of Reason, over what might be described as his Fall from Grace; the goat dies in cushioning Vendredi's fall from the precipice.

Andoar's carcass provides the raw materials for Vendredi's two most enduring creations, each of which portend two distinct paths in the history of mankind. Firstly, from the dried out, epilated goat's hide he fabricates a kite. In that it probably represents man's first conquest of the ether, the flying of the kite prefigures not only the history of aviation but also the spirit of exploration and discovery that has resulted in men walking on the moon. Reclining on the beach with the cord attached to his left ankle, Vendredi delights in the measure of control he can exert over atmospheric forces, 'cette choréographie aérienne, car Andoar, fidèle et lointain cavalier, répondait à chacun de ses mouvements par des hochements, des voltes et des piqués' (V, 205). But it is too near to his Achilles heel; this fascination with the human mastery of the elements lures Vendredi away and on to the *Whitebird*, to become one of the first victims of the ideal we call Progress. The irony, of course, is that Vendredi has already become Robinson's ideal. The Greek myth tells us that from the bloody issue of Kronos' sickle and the ravages of time there rose from the waves the goddess Aphrodite, the incarnation of immortal beauty. Through his fundamental *vénusté*, signalled by the Tarot and eventually recuperated in the narrative of the log-book (V, 208), Vendredi is established as the myth archetype, the personification of the Romantic idyll, that ultimate retreat from the contingencies of time and need which is Speranza. Hence the significance of the second creation, in which Vendredi takes down the separated membrane of the goat's intestine, previously hung on a tree to tauten, and proceeds to string Andoar's ant-eaten skull as one would nowadays a tennis racket. The result is an aeolian harp, 'le seul instrument dont la musique au lieu de se développer dans le temps s'inscrit tout entière dans l'instant' (V, 227), which Vendredi judiciously positions in a dead cypress tree, to await the coming of the wind.

Thus, the enigmatic creativity of Vendredi, which the reader is encouraged to think of as mysterious and magical, has a quite different, parabolesque function. The slaying of the goat equates to the death of an old order in which absolute Old Testament values, and especially the theological duality of Good and Evil, give way to the values of the Enlightenment. The apotheosis of goat as aeolian harp, moreover, suggests that, via Vendredi, Robinson has reached a state of consciousness, of communion with the natural world that brings him close to the thinking of the high priests of eighteenth-century romanticism, Rousseau and Goethe. The magic of the aeolian harp, which is not lost on Robinson, is that its music is 'véritablement élémentaire, inhumaine' (V, 209). By dint of its functioning independently of the human agent, and in consort with the natural elements, the aeolian harp is elevated to a mythical level. In Coleridge's poem, it is presented as the symbol of symbolism. Having instigated a putative history of knowledge, Vendredi himself remains an empty vessel. He is nothing more than Robinson's alter-ego, a series of figures conveying the evolution of Robinson's thinking and the changing state of the relations between Robinson and the island. Each successive incarnation—primitive savage, loyal servant, witch-doctor, Rousseau Man—reflects significant changes in Robinson's mental and emotional constitution. However, Vendredi is burdened with a heavy symbolism. Interestingly, his role as symbol of the Other is eventually usurped as, with the arrival of the would-be rescue ship, Tournier's narrative rejoins that of Defoe.

In *Vendredi* the concept of time which initially dictates Robinson's *modus operandi* is slowly superseded by a different order corresponding to the spatial configurations of the island. This transition is complete following the explosion in the cave. Robinson's past, History, is now irrelevant; his existence is entirely governed by geographical, geological and meteorological factors; that is, until the crew of the *Whitebird* disembarks. Robinson's perception of the crew is recorded in conceptual terms, in the non-naturalistic manner the reader has now come to expect of his narrators (V, 238–39). Leibniz's concept of the monad figures prominently at this point in the narrative. The Leibnizian monad defines the possibility of a distinct, coherent world incarcerated within each individual human being, the values and beliefs of which that human being will seek to impose upon the worlds of others circulating around him. What would therefore link one monad to another is a shared concept of time, represented by the uniform temporal scales—on calendars, sun-dials, clocks etc.—extrapolated from the observable symptoms of the dual rotation and revolution of the Earth, which successive civilisations have applied to the human condition. For Robinson the arrival of the *Whitebird* acts as a sudden reminder of his own mortality. It signifies incontrovertibly the return of time:

> Robinson mesura tout à coup le poids extraordinaire des quelques instants qui restaient avant que l'homme de proue croche dans les rochers avec sa gaffe. Comme un mourant avant de rendre l'âme, il embrassait d'une vision panoramique toute sa vie dans l'île, l'*Evasion*, la souille, l'organisation frénétique de Speranza, la grotte, la combe, la survenue de Vendredi, l'explosion, et surtout cette vaste plage de temps, vierge de toute mesure, où sa métamorphose solaire s'était accomplie dans un calme bonheur. (V, 234)

His first impulse is to measure this time:

> Le cerveau de Robinson travailla à vive allure. Le naufrage de la *Virginie* avait eu lieu le 30 septembre 1759. Il y avait exactement vingt-huit ans, deux mois et dix-neuf jours. (V, 235)

Although the presence of other human beings on Spéranza allows Robinson to measure in more conventional philosophical terms than hitherto the value of *autrui*—'C'était cela autrui: un possible qui s'acharne à passer pour réel' (V, 239)—he also sees in it the future devastation of the fragile ecosystem represented by Speranza (V, 239), and consequently his own demise. However, Robinson's subsequent decision to remain on the island is motivated primarily by his aversion to temporal structures, which incorporate his fear of death and need to believe in some sort of after-life, 'il y était poussé par son refus panique du tourbillon de temps, dégradant et mortel' (V, 245). Of course, this metaphysic is illusory. Robinson's vision of Speranza is grounded in the idea of a communal existence. When he discovers that Vendredi has stowed away on the *Whitebird* and he faces once again the prospect of solitude, there is only one option left for him to take. About to descend for the second and last time into the grotto, his passage is suddenly blocked by another representation of the self, a vision of young Robinson in the shape of the ship's boy from the *Whitebird*, and the promise of eternity is renewed.[53]

The repetition of the sunrise and Robinson's 'extase solaire' relayed on the last page of the novel have encouraged critics to read the episode of the *Whitebird* as a temporary blip in the process of interiorisation, realised in the breaking of each new dawn as both the repetition of a past event and an absolute beginning, that leads Robinson ever closer to the perception of the Ideal.[54] This is not necessarily the case. The *Whitebird* episode should serve to remind the reader that his or her first point of reference is Defoe's text. Thus, the sequence narrating Robinson's discourse with the officers of the *Whitebird* is important because it is precisely at this point that the full extent of the temporal disjunction between the two texts is revealed. We already know that the shipwreck in *Robinson Crusoe* occurs on 30 September 1659 (RC, 70), whereas in *Vendredi* it takes place exactly 100 years later (V, 10). The *décalage* would appear to be consistent with our reading of *Vendredi*; 1759 is the year when the first edition of Rousseau's *Emile* was published, a text which, its author acknowledged, was profoundly influenced by Defoe's novel. However, the rescue ship in *Robinson Crusoe* arrives in 1686; in *Vendredi* the *Whitebird* weighs anchor on 19 December 1787. Salkin Sbiroli interprets this 'différence curieuse' as the 'dernière dérision du texte de Defoe';[55] Robinson's precision timekeeping that lapses for one day only in Defoe's novel is a whole year out in *Vendredi*. But the time difference is not an accidental one. The shipwrecks both occur at the end of September, and both rescue ships arrive on the same date, 19 December. Rather than deflecting the reader's attention from the temporal lacunae, these coincidences attract it to them. Tournier's explanation, tucked away in the introductory sequence of *Vendredi ou La vie sauvage*, is revealing. The narrator writes:

> On était au milieu du XVIIIe siècle, alors que beaucoup d'Européens— principalement des Anglais—allaient s'installer en Amérique pour faire fortune. Robinson avait laissé à York sa femme et ses deux enfants, pour explorer l'Amérique du Sud et voir s'il ne pourrait pas organiser des échanges commerciaux fructueux entre sa patrie et le Chili.[56]

He mentions *en passant* an oft overlooked aspect to Robinson's character, his job. Robinson Crusoe was one of the first commercial travellers.

In *Les Mots et les choses* Foucault makes the remarkable claim that towards the end of the eighteenth century, western Europe was the site of an intellectual earthquake, a revolution in the *épistème*, or way in which thoughts are formed, the cultural and political effects of which were beyond anything dreamt up by the actual French revolutionaries. Foucault is able to chart in the histories of such widely divergent disciplines as philology and the natural sciences a transference from a dominant discourse founded on the perception of similarities and analogies to a new, and much less stable configuration, in which those resemblances displayed through the history of language are ordered *successively*. The most tangible by-product of this massive shift in conceptual patterns of thinking was the development of a new science of economics. Prior to this, Foucault asserts, the concept of money was inextricably linked to its representation in the form of gold and silver coins, and its value therefore determined by the preciosity of the metal. However, with the advent of seventeenth- and eighteenth-century mercantilism, by which time the concept of value had become fixed by the stocks of gold and silver held by each trading nation, all forms of wealth could be translated into currency. The value of the monetary sign was then determined by the inscription of the monarch's head on the coin, and no longer by its intrinsic worth as a piece of gold or silver. As Foucault puts it: 'Du coup le rapport si étroitement fixé au 16ème siècle est retourné: la monnaie (et jusqu'au métal dont elle est faite) reçoit sa valeur de sa pure fonction de signe.'[57] This formatting of the system of exchanges according to Cartesian principles therefore made possible the worldwide trade boom of the seventeenth and eighteenth centuries. Yet already by the end of the seventeenth century, when money was first considered as a security and assimilated to credit, the idea of temporality in the analysis of wealth had come into being. Foucault theorises it accordingly, '. . . il fallait bien alors que la durée de la créance, la rapidité avec laquelle elle venait à échoir, le nombre de mains entres lesquelles elle passait pendant un temps donné, deviennent des variables caractéristiques de son pouvoir représentatif'.[58]

In the second half of the eighteenth century, the analysis of wealth was given a new dimension by Adam Smith. Smith distinguishes between the representation of objects of need and objects of desire. Objects of need, he argued, have two representations, one that shows up in the normal way within the system of exchanges but also a second, that accrues from the necessity value of the object. This second representation is in the form of the work or labour required to produce the object, the constitutive ordering principle of which is time. Smith paves the way for a new ethics of economics, based on the conceptual value of work. The notion of labour costs was to dominate the thinking of classical economist David Ricardo who, according to Foucault, 'distingue pour la première fois d'une manière radicale, cette force, cette peine, ce temps de l'ouvrier qui s'achètent et se vendent, et cette activité qui est à l'origine de la valeur des choses'.[59] For Ricardo, if the quality of work involved in manufacturing the item is the factor that determines its price, it is not only because the price can be represented in units of work (which is essentially Smith's thesis); more than this, it is because work/labour as an activity of production is the 'source of all value'. And it is impossible to define this value in terms of the system of equivalences pertaining to the first trading era, which is based on the relative value of one item of merchandise compared to the next. Ricardo asserts that by the end of the eighteenth century, value is no longer conceived as a sign, but as a product. He demonstrates the theory simply by pointing out that the value of an item is proportional to the amount of work required to produce it; however, this value does not vacillate according to increases or cuts in salary, against which work/labour is exchanged like any other commodity. The system of exchanges retains its power of representation, but it is assimilated to the order of labour, which cannot be defined by a process of exchange.

The fundamental difference in Tournier's treatment of the Robinson Crusoe story, which entails the curious one hundred and one-year *retardement*, can be seen in the context of these developments outlined in Foucault's writing. The first Robinson, a seventeenth-century trader, is imbued with the mercantilist spirit; note the accumulation of nouns designating prospective trade agreements on pages 39–41 of Defoe's novel. However, the narrative contains no detail relating to the economic process or its effects. Instead there is much speculation on Robinson's part over potential openings for trade in the New World. In *Vendredi*, however, we see perfectly contrasting discourses representing the evolving dichotomy of late eighteenth-century economic thought, which was to lead to the polarisation of economics in the next with the imposition of Marxist and Capitalist models. In an early entry to the log-book we find a sophisticated eulogy of proto-capitalist man, framed in the uncompromising language of the moralist. Robinson proclaims his love of money in unambiguous terms:

> Je mesure aujourd'hui la folie et la méchanceté de ceux qui calomnient cette institution divine: l'argent! L'argent spiritualise tout ce qu'il touche en lui apportant une dimension à la fois rationnelle—mesurable—et universelle— puisqu'un bien monnayé devient virtuellement accessible à tous les hommes. La vénalité est une vertu cardinale. (V, 61–62)

The problem for Robinson is that there is no-one to buy his produce, and therefore no need for the existence of money. Rightly, he perceives the true nature of his deprivation. The tragedy of his situation lies in his indefinite isolation from the vital rationale of his age, the positivistic value of money. At the same time we read a consistent sub-text to the narrative which emphasises the physical involvement of the human agent in the production of commodities and the manufacture of goods. Tournier plies his reader with much detail of the ways in which Robinson constructs his writing materials, shelter, his methods of planting crops etc. Similarly, the skills, knowledge and timing involved in Vendredi's meaningful work—the manufacturing process of the arrows, the kite and the aeolian harp—are stressed. Most cleverly, perhaps, Tournier caps Robinson's exposition of capitalist morality in the first-person narrative of the log-book with a passage in the plural, third person, describing in detail his instigation and cultivation of several plantations, including the establishment of an apiary and a fish farm. This contrary, heterodiegetic narrative emphasises labour costs, calculated in terms of the extreme discipline and sheer effort of work required to ensure success (V, 63).

The one hundred and one years separating this Robinson from his forbear is important on account of these contributions to the history of knowledge from the classical economists, who brought to light the hidden agenda in the history of our industrial age that was to be fully revealed by Marx and was hitherto to inspire the modern labour movement. Thus, the association of time and labour is an important feature of Tournier's novel. When the clepsydra accidentally stops, Robinson is 'en vacances', and his mood euphoric (V, 93). Later we are told that the inertia of the clepsydra is automatically associated in Vendredi's mind with the absence of the Governor (V, 157), implying that he sees it as the chronometer of his own duties, or work. Most of all, Vendredi's dehumanising slavery is contrasted with the precision, skill and close attention required to produce the aeolian harp. The narrative endows this process with the dignity of labour: 'Dès lors sa peine et son temps ne comptaient plus, sa patience et ses soins n'avaient plus de limite' (V, 207).

It is perhaps inevitable that a Robinson Crusoe rediscovering his desert island in the context of a twentieth-century fictional narrative should carry with him the weight of the industrial revolution and the intimation of its forthcoming consequences. But *Vendredi* is also a text which resists narrow interpretations. The theme of the novel is the exploration of the Other, and the Other encompasses that which is beyond the experience, and therefore the present understanding of the subject. It is what philosophers sometimes refer to as 'sense'. Tournier's second novel, *Le Roi des aulnes*, tackles a different Other which manifests itself within the realm of human experience. The two novels were written in tandem; however, the passage from first to second incorporates a switch, from the sense to the reference of metaphor.

CHAPTER THREE
The Drive for Reference

In the 1970s two well-known French philosophers clashed swords. Their *querelle* concerned the seemingly arcane issue of metaphoric reference. As we have seen, Paul Ricoeur argues convincingly in *La Métaphore vive* that metaphor is a cognitive tool, that it helps in certain circumstances to articulate our experience of the world. Ricoeur's analysis is anchored to the established phenomenological precepts of Kant and Husserl, for in order that metaphor may refer, its transgressive character must ultimately be tamed by the master discourse of philosophy. However, according to Jacques Derrida's deconstructive practice, the philosopher's discourse is itself shot through with metaphor. It can have no independent, 'commenting' authority for it is contradicted repeatedly by the twists and turns of its own metaphorical language. Derrida argues that it is not possible even to 'illuminate' the presuppositions that subtend his own discourse on metaphor, given that metaphorical practice is infinitely regressive and therefore does not allow us to locate the source of light in a fixed, clearly determined centre. Flowers turn towards the sun. This heliotropic movement is, Derrida suggests, the paradigm of linguistic tropes, but the sun is also not a stable entity. It sets, is eclipsed, and light is reflected from the stars. The sun is caught up in its own troping. The question is whether metaphor can refer to something other than another metaphor. Derrida thinks not. Does metaphor, through language or cognitive psychology, engage somehow with a world outside the text? Ricoeur thinks that it must. The philosophers' debate reifies the most frequently rehearsed argument about the status of art and literature. Aestheticism, or the primacy of aesthetic principles, and the contextualisation of art through history make competing demands on the person of the artist. Rarely has the issue been so finely balanced, the tension so palpably evident, as in the writing of— and subsequent writing on—Tournier's second and most controversial novel, *Le Roi des aulnes*.

THE *GEIST* IN THE MACHINE

Le Roi des aulnes renders a portrayal of Nazism which, on account of the seemingly uncritical perspective informing the narrative and of the context (a purely fictive one) in which this information is given, has been seen as dangerously ambivalent. Contemporary reviewers questioned the motives of a writer who apparently sought to aestheticise Nazism, and could so do by using his chosen genre as a sort of protective shield.[1] However, since 1970 Tournier critics and scholars have implicitly rejected these accusations, no doubt on the grounds of bad taste, preferring instead to focus on other aspects of the text.[2] The result is that the response that Tournier himself clearly solicited through this work has not been forthcoming. His presentation of Nazism in *Le Roi des aulnes* is carefully judged, and it is based on comprehensive historical research. Therefore it makes specific demands on its readership, who are asked to evaluate the contribution of this novel (and others in a similar vein, notably Gunther Grass's *The Tin Drum*) to our understanding of an issue that should once again be taxing the minds of European citizens.

That consideration of this theme should be given priority in any reading of *Le Roi des aulnes* is evinced by the author's own comments on the composition of his work. In *Le Vent Paraclet* Tournier chronicles the difficulties he faced and anxieties he felt in trying to present a genuine image of Nazism in the text of his fiction.[3] Tournier's protracted stumblings over the continuation of *Le Roi des aulnes* are instructive. Unlike other roughly contemporary European novelists, notably Primo Levi and Jorge Semprun, he did not personally experience the horror of Nazi persecution. This experiential deficit does not preclude him from writing on Nazism and the camps, but it does mean that any such 'unauthorised' (without the authority of experience) representation of events from the Second World War era in a work of fiction becomes a delicate enterprise. However, Tournier's initial reluctance to proceed with the writing of the novel stems from the impediments it inevitably presented to the satisfaction of a strongly held, philosopher's desire, that the world (as he sees it) should support a metaphysical system. As we have seen, Tournier's first published novel, *Vendredi ou les limbes du Pacifique*, reifies a metaphysics which privileges the Romantic ideal of the fundamental intransitivity of the symbol. The parallel evolution of *Le Roi des aulnes* with *Vendredi*— both novels shared the same ten-year gestation period—indicates that

Tournier was not only interested in situating his conception of this romanticist ideology on Robinson's island, but also in restoring it to its original locale, to Germany, viewed primarily in terms of that country's philosophical and literary heritage. However, whilst writing *Le Roi des aulnes* some thirteen years after the end of the war, Tournier is confronted with the spectre of the *Volksgeist*, the absorption of an entire cultural tradition into the most fervent and catastrophic of all nationalisms. Not surprisingly, given the apparent political consequences of the Romantic aesthetic he appreciates, he is stopped in his tracks.

How deep into the rich subsoil of the German Romantic tradition do the roots of Nazism extend? It is a question to which there can be no clearly defined answer. However, Alain Finkielkraut traces the early stages in the cultural development of a *Volksgeist* in his book, *La Défaite de la pensée*. The inference is, though Finkielkraut does not state it explicitly, that Nazism is determined by well-established historical and cultural forces. He refers to the volte-face on the issue of nationalism performed by Goethe, seen now, as then, as the epitome of German Romanticism. The young Goethe was imbued with the vision normally attributed to Herder of a eurocentric culture defined by the supremacy of German architecture, philosophy and literature, radiating out from the nation-centre. This nationalism is prominent in Goethe's 1772 essay, *Architecture allemande*, in which he sets down the formula: 'L'art caractéristique est le seul art véritable'. However, it fades rapidly. In 1808, two years after the Battle of Jena, Goethe was invited to give his opinion on a prospective volume of exemplary German poetry. In a move which, in the light of the dominant ethos of the time, would have been regarded as an act of treason coming from any other than he, Goethe made a single recommendation to the editors: that they should include in the anthology translations of some non-German works. For Goethe had by then decided that, as literature was capable of transcending differences of time, race, language and culture, this is what the writer should aim to do, and he never rescinded this view.[4]

Tournier would clearly like to write with the panoptic eye of a twentieth-century Goethe, and it is in deference to these lofty principles that he is sometimes inclined to be over-generous in praise of thinkers who are, in current jargon, 'politically incorrect'. For example, in contrast to Finkielkraut, Tournier portrays Herder as a man driven by an insatiable curiosity for knowledge of the world outside Germany, a curiosity reflected in his work on world languages and a predilection for the then exotic Shakespeare that puts him in the same camp as Diderot, Lessing, D'Alembert and the other eighteenth-century Encyclopedists.[5] But it is also true that Tournier, writing some 200 years later and with the benefit of 20/20 hindsight, does not shirk his responsibility as an artist of his time. When, with the writing of *Le Roi des aulnes*, he finally crosses the threshold of 1939, Tournier withholds nothing. Neither his protagonist Tiffauges nor his reader is spared the details of Nazi Germany; each encounters its darkest secrets.

What allowed Tournier to proceed with *Le Roi des aulnes* is the realisation that, in this case, there can be no aesthetic value in an ethical vacuum. His text had not only to symbolise Nazi Germany,[6] it had also to identify the historical phenomenon and represent it for the political force that it was and still is. And this transition, from the symbolic to the referential, is dramatised in the text.

We can see how if we concentrate on two key descriptive tags. Tournier's Ogre is *sinistre*. Subsuming the many mythological and folkloric resonances connected with the Ogre archetype, Tiffauges is essentially malevolent, seen and treated by others as a harmful influence, or at least as a threat. But *sinistre* also denotes his left-handedness and the inception of his diary, which is logically entitled the *Ecrits sinistres*. Having damaged his right hand in an accident at the garage, Tiffauges discovers whilst doodling a few days later that he can write with his left, and the *Ecrits* are born, a mutant form 'd'un graphisme étrange, étranger, un peu grimaçant, dépourvu de toute ressemblance avec mon écriture habituelle, celle de ma main droite' (RA, 17).[7] The *Ecrits sinistres*, this eruption of an individuated first person form within the heterodiegetic construct of Tournier's narrative, signify the double function of Tiffauges' character. In the first instance they give an essentialist vision of a world which is ultimately tied to the will of the subject. The *Ecrits* are patently authoritative. However, they also reveal Tiffauges to be an inveterate reader of signs. 'Tout est signe!' (RA, 15), he exclaims, and indeed everything is: Nestor's gyroscope, the Rhineland pigeons, the deer droppings that fascinate Göring, they are all physical signs, jealous guardians of some innate essence. The *Ecrits sinistres* therefore announce the mode of the narrative to follow, which will be hermeneutic. We readers follow in the wake of Tiffauges attempting to decipher the signs, as he follows in the wake of his own 'ogrish' prophesying. This quest structure is crucially disrupted by the figure of History. In the first diary entry the Ogre writes: 'Je crois, oui, à ma nature féerique, je veux dire à cette connivence secrète qui mêle en profondeur mon aventure personnelle au cours des choses, et lui permet de l'incliner dans son sens' (RA, 13). These apparently eccentric words acquire infinitely greater significance some two hundred pages on, when they are reiterated in the third person: 'Personne n'avait autant que lui la conscience de son destin, un destin rectiligne, imperturbable, inflexible qui ordonnait à ses seules fins les événements mondiaux les plus grandioses' (RA, 249). Even those readers with only a superficial knowledge of twentieth-century European history will already know at this point what these 'événements mondiaux' entail. However, Tiffauges does not perceive the political consequences of his world-view until a much later stage in his story. This intrusion of History into the narrative of fiction serves to reinforce a strong parallelism, in which the conglomeration of symbols populating Tiffauges' fantastic world and presented via the *Ecrits sinistres* with some intellectual dexterity is seen to correspond to the powerful essentialist rhetoric disseminated throughout the 1930s by Goebbels' propaganda machine.

The other key term is the proper noun 'Canada', which conjures up for Tiffauges the image of a mythological dreamland. He learns later that 'Canada' was the name given by the inmates of Auschwitz to the treasure house where the personal effects of the gas victims were hoarded. Immediately the referential claims hitherto absent from what are to Tiffauges the enticingly sensual signs of the Napola, the elite Hitler Youth training institution cut off from both the realities of everyday life and the political reality of the impending Russian invasion of Germany, are revealed. The shower-heads, the shorn locks of the *Jungmannen* on the barber's floor, and the mass groupings of naked bodies each have their correlate in the machine of death simultaneously in progress in the Nazi death camps: institutions which were also secretly maintained and kept out of the sight of ordinary people.[8] Tiffauges receives this staggering piece of information from Ephraïm, the Jewish boy he finds dying at the roadside and subsequently nurses back to health. Ephraïm provides the vital channel of communication through which Tiffauges perceives both the sense of Canada—it denotes still, even when used in the context of the concentration camps, a place where treasured items may be found—and its reference— Hitler's Final Solution. Thus, he comes to 'know' the truth about the Nazi regime.

Ephraïm's revelation makes sense of the series of tête-à-têtes between Tiffauges and the disaffected Kommandeur of Kaltenborn.

The Kommandeur, a slightly manic Doomsday seer, lectures Tiffauges on the nature and function of the symbol in Nazi Germany. 'Le symbole bafoué devient *diabole*' (RA, 473), he declares. Colin Davis points out that the significance of this neologism derives from the Greek word *diabolos*, meaning that which disunifies. The symbol disunifies in the sense that it short-circuits the ordinary relationship between sign and referent, asserting firstly its supremacy and then its independence from any need to signify. In the Kommandeur's words the symbol 'acquiert son autonomie, il échappe à la chose symbolisée, et ... il la prend lui-même en charge' (RA, 321). The proliferation of diabolical symbols—the Kommandeur cites the swastika (an inversion of the Maltese Cross, traditional symbol of peace and security) and the Prussian eagle of the Third Reich (formerly a heraldic emblem reproduced as a symbol of Nazism with its head pointing in the opposite direction) as examples of these—invites the possibility of apocalypse. This is the measure of the threat posed by Nazi Germany, described by the Kommandeur as 'le produit des symboles eux-mêmes qui mènent souverainement le jeu' (RA, 322), and by Davis as a 'symbolic pantheon deployed independently of all human signification'.[9]

What the Kommandeur achieves by harnessing his discourse on the autonomy of the symbol and the attack on the notion of an intelligible world constituted by this autonomy to the contemporary reality of Nazi Germany is in inverse proportion to Tiffauges' seduction away from the actual world of fellow human beings by symbols in general, and by the ultimate symbol of Germany itself; for Tiffauges, 'l'Allemagne se dévoilait comme une terre promise, comme le pays des essences pures' (RA, 193). His encounter with Ephraïm is, then, the single most important event in the narrative, because it gives added meaning to everything that has come before. The narrative has taken Tiffauges from a concept of the sign as pure meaning—the equivocal *sinistre* gives us both sides of the Ogre's atemporal essence—to that of the sign as a means towards the truthful apprehension of a political reality. The first view is founded on the primacy of the symbol and favours subjective perception, the second on viable communication and the possibility of reference. This decisive shift from the sensing of the thing to the grasping of its reference occurs when Ephraïm first utters the word 'Canada':[10] 'Lorsque Ephraïm prononça pour la première fois le mot Canada, Tiffauges comprit que la promulgation de la grande inversion maligne venait de retentir' (RA, 556). This is the significant moment when Tiffauges disclaims his essentially stable view of a world

subject to a series of malign and benign inversions. Having intentionally sought out the plain of eastern Prussia, where, in the cold and
penetrating hyperborean light, 'tous les symboles brillaient d'un éclat
inégale' (RA, 192), he is taken beyond the allure of his chosen destination. All these privileged moments in the course of his quest are
suddenly transformed into a sequence of minute reflections that add up
to a 'monstrueuse analogie', the *contresemblance* contained in the
Jewish child's reference to Canada.

This neat reading solves Tournier's ethical dilemma but obscures
the real question, which is to ask how it is that symbolism, whether
expressed pictorially or linguistically, can be so powerful, so influential
on such a grand historical scale. The answer lies outside the parameters
of a postmodern culture, which tends to exclude ideas about the real
impact of rhetoric on history, or indeed on any narrative event, from its
theses, since logically these lines of inquiry can lead only to a set of
unverifiable, psychological assumptions, concerning such matters as the
appeal of Nazism. However, we are obliged to consider the effectiveness of the symbolism in *Le Roi des aulnes*. In the opening line—'Tu es
un ogre, me disait parfois Rachel. Un Ogre?' (RA, 13)—the symbol and
major theme of the novel is introduced as Flaubert would have wished
it, almost casually, in a reflective moment. The narrator wonders why
his girlfriend should describe him as an ogre. After all the Ogre is the
giant at the top of Jack's beanstalk or the troll under the bridge, the
Bogeyman in little children's nightmares. This representation in central
and north European folklore of the Ogre as inherently harmful to
human society is of course consistent with its etymology; his mythological avatar is Orcus, the Roman God of the Underworld. Significantly, in the transition from mythology into history the archetype of
the Ogre has become associated with cultural and theological difference. History is littered with infamous Ogres—Genghis Khan, Ivan the
Terrible, and the excommunicated Henry VIII all spring to mind. In
eschatology the image of the Ogre prefigures Satan and the final battle
between Evil and Good when the world itself will be at stake. In this
world, fragmented by a plurality of cultures, it is always identified with
the Other, that which, coming from the outside, threatens to invade the
cultural home. In each case the Ogre incarnates a strongly negative
persona; that is, until the rise of fascism in the first part of the twentieth-century.

Le Roi des aulnes opens a new perspective on the archetype of the
Ogre; Tournier suggests that the Ogre, far from being an alien force

menacing societies from the exterior, is a creature of immanence. He reminds us of the etymology of the word 'monstre': *monstrum— monstrare—montrer* (RA, 14). The monster is that which is shown. People have always gathered to watch freak shows. The traditional fairground exhibitions have been supplanted by big screen versions, but the Victorians' fascination with the pitiful Elephant Man and our more recent attraction to the macabre Freddy of *Nightmare on Elm Street* (Parts I, II, III and IV) are rooted in a common impulse. Tiffauges excites the same public curiosity in *Le Roi des aulnes*; he has the same monstrous quality. Perhaps a similar urge once drove ordinary Germans out of their homes to hear Adolf Hitler speak. The newsreel footage shows how Hitler would stand in silent contemplation of an audience apparently mesmerised by his presence sometimes for as long as forty minutes before he uttered a word. To some extent the content of his speech, the verbal rhetoric for which he was famed, was, though still important, subsidiary to the mixture of awe and fear inspired by this 'demonstrability'.

If Tournier is at pains to stress the physical characteristics and behavioural traits of his Ogre—the enormous stature, the under-developed penis, a voracious appetite for fresh meat, and, most significantly, the sensitive, bearing hands—it is not done merely so that we are able to recognise Tiffauges' fellow-travellers depicted in this text (Nestor, his schooldays mentor, Weidmann the mass murderer, and of course Göring himself) for what they are; these characteristics are emphasised because they are symbolic. The Ogre does indeed crave flesh, but his gentle ingestion is more symbolic than real. It corresponds to a spiritual anthropophagy, the devouring of human reason. Once again, the importance of the *Ecrits sinistres* to the narrative of *Le Roi des aulnes* is all too evident. And what the inception of the diary comes to represent is the assimilation of the mind to the body, and consequent expression of a radical essentialist philosophy.

The political point Tournier wanted to make in *Le Roi des aulnes* is that Nazism comes from within. It is not something that can be intellectually siphoned off, or dismissed as a nihilistic reaction to extra-ordinary economic hardships accentuated by the actions of incompe-tent and corrupt politicians. The Ogre is (in) the garage mechanic; *Le Roi des aulnes* forces us to face the pessimistic reality that what we now know and remember as fascism, or Nazism, is not the product of external historical circumstances, with all the reassuring distancing and unburdening of individual responsibility that this diagnosis implies, but the mobilisation, in thought, of something which may form part of the human condition. Fascism was accommodated (to differing degrees) in all the major European countries during the 1930s precisely because it was a popular movement that came not from within an exclusively nationalistic framework, but from a common cultural consensus. During and after the Second World War allied propaganda depicted Hitler, Mussolini and their acolytes as Ogres, and in the early years of the Cold War they were replaced by Stalin. However, it was only in 1990 that the Ogre reverted fully to type, as the features of Iraq's Saddam Hussein came to dominate the screens of the world's media. For the Americans, the British and the French it was much easier to wage the Gulf War, for the adversary was no longer, as Hitler initially seemed to be, the enemy from within. It was no longer a question of having to get to grips with the realisation that a common cultural heritage would not prevent the old continent from being split asunder. Saddam merely threatened the oil supplies of the west.

We ignore at our peril the current signs of a Nazi renaissance at the heart of Europe. But it takes more than the vicious expression of xenophobic attitudes for it to succeed. The political volatility of Europe in the first half of this century was reflected in the fashion for radical artistic movements, firstly Marinetti's Futurists and then Breton's Surrealists, that found cause to celebrate a cult of youth. More importantly, though less obviously, these movements issued a challenge to the old philosophical certainties, a challenge which was spectacularly upheld by one of the foremost of modern philosophers. In *Le Roi des aulnes* Tournier parades a number of ogrish figures; it may be that the most important of these is the least visible, Hannah Arendt's 'secret king of thought', the German philosopher Martin Heidegger. The radicalism of the age found its most cogent expression in the devastating assault on the Cartesian cogito, and on the sanitised view of the world implicit in all empiricist philosophy, staged through Heidegger's work.

There is no longer any disputing the fact that Heidegger was, at one time, a Nazi.[11] What is at issue is the extent to which Heideggerian philosophy is imbricated with Nazism. This is a major question which has bedevilled the European intellectual community; it is my contention that the narrator of Tournier's *Le Roi des aulnes* instantly recognises it as such. The upper case repetition of Ogre in the opening lines of the novel echoes Heidegger's fundamental distinction between being and Being (the German terms are *das Seiende* and *das Sein*), with the question mark caress at the first intake of the reader's breath an indication that the narrative will read at one level as a specifically Heideggerian coming-into-Being. The genesis of Being, of this axiom which underpins Heidegger's edifice of thought, is most clearly expressed in the lecture he gave in 1955 to a colloquium in France entitled *Was ist das—die Philosophie?*

> All being is in Being. To hear such a thing sounds trivial to our ear, if not, indeed, offensive, for no-one needs to bother about the fact that being belongs to Being. All the world knows that being is that which is. What else remains for being but to be? And yet, just this fact that being is gathered together in Being, that in the appearance of Being being appears, astonished the Greeks and first astonished them and them alone.[12]

This astonishment (*Stimmung*) at the fact that all things are, that there is a universal and totally determinant attribute to things which is that of existence, is, or so Heidegger claims, the catalyst for thought, the source of what we should understand by 'philosophy'. The concept of *philosophia* derives from 'philosophus', a term coined by the pre-Socratic thinker Heraclitus, and it means approximately, 'he who loves the *sophon*'. According to Heraclitus' own conception, says Heidegger, *sophon* surrenders the truth of Being, namely that 'One is all' (*Panta ta onta*). Heidegger maintains that from this point in the history of western civilisation 'philosophy' became somehow estranged from its proper meaning. The heritage of Aristotle and Plato is not 'philosophy', he argues, but Reason, which is non-being. The latter, this self-sufficient mode of thinking that purports to stand aloof from human existence, reaches the pinnacle of its powers with Kant, for whom Reason was the supreme human resource. However, in *Le Roi des aulnes* philosophy is no longer the property of *ratio*; it has been appropriated, usurped by the Ogre. Tiffauges boasts of being there, in the very beginning, 'Or moi, j'étais là déjà, il y a mille ans, il y a cent mille ans ... l'être et moi, nous cheminons depuis si longtemps côte à côte' (RA, 13–14).

The Ogre, by virtue of its very essence which is expounded in the opening paragraphs of the novel, illuminates Heidegger's concept of *In-der-Welt-sein* with the vision of antiquity, when Greek man first questioned Being. This necessary return to origins underlines the revolutionary zeal of Heidegger's metaphysics. But it is only the first step. For a being which questions its own existence (*Sein*) by means of language becomes immediately aware of its *Dasein*, of its existence in the world, amongst others. And the essential mode of this existence is time. In Heidegger's terms 'we live time'. Time is the marker of human experience; hence the title of his opus, *Sein und Zeit*.[13] In the closing chapters of *Sein und Zeit* Heidegger articulates the temporality of this quest for authentic existence in the form of a theory of history. The theory ensues from the necessary assimilation of the individual's fate (*Schicksal*) into a collective destiny (*Geschick*) which is garnered from a common heritage (*Erbe*). The fact that this assimilation is necessary follows from the ontological premise of *Dasein*, that *Dasein* is a Being with others. The pivotal term in this nexus is the verb *schicken*, meaning 'to send'. Fate is that which is sent to *Dasein*; *Geschick* is the 'sending'. This process essentially governs the form in which the future will come to pass for each individual. This future, his future, is meaningful only if it is founded on an *Erbe*, an inheritance. Tiffauges, who has a penchant for outmoded systems of transport, also sees the future as a recollection of, or a regression into, the past. He writes: 'Il est bien caractéristique de notre temps que le progrès se fasse désormais à *rebours*' (RA, 106). Professor Keil, brought from Königsberg (Kant's town) to examine the exhumed erl-King, lends intellectual credibility to ogrish vision when he maintains in his account of the ancient Germans that the future is predicated on the rediscovery of the past: 'Mais plus nous avançons dans le temps, plus le passé se rapproche de nous' (RA, 296).

Astute Heidegger specialists like William Richardson and George Steiner have shown how the individual's pursuit of authentic existence logically entails the elaboration of a concept of common destiny. Steiner especially argues that Heidegger's theory of historicality outlined in the final sections of *Sein und Zeit* provides a more than adequate metaphysical framework for an ideology of National Socialism.[14] However, as Tiffauges progresses towards the land of his inheritance, as the course of history itself is bent ever more into line with the dictates of the Ogre's personal destiny, so another voice begins to make itself heard in the narrative of *Le Roi des aulnes*. The most important instrument in the Ogre's intellectual apparatus, to the extent that it sometimes seems to enjoy a discursive life of its own beyond the concerns and confines of the specific narrative discourse in which it is articulated, is the concept of *l'inversion*. *L'inversion* operates a change in the meaning of the sign symbol. When the Ogre bears the child, the extra weight is transmuted into euphoric lightness, and Tiffauges lauds this 'Inversion bénigne, bénéfique, divine...' (RA, 133). However, when at a later point in the narrative he holds the body of the decapitated Hellmut in his arms, the weight of the corpse bears down intolerably, and he discovers the nature of *l'inversion maligne* (RA, 539). This discovery signals the ontological demise of the Ogre's quest.

The concept of *l'inversion* is privileged in the narrative of *Le Roi des aulnes* because it is revelatory of the fullness of the symbol and concomitant failure of essentialist metaphysics. *L'inversion maligne* demonstrates the perversion of Heidegger's thought, redolent of his strictures against the autonomous existence of the human mind, a perversion resulting from an absolute refusal to rationalise. This irrationality became more pronounced in Heidegger's work after the war, when he attempted occasionally to relate his philosophy to contemporary issues, once famously describing the debate over the atom bomb as a journalistic footnote to a crisis whose real source is 'the forgetting of Being' at the inception of the intellectual history of the west.[15] In *Le Roi des aulnes*, the old Kommandeur of Kaltenborn indeed reveals the bastardisation of teutonic lore by Goebbels' team, but any attempt to rediscover a pure tradition, consonant with Heidegger's desire to recover Being, is also shown to be utterly flawed. The philosophical imperative commanding both the *Ecrits sinistres* and the Kommandeur's discourse is fundamentally anti-Cartesian; it creates no distance from which to observe.

Tournier manages the situation with aplomb, allowing his reader the scope to read analytically through a clever, self-conscious use of metaphor. More usefully with *Le Roi des aulnes* than with *Vendredi*— partly because the stakes are so high—Tournier's procedures can be garnered to a theory of metaphor. Here Ricoeur's conception of metaphor in its radical copula form is crucial. The meaningful 'is' of the metaphoric equation inscribes an ontological commitment which is endowed with the value of paradox, the truthful 'is not' given by the occluded reference.[16] This tension is presented narratologically in *Le Roi des aulnes* with the deployment of the technique of *mise en abyme*. The narrative of 'Tiffauges le colombophile' (RA, 211–46) is a judiciously placed *mise en abyme*. On reaching the end of the book the reader perceives that the story of the Rhineland pigeons duplicates symbolically an important chain of events which occurs at a later time. The story then becomes a fable. The sacred communion between Tiffauges and his brood is forecast to be the 'signature de l'être ... cette union du signe et de la chair qui était pour lui la fin dernière des choses' (RA, 216); however, the sequence in which this meaningful union is narrated constitutes a formalistic, structural device, deliberately planted for a different purpose. The *mise en abyme*, which is recognised retrospectively, filters the grand historical narrative succeeding it through a much sharper lens. Should the reader return to it, he will encounter a less ambiguous expression of the author's intentions, sympathies, and interests. Vercors adopts a similar technique in *Le Silence de la mer*. By focusing the question of how to resist the Nazi occupation of France on the interaction between three characters living cheek by jowl in a billeted household, Vercors throws into relief the fear, anxiety and moral compunction contingent to a debate which is pursued only in the most abstract of ways in the historical narrative of international events.

Jacques Derrida's subtle discussion of Heidegger's Nazism provides an interesting footnote to Tournier's treatment of the theme in *Le Roi des aulnes*.[17] Heidegger believes in the revelatory possibilities of etymology, on the grounds that the antique Vulgate, and particularly the antique German rather than Greek Vulgate, is richest in sense, for it bears existential witness to a moment in time when Being first spoke to Man. In diligent acceptance of Heidegger's method, Derrida applies a linguistic litmus test to each occurrence in Heidegger's collected works of the word *Geist*. He finds that the meaning of the term depends entirely on its rhetorical function. Derrida ascertains that, although *Geist* features regularly in Heidegger's writings, it seldom contains the sense of wholesale commitment that marks his use of it in the infamous Rectoral Address of 1933 and the years following. Elsewhere the word is either wrapped in quotation marks, or buried in a context that warns us not to read it as a privileged term in the company of others like *Dasein* or *Denken*. However, Derrida argues that it is in texts like the Rectoral Address, where *Geist* regains its essentialist definition, that Heidegger's thinking is drawn into the orbit of National Socialist ideology. At this historical moment of the utterance the quotation marks are lifted, and the word emanates a rhetorical force which is consonant with its etymology; the old German *Gheis* suggests fire, conflagration—a spiritualised ardour. Here Derrida is playing on the substantial gap he has opened up between the German *Geist* and its supposed equivalent in the French language, 'esprit'. The latter connotes, of course, an entirely different philosophical tradition. The Derridean antennae thus uncover the figurative foundation in Heidegger's texts of a nationalist concept. *Gheis*, in Heidegger's narrative, is the spirit of nationalism expressed as fire, one of the four natural elements. Tournier is careful to include a description of a ritualistic celebration of German identity in *Le Roi des aulnes*. The words of the chorus sung by the élite recruits as they celebrate the summer solstice on the waterside at Lake Spirding seem to confirm the rhetorical presence of fire as a vehicle for Nazi expression of the national identity. The following words are italicised in Tournier's text:

> Nous sommes le feu et le bûcher. Nous sommes la flamme et l'étincelle. Nous sommes la lumière et la chaleur qui font reculer l'obscur, le froid et l'humide. (RA, 301)

At the end of the novel the Ogre sheds at last his archetypal skin. In flight like Aeneas from burning Troy, though with Ephraïm on his shoulders, Tiffauges loses his philosopher's glasses. The narrative paints an amusing picture, as the misshapen giant careers through the marshland having had his ears adapted as a steering wheel by his precocious driver. When this 'Cheval d'Israël' comes to an abrupt halt, paralysed by his fear of impending apocalypse, he is prompted to continue by the threat of having his ears pulled off. At the same time the burden of his responsibility, the sense of his Being, is finally lifted: 'Tiffauges obéit docilement, et ne fut dès lors qu'un petit enfant entre les pieds et les mains du Porte-étoile' (RA, 578). Something vaguely spiritual and yet comical at the same time, amenable to the cluster of meanings gathered into the French word 'esprit', has occurred. Tournier's serious investigation into the Nazi phenomenon collapses into comic irony; and yet it is perhaps not such a bad idea that a novel in which so much is invested in the power and darkness of the symbol should end in the light of Reason.

PHORIE AND *MÉTA-PHORIE*

If the idea of a philosophical coherence to *Le Roi des aulnes* is debatable on its own terms, it certainly projects a false image of its creator. In common with many other twentieth-century thinkers, Tournier is dismissive of a liberal, humanist agenda which he sees as having become infested with a bourgeois ideology. In a diary entry dated 6 May 1938, Tiffauges records his disgust at seeing the portrait photographs of all twenty-two of the newly elected ministerial cabinet: 'Etonnante et patibulaire galerie! La bassesse, l'abjection et la bêtise s'incarnent diversement en ces vingt-deux visages' (RA, 121).[18] Diametrically opposed to this scene of bourgeois corruption represented by the rogues' gallery is the example of Tiffauges, who, let us remember, harbours little of the Ogre's traditional aggression. Rather, Tiffauges has more in common with a Quasimodo, or a King Kong, or better still Klaus Kinski's classic Nosferatu, tender, misunderstood monsters, exuding pathos and generally victims of the brutal, vengeful and anonymous crowd. Speaking of the inspiration for his creation, Tournier says:

> Ce n'était pas la guerre d'un lion que je voulais raconter. Celle d'un pauvre géant au contraire, un ogre affamé de tendresse, myope et visionnaire, joignant sans cesse ses énormes mains en berceau pour y recueillir quelque petit enfant.[19]

Conversely, humanity in *Le Roi des aulnes* is personified by the grotesque figure of Mme Eugénie, perched on top of a precarious pile of trestles and chairs in order to get a clear view of Weidmann's execution.[20] This scene recalls those events of greater moment in French history over the last two hundred years bearing the imprint of the Terror, when the crowd gathered to watch their corporate guilt expunged as the heads of hapless scapegoats plopped into the basket beneath the guillotine. Excessive pride in the Revolution and the hypocrisy of the 'Épuration' nearly 200 years later seem to grate on Tournier. His comments on the indictment and subsequent execution of collaborationist writer Robert Brasillach indicate a deeply felt cynicism.[21]

Tournier's unqualified rejection of western liberalism, juxtaposed with his overtly sympathetic portrayal of the Ogre in *Le Roi des aulnes*, has been the source of considerable disquiet in some literary and journalistic circles. On a television show, Tournier was relentlessly pursued on his allegedly ambivalent attitude towards Nazi atrocities (in the light of a book first published more than twenty years ago) by a dogged interviewer, who was eventually placated, but only after the author had supplied wholesale denunciations of *Mein Kampf*, Goebbels' collected speeches, and Nietzschean philosophy.[22] It would appear that Tournier finds it difficult to talk about this subject in any other language than in the language of his fiction. Even then, the genesis of the fiction, as recounted in *Le Vent Paraclet*, is characterised by anguish and contradiction.

More than anything else that Tournier has ever written, *Le Roi des aulnes* (perhaps inevitably) promotes, reasserts even, the value of art, in a philosophical sense, to society. The concern with representation is contingent to the theme of the novel. It is bound to be provocative, even more so when the author, in his postscriptum interpretation of his own novel, suddenly changes tack. Having asserted his problems in talking about Nazism, Tournier then denies that it is the major theme of the novel. Over the chapter in *Le Vent Paraclet* entitled 'Le Roi des aulnes', there is a perceptible shift from a view of the fictional narrative as a centrifugal dynamic which places it in constant relation with an external referent to the opposite view, of the narrative as an interiorising entity, a centripetal force which stresses the internal coherence of the text. The greater part of this chapter, approximately three-quarters of the whole, is dedicated to the exposition of the first view. Tournier dwells on his own personal experience of Nazism, and then talks extensively about the inception of the text, highlighting the reasons for his choice of the Ogre symbol and the appropriateness of this symbol as a vehicle for a novel about Nazism. His retreat, that of an author perhaps cowed by the totalising narrative of History, is spectacular. The vision of a novel bristling with symbolic significance is reduced to the notion of a self-generating narrative: 'C'est une énergie *sui generis* qui l'anime' (VP, 126). Although he warns against the 'froideur' and 'indifférence' of excessive formalism, Tournier now appeals first and foremost to the untranslatable beauty of aesthetic form. In this he claims as his master model and inspiration for *Le Roi des aulnes*, Bach's *Art of the Fugue*:

> Car cette oeuvre possède une charge à la fois humaine et cosmique d'autant plus riche, d'autant plus émouvante qu'elle est soumise à une contrainte formelle plus impitoyable. On dirait que cette construction monumentale est portée à incandescence par la violence des règles du jeu contrapuntique, comme le courant électrique éclate en lumière aveuglante à condition de passer dans un filament diaphane, enfermé lui-même dans une ampoule vide. J'aurai réussi *Le Roi des aulnes* si cette architecture apparemment adossée à la terre, aux hommes et aux bêtes émouvait, effrayait et amusait, d'autant plus qu'elle est en vérité suspendue à ses seules et secrètes vertus, et soumise à un ordre qui ne découle que d'elle-même. (VP, 127)

The variations on the unitary theme of Bach's *Art of the Fugue* correspond to the permutations in the narrative of *Le Roi des aulnes* of *la phorie*, a concept deriving from the Ancient Greek word meaning 'to carry'. In its most concrete form *la phorie* embraces the act of bearing. Tournier delights in the original simplicity of the term, as he describes how it became the *moteur générateur* of his narrative: 'Partant du thème phorique—simple comme le simple geste de poser un enfant sur son épaule—j'ai essayé d'édifier une architecture romanesque par un déploiement purement technique empruntant ses figures successives à une logique profonde' (VP, 126). Thus, Tiffauges passes through various phoric states, until eventually he fulfils his own prophecy becoming, like Atlas, the 'astrophore', carrying on his shoulders 'une étoile plus radieuse et plus dorée que celle des rois mages' (VP, 136). This perfect fusion of the terrestial and the celestial revealed in the closing image of the glittering night sky suggests a Mallarméan celebration of pure form.[23] However, Tournier does not want us to regard these successive movements of the phoric narrative as a series of coat-hangers over which Tiffauges' remarkable story is slung. On the contrary, the manifestations of *la phorie*, 'toujours couverte par le léger manteau de la psychologie et de l'histoire' (VP, 126), are, he says, the essence of the novel. *La phorie* is 'le seul véritable sujet du roman', and the 'perversion propre à Tiffauges et grand geste de l'Ogre' (VP, 120). Equally, in line with his admiration for the 'charge à la fois humaine et cosmique' of Bach's fugue, the conceptual basis of *la phorie* extends beyond the technical proficiency of Tournier's narrative, for it connotes as well that most exquisite of human sensations, euphoria (*l'eu-phorie*). A feeling of euphoria accompanies the phoric act. So, from an early stage in the narrative the euphoria associated with bearing somebody, or, less often, being borne, is confirmed as the pleasure principle which dominates the life of the sexually inadequate Tiffauges. Interestingly, feelings of euphoria stem from the 'fond équivoque' of the phoric act, which is documented in the *Ecrits sinistres* in the context of a meditation on the role of the head porter in the Christian tradition, Saint Christopher:

> L'Enfant Jésus sur les épaules de Christophe est à la fois *porté* et *emporté*. C'est là tout son rayonnement. Il est enlevé de vive force, et très humblement et péniblement soutenu au-dessus des flots grondants. Et toute la gloire de Christophe est d'être à la fois bête de somme et ostensoir. (RA, 85–86, italics mine)

The phoric act necessarily involves an object which is carried, 'porté' in the most physical sense of the word, and at the same time taken away, or 'emporté'. Therefore, the feeling of euphoria associated with the subject-bearer, where the carrying is also a taking away, is transitory. Goethe's poem is the textualised origin of the phoric act in *Le Roi des aulnes*. The 'enlèvement' that takes place in it results in the death of the child. In the phoric equation therefore, the physical presence of the 'enfant porté' is counterbalanced by the absence, or death, of the 'enfant emporté'. Euphoria is often used to describe the feeling of awe experienced by the Romantic poet, as he contemplates the beauty of the natural world, a beauty which is harnessed fleetingly in the words of a poem, but only fleetingly because in the Romantics' eyes the work of art can never fully transcend the magnificence of its inspiration. Likewise, the reader may be 'transported' momentarily by the evocative power of the verse in the knowledge that it contains nothing of the essence of the original model.

The extended service to which Tournier puts his discovery forces the reader to confront the essential ambiguity of the literary text. Jakobson's deepening of the 'fundamental dichotomy of signs and objects' promoted by the poetic function entails, as we have seen, Ricoeur's splitting of the literary reference. In the cold, detached world of textual analysis *la phorie* informs a technique of narration. However, at its root it is a brute concept imbibing the warmth of human contact. As such *la phorie* connotes the close proximity of author and reader, each of whom is grappling with the same set of rules, structures and meanings articulated through the single organ of the text. In *Le Vent Paraclet* and in the fiction of *Le Roi des aulnes* itself, Tournier demonstrates how the linguistic ramifications of *la phorie* govern the narration of events. My contention is that *la phorie*, or the writing of *Le Roi des aulnes*, is not the only subject of the novel, for we must also consider *la méta-phorie*, a neologism which asks after the meaning of the act, and concerns the reading of the narrative. *La phorie* signifies the carriage of something, *la méta-phorie* the carriage of meaning. The attention which Tournier lavishes on the concept allows us to make a declaration, which we have been building up to for some time: that the reading of a literary text puts into extended practice the same conceptual process by which we 'understand' the simple metaphorical expression. Thus, although Tournier anchors the concept to a set of formal procedures, he indicates, by comparing it to Bach's *Art of the Fugue*, that *la phorie* has the same capacity for dialectical regeneration as the terms in Lévi-Strauss's mythical topoi. In *Le Roi des aulnes*, *la phorie* mediates between the impossible demands presented by the 'référent obligé', and the possibility of gaining meaning through literary form. *La méta-phorie* establishes the notion that the reading process itself is fundamentally metaphorical.

Tournier readers have been tormented by two unsolved mysteries in *Le Roi des aulnes*. One of these surrounds the meaning of the ending which has left many commentators baffled; the other is concerned with the identity of the person(s) who impaled Haïo, Haro and Lothar on the ceremonial swords. The question is posed rhetorically in *Le Vent Paraclet*. Tournier's reply is fascinating: 'Qui? Mais tout le roman, bien sûr, la poussée irrésistible d'une masse de petits faits et notations accumulés sur les quatre cents pages qui précèdent!' (VP, 126). The fate of Lothar and the twins is a product of the narrative itself, prophesied by Nestor ('Il faudrait réunir d'un trait alpha et oméga' [RA, 63]), prefigured with the roasting of the pigeons, and premeditated in the discourse of the Kommandeur and the design of his heraldic emblem showing the 'Trois pages de gueule dressés en pal' (RA, 493). Thus, the murder of the children, like all the other improbable events in Tiffauges' story, from the materialisation of the elk to the transformation of the hunted faun into Lothar, reaffirm the status of the text as a narrative of fiction. But what can fictions tell us? They may indicate the extent to which myths are still prominent (especially in advanced societies) and also the extent to which we all fictionalise our individual lives. However, in the context of a narrative like *Le Roi des aulnes*, the fiction probes deeper. It identifies the significant role of the imagination in our recollection of the past, a past which escapes us as soon as it leaves the shadow of the immediate present. Therefore, the historical fiction will ask serious questions of the empirical historian whose enterprise is geared precisely to the eradication of all fictions. To what extent does the historian's methodology involve the prejudicial selection of features, the search for keys to understanding in the reportage of crisis events? How far does he rely on an intuitive rationalisation, and how far is the theoretical paucity of this approach compensated by the historian's infamous empathy? Here fictions can play significant roles. By presenting the image of the three Hitler youth impaled grotesquely on the instruments of their supposed heritage, the killing of three innocents who were also the supreme icons of a pathological political phenomenon, Tournier seems to be saying that there are some phenomena—and here the implied reference is to the phenomenon of Nazi Germany—that resist rational explanation.

In his chapter on *Le Roi des aulnes* Martin Roberts shows how the incident is neither psychologically nor ideologically motivated; rather it is an aesthetic inevitability. Roberts argues that *Le Roi des aulnes* is composed of a complex, interlocking system of prefigurative chains. In respect of the murder of the three Hitler youth, distinct referential fields are demarcated. There is a pronounced 'cri' motif. A number of references to unarticulated sound circulate around the Ogre's characteristic 'brame'. The reader's attention is especially caught by the hubbub of children's voices in local schoolyards, a sound which is manufactured as well as real because Tiffauges has chosen to record it on tape. This gently perverse out-of-the-ordinariness is echoed one day as Tiffauges passes a school playground by a piercing shriek that roots him instantly to the spot. The 'cri' becomes associated with pain and death; the death knell sounded at the end of the day's hunt at Rominten (RA, 324–25), and of course the screams of the Jungmannen impaled on the swords (RA, 574).

Apparently idiosyncratic mythological or literary references act as bridges between referential fields. In this case, Tournier's three victims recall Shadrach, Meshach and Abed-nego, the three Hebrews who are delivered from the fire having been cast into the furnace for refusing to worship Nebuchadnezzar's golden image (Dan. 3). The Old Testament story is filtered through Stockhausen's *Gesang der Jünglinge*. Modifications introduced by Stockhausen—he suggests that the victims are young men rather than adults and that children's voices are heard—make his piece more conducive to Tournier's project. Tiffauges recounts in his *Ecrits* how he is moved by a Mass given for the Holy Innocents. Furthermore, he meditates on the nature of the children's suffering and explicitly links the 'grande et terrible tuerie' at Bethlehem with the 'symphonies de cris d'enfants' recorded in the schoolyards, and therefore with Stockhausen's piece. The two biblical references, Old and New Testament, combine to reinforce the association between the 'cri' motif and the visions of massacre which also punctuate the narrative; the reference to the Massacre of the Innocents anticipates the deer slaughtered by Göring, the twelve hundred hares bagged at the Nazi hunting party, and of course, the culminating massacre of the three Jungmannen. Such is Tournier's attention to detail that he plants a number of impalement references, in order, as it were, to seal the specific fate of his Holy Trinity. The obvious allegory of the pigeons is complemented by separate incidents of two dead horses, one gored by a boar (RA, 312), the other impaled on the shaft of a cart (RA, 529). The impalement sequence is founded by another reference, this time to an obscure legend, told to Tiffauges by his alter-ego Nestor. The Baron des Adrets was a nobleman alive during the Wars of Religion in sixteenth-century France who took a perverse pleasure—'l'euphorie cadente' (RA, 82)—in watching blindfolded prisoners stumble off a parapet to their deaths, the final touch being provided by the thicket of lances placed below to cushion their fall.

Tournier's preparation for his subliminal ending is more subtle, though this time it relates to a single episode, the discovery of the peat man which occurs towards the end of Tiffauges' incarceration at Moorhof. As Roberts notes, the discovery occurs while Tiffauges is absent in the forest. On his return the news is broken to him with some relief by the Lieutenant at the camp who had feared that the corpse was his, 'd'autant plus que la description qu'on m'en a donnée par téléphone correspond assez à ton signalement' (RA, 291). At the autopsy the rhapsodic Professeur Keil breaks into Goethe's ballad and is interrupted just as he utters the word 'enfant' by a messenger who reports that a second body has been discovered (RA, 295). The second discovery turns out to be a bodiless head. Keil's descriptions of the 'petite tête' (RA, 295) and the 'petit visage émacié, puéril et triste' (RA, 297) indicate that it is that of a child. In a scintillating piece of scholarship Roberts elucidates a number of correspondences, relating to peculiar headgear, the lightness of the head, inexplicable references to it being that of a 'bagnard', and the shepherd's cloak preserved with it, which allow us to identify the peat child as Ephraïm, a character in Tournier's fiction whom the reader has yet to meet.[24] Similarly, the mystery of the blindfold embossed with a six-pointed star worn by the *homme des tourbières*—a detail which is curiously absent from the Professor's summative lecture—is retrospectively solved.

The inference then according to Roberts is that the father and child in Goethe's ballad, the *homme des tourbières* and the accompanying head, and eventually Tiffauges and Ephraïm, all form part of the same aesthetic continuum. Tiffauges' descent into the marsh is therefore the 'final piece in a prefigurative *jeu de construction*' without which the entire referential construct would collapse, and it is in this overridingly aesthetic sense that Tournier's ending may be considered as *necessary*. As Roberts stipulates, it is pointless to speculate as to why Tiffauges allowed himself to sink into the marsh, 'since the "motive" for his action, if there is one, is not psychological but aesthetic'.[25] Moreover, Roberts is critical of Tournier's representation of the final impalement scene. Tournier is obliged to accord to this event a special significance as it is also the realisation of numerous prefigurative references given in the preceding pages. However, by choosing to describe the scene with 'voyeuristic minuteness', he effectively transforms it into a spectacle. It is not that he trivialises the event, but that the close description may anaesthetise the reader to the violence. Perversely, Tournier is accused of a kind of aesthetic sensationalism. In his over-interested descriptions of the atrocity, whether it be the impalement of the three *Jungmannen* or the disintegration of Arnim le Souabe, he is positioned at one small remove from the ghastly Mme Eugénie, straining excitedly to get a better view of Weidmann's execution.

Roberts' criticism of what amounts to Tournier's pronounced naturalistic tendencies is the tangible expression of the former's more general anxiety over *Le Roi des aulnes*: namely, that a novel which articulates such a sophisticated (and largely unchallenged) view of history as self-generating and deterministic risks giving the impression that the historical reality to which it refers is equally self-generating. No less an authority than Paul de Man has argued that whenever Art, or artistic processes, are privileged, there is a danger that basic ethical and philosophical tenets may be diminished: De Man writes 'The aesthetic is, by definition, a seductive notion that appeals to the pleasure principle, a eudaimonic judgment that can displace and conceal values of truth and falsehood likely to be more resilient to desire than values of pleasure and pain'.[26] However, in the case of *Le Roi des aulnes*, Roberts neither accounts fully for the symbolic value of the references he cites, nor does he weight them in terms of their importance to the narrative. For example, the rejection of idolatry which is generally understood as the meaning of the biblical story of Nebuchadnezzar and the Hebrews in the fire is expressly linked to political tyranny. Thus, the symbolics of the story neatly adumbrate three dimensions of modern Nazism: Nebuchadnezzar's gold connotes Nazi iconography and the Nazis' love of icons, his autocracy Nazi totalitarianism, and his casting of the Hebrews into the furnace—the parallel with the death camps is obvious—their disgusting anti-Semitism.

Both the impalement episodes and Tournier's celebrated ending are overlaid with Christian symbolics. In addition to the Massacre of the Innocents, the heraldic design of Kaltenborn suggests the crucifixon, an image which is then grotesquely substantiated by the impalement of the boy wonder, Lothar, flanked by the twins. At the climax to the novel Tiffauges' slow descent into the peat bog contrasts with the transmigration of his charge, Ephraïm, into a Star of David shimmering in the night sky. The reader's expectation, surely, is that this supernatural event follows on in some way from the forging of the relationship between Tiffauges and Ephraïm, and, more importantly, the attendant circumstances of their coming-together. The most plausible of symbolic representations would cast Tiffauges as an unlikely Messiah, bearing the sins of the world on his shoulders, the inference being that only a Second Coming could provide redemption for mankind in the wake of the Holocaust. Through and in spite of the numerous inversions, malign as well as benign, *Le Roi des aulnes* ultimately keeps faith with the symbolics of the Christian tradition and the promise of the

Resurrection. Just as Christ bore his cross on his way to the hill where he died borne by the Cross, so Tiffauges, bowed under the weight of the Jewish child (assuming the responsibility in which we all share), wades into the weightlessness of the marshes. Sublime though the ending may be, the symmetry is not yet restored. Only in the future can this be, when Tiffauges finally reaches his posthumous destiny as the next Erl-King, when his exhumed body, embalmed in the peat, will tell its tale, and Tiffauges, the monster, will be put on display once more, this time as a concrete symbol of history.

TOWARDS THE OTHER

Tournier's obsession with structural motifs in *Le Roi des aulnes* reflects a subliminal anxiety about the role and function of language, conveying a sense of the author's responsibility as a communicator. In a survey which pays especially detailed attention to *Le Roi des aulnes* and *Les Météores*,Walter Redfern reveals Tournier to be an inveterate punner. He argues not that Tournier's work is strewn with wise-cracking puns but that his fiction is orchestrated by an inexhaustible polysemy. Redfern is keen to spot the 'original' pun in the narrative, which is identified as the generative unit of an expansive semantic configuration. To take an example from *Les Météores*, the surname of one of Alexandre's schoolmates is 'Ganeça'. The word 'Ganeça' occupies the nodal point of a semantic cell which multiplies in the course of our reading so as to inform the thematic progression of the novel. Diversifying from the proper noun, Redfern leads us on a tour of Indian legend during which the stuff of Alexandre's life, the 'ordures ménagères' over which he rules, and his militant homosexuality, reaches mythical status.[27]

Such chiasmic liaisons allow for an extraordinary breadth of reference, implying that Tournier's is a less careful, and certainly less systematic form of cultural *bricolage* than Roberts would have us believe. In *Le Roi des aulnes* the uncrowned king of the Collège St Christophe, who exerts a Socratic influence over the young Tiffauges, is called Nestor. In Greek mythology Nestor, friend of Hercules, was granted a life of three centuries and combined the roles of warrior and wise man. In Christian history Nestorius, the patriarch of Constantinople, is supposed to have denied that Christ was the son of God, calling him instead 'Theophorus', or bearer of God. In Joyce's *Ulysses*, the 'Nestor' episode takes place in a school, the subject is history, and the dominant symbol is a horse. As Redfern stipulates, all of these external references are 'internalised in Tournier's fictional character and situation'.[28] Therefore, superimposed on the form of punning alluding to the significance of themes to be 'picked up' later in the text (an obvious example would be the message 'A T pour la vie' tatooed on Pelsenaire's inner thigh[29]) we find in *Le Roi des aulnes* an inflated punning on proper names which 'authorises' a covert intertextuality.[30]

Redfern recognises that the value of punning depends on the connivance and skill of the reader.[31] Tournier is, as we know, a supporter of the pun. The pun allows the writer to yoke together far-flung concepts and features, creating a huge area into which he can then move. In soldering such distant affinities, the pun facilitates creativity. And to the extent that this creativity may give rise to the creation of new meanings, the pun is metaphorical.[32] The pun extends to what we have called the *épochè* of the metaphorical expression. It is the site of absolute semantic difference grasped through similitude in language. Puns offer fertile ground to writers, who, in their vigilant quest for avenues of fiction, are obliged to collapse the structures of everyday life. To imagine is to address oneself to what is not, literally to live in one's dreams. But the reader's job is different. He endeavours to re-constitute a world through the lens of the fiction, and this work is finite. At some point, whether he is aware of it or not, the reader will re-impose limits on the play of language. If the beauty of the ruins is to be preserved, then their restoration is a necessity. This is the contribution of the reader, in whom all the cognitive possibilities of metaphor are invested. The scope of the pun, on the other hand, is limited. It postures as the *agent provocateur* of metaphor, but it has no role to play in the symbolics of language.

Redfern's eulogy of Tournier's punning takes no account of these limitations. In his article any lexical ambiguity—pun, oxymoron, metaphor—is liable to be unquestioningly applied to the symbolic relationships Tiffauges maintains to the world at large, as well as to his characteristic inversions of these relationships. The nominal punning on Nestor and Tiffauges takes root in the flesh. Nestor is described, on account of his unusual appearance, as 'Physically ... an oxymoron ... an adult dwarf or a giant baby?', and Tiffauges as 'an existential pun ... for ever ready to *take off* from reality'.[33] Frege argues that for us to talk of the sense of a particular word, we must be able to determine its sense in all the possible contexts in which it might be used. Extensive punning must, therefore, degenerate into non-sense. Punning schemas are thus disassociated from the interpretive process. As Redfern acknowledges, a novelist's punning is always circumscribed within the individual reading of the text. The efficacy of the pun depends on its being recognised. In texts where the semantic orientation is determined by a significant incidence of puns, any meaning which may then accrue is arbitrary. In a text like *Le Roi des aulnes*, punning trails will inevitably be overshadowed by the propagandist influence exerted by Tiffauges, whose primary function is to communicate a singular, rather than a differential view of a world, that contrasts to the way in which we conventionally apprehend it, in life, and through the history books.[34] In this process of understanding, and responding, puns play a negative, warning role. At most, we can say that the pun is the equivalent of the sense of the focal word within a metaphoric frame. That said, it does not define the figure; rather it signifies the contradictory half of metaphor, connoting the philosophical paradox which is then stated explicitly in the form of the radical copula. The etymological origin of the word 'paradox' (from the ancient Greek *para doxan*, meaning 'alongside, or beyond opinion') suggests that a paradox is something which opposes existing notions. Therefore, the paradox must contain the germ of an alternative to the conventional, which may potentially flower into a different system, or a new form of knowledge. Perhaps it is on account of this challenge to existing hierachies that the pun has always been maligned in 'higher', resolutely traditional literary circles. In this sense also, it acts as a supplement to the more systematic percolation through conventional speech of metaphor. However, although the pun may trigger the metaphoric process, it may also backfire. Left to its own devices the pun equates to absolute, alienating difference.

For a brief period of time in *Le Roi des aulnes* Tiffauges is held in the POW camp at Moorhof. As many other writers (and film-makers) have done, Tournier lingers on the idea of the prison as a simple, analogue model of human society. The belief is that the state of captivity and accompanying material deprivation stimulates the imagination in a way which would simply not occur in the free world. This labour (of the imagination) may be directed towards the concoction of ever more ingenious escapes (from Colditz); on the other hand it may be channelled into the realisation of great works, Genet's *Notre-Dame des fleurs* or Gramsci's *The Prison Note-books*. The open-air POW camps of the Second World War are especially conducive to the development of an imaginative or sophisticated discourse. Where there is ample scope for social intercourse, but nothing much to do other than work, talking becomes an art form in itself. One of the inmates at Moorhof, who is gifted with an extraordinary verbal virtuosity, gives talk shows. The virtuoso is characterised by his name, Phiphi de Pantin, a walking tautology, a nonsense person or non-entity, the jester of the court. His role is that of the clown, the punster, the fool even, 'qui fatiguait tout le monde de ses calembours et de ses grimaces' (RA, 259). The morning after his most colourful linguistic show to date Phiphi is found dead, hanging from a telegraph pole.

In the context of the novel as read up to this point, of the magnetised narrative drawing Tiffauges ever nearer to the Napola at Kaltenborn and his confrontation with the Nazi myth, Phiphi's suicide may seem incidental. However, Tournier has a habit of according significance to his marginal characters, particularly those with suggestive or allusive names. Phiphi's death is important, because it concerns a fundamental question about language and meaning. The punster's language will always turn in on itself. When this 'en/déchaînement' figures in the discursive situation of the POW camp, it has tragic consequences. Colin MacCabe has written about discourse as a means by which we 'move away from a conception of language as a set of significant oppositions independent of the speaking subject (Saussure's *langue*) to focus on the position of the speaking subject within the utterance'.[35] For lack of any knowing receptacle, Phiphi's verbal ejaculations rebound upon himself. As the acknowledged speaking subject he finds that he talks in a language which has no meaning other than to make people laugh. The other prisoners fail to appreciate that, bizarre though it may seem, Phiphi's 'feu d'artifice' desperately demands an object. On the eve of his death, the narrator recalls him being 'si déchaîné que ses camarades le tarabustèrent pour lui faire avouer qu'il avait trouvé du vin' (RA, 272). Divorced from a common model of communication, Phiphi is shut out from reality, and he dies.

Phiphi's story carries the message that language should never be considered an entirely autonomous entity. For the punning novelist, words will always speak much louder than actions, because words and the workings of language generally are his first and last love. For Tournier words are signs which express and enhance actions in a particular way, a way which compares and contrasts with the representative value of other signs, like the photographic image or the physical gesture. The identity and different functions of these signs are fixed by a conceptual value common to them all; they refer to things which are already there in the world.

In his *Essai sur l'origine des langues*, Rousseau conceives of a distinction between proper and figurative language which relates to the intellectual and emotional planes of human existence. Raw, unarticulated sound is ostensibly a cry of passion: fear, anger or love. But it is not a unitary entity. Differences of pitch, tone, and the capacity to form a significant range of different sounds, are natural features of the human organism. Rousseau ventures that the savage's perception of this acoustic difference originally laid the basis for the first language. This would have been a kind of poetic tongue, modulated through a series of phonic similarities and disparities. It would have been a language inextricably tied to the expression of instinctual desires, needs and emotions. Nobody knows how such a language might have become *the* vehicle for the expression of ideas, and Rousseau does not even attempt to provide an answer. He merely establishes an absolute precedence: 'Voilà comment le mot figuré naît avant le mot propre, lorsque la passion nous fascine les yeux et que la première idée qu'elle nous offre n'est pas celle de la vérité'.[36] The language of passion came before the language of reason, and 'never the twain shall meet'. In between there is an historical black hole. However, Tiffauges partially exists outside history. 'L'en deçà vaut bien l'au-delà,' he writes in the first entry of the *Ecrits sinistres*, 'd'autant plus qu'il en détient probablement la clé' (RA, 13). The attention given to the incidence of non-verbal sound in *Le Roi des aulnes* is a persistent sign of his mythical essence.

This 'cri fondamental' echoes throughout Tournier's fiction, but it intrudes most heavily into *Le Roi des aulnes* where Tiffauges is both a receiver and transmitter of non-verbal sound.[37] Tiffauges' own version of the cry, the Ogre's 'brame', signals the inarticulate suffering and despair of the freak who is eternally ostracised from human society: 'En lui s'exhale tout l'ennui de vivre et toute l'angoisse de mourir' (RA, 73). Although we have seen how in Roberts' reconstruction of Tournier's magpie method of composition non-verbal sound is equated squarely with pain, the emphasis on raw sound in general may suggest depths of emotion and feeling which exist beyond language. Incisive literary criticism is careful to eschew any banal psychologising of the text. Yet rhetoric has always been defined as a strategy of discourse aimed at persuading and pleasing, and classical tragedy as a cathartic experience for the audience. Both are art forms that act directly on a collective psyche. The same is surely true of the modern novel; the more successful it is in commercial terms, the more important this action becomes. Tournier knows that to read dispassionately is not to read at all. But how does the author arrive at an emotive level of communication? How does he transcend the objectifying, distancing, printed word, when this self-same written sign is the only tool at his disposal with which to do it?

Paul Ricoeur is one of the few modern philosopher–linguists who is prepared to entertain a notion of 'feeling' within the theoretical framework of his analysis. But even this most intrepid of thinkers is concerned lest we misconstrue his initiative as an attempt to establish a 'new kind of intentionism—and the worst kind!—in the form of a new emotional realism'.[38] Nevertheless, he recognises that imagination and feeling have always been closely linked in classical theories of metaphor, and therefore that a theory of metaphor cannot be complete unless it gives an account of the 'place and role of feeling' in the metaphoric process. Ricoeur argues that 'To *feel*, in the emotional sense of the word, is to make *ours* what has been put at a distance by thought in its objectifying phase'.[39] The literary narrative is the representation of thought at its most objective. Therefore, to feel the impact of that which is communicated in writing is to go back, to regress to the concrete milieu in which and through which we see similarities. It is to encroach on the domain of the writer. The most successful authors are those who are prepared to bare their souls, to expose the monstrous nature of their imaginations.

In *Le Roi des aulnes*, the most emotionally troubling scene is the one in which Tiffauges witnesses at close hand the death of Arnim le Souabe.[40] The image of the fatal explosion is reproduced metaphorically in the text, but only after it has been reported in terms of the instantaneous effect it produces on the narrator, Tiffauges, who is standing a few yards away. The sequence begins with a routine description of the training exercise. Having supervised the distribution of the mines, Tiffauges heads off after the final recipient, Arnim, who is ominously described as 'le dernier porteur'. The narrative then displays a number of techniques commonly used by film directors to increase suspense prior to a significant event. There is a rapid increase in narrative time. As the time in the story of Arnim's death ticks away before the fatal instant, the space accorded to the narrative is extended. Thus, each successive movement made by Arnim is recorded in the accumulation of active third person verb forms. We are also mindful of the inexorable background movement of the subject (Tiffauges) towards the object (Arnim). Attention is focused ever more sharply on the figure of the boy. A similar effect would be attained in filmic discourse via the judicious combination of a slow motion camera and a zoom lens. Language signifies in subtler ways. Several interjections on the part of the first person narrator disturb the flow of active third person forms, dissipating the tension slightly so as to mimic the stop-start movement of the struggling mine-carrier. The effective increase in narrative time is not maintained consistently; rather, in this relatively short space of time (one paragraph only) the narrative conforms to a fluctuating rhythm, that is, until Arnim catches sight of the approaching Tiffauges, 'il s'arrêta à nouveau, et, m'apercevant, il sourit et gonfla ses joues pour exprimer sa fatigue' (RA, 543). Then, at the point where the subject enters fully into the frame, the third person descriptive mode is resumed.

The explosion, like the one in *Vendredi*, transforms the life of the main character. Initially it is presented through the perspective of the eyewitness, redescribing the incident as if he were making a police statement. Paradoxically, this experiential account merely serves to distance the reader, who has been brought cleverly into the action and up close to the event by the narratorial deployment of suspense-building techniques. It is only when the flat realism of the aftermath cedes to the figurative representation of the event that the reader starts to experience real horror.[41] Hester's 'gestalt switch', the transition from the proper to the metaphorical mode, is signalled by the narrator who refers to the event as 'ce farouche baptême'. If reduced to a matter of semantics, the metaphorical narrative represents the youth being blown to bits in a series of vivid images: as an immense, rising sun; as a purple hurricane hurling Tiffauges to the ground; as a scarlet cyclone driving his face into the soil; and as the crimson coat of the monarch draped over the shoulders of the Erl-King. The metaphors perform the most dramatic revelation of Tiffauges as the Ogre, via the ultimate *inversion maligne*; Tiffauges is literally showered with the insides of Arnim's body. His transformation is secured by a further simile comparing the event to the conversion of Saul on the road to Damascus. However, the importance of this episode does not lie in its confirmation of the reader's interpretive faculties. It denotes rather the failure of ordinary language to represent the event. The entry of metaphor into the narrative discourse activates an emotional response on the part of the reader. The reader does not feel this emotion directly. Rather it is delayed. What the reader experiences is the violence done to language by metaphor, and its re-creation through metaphor in the domain of his or her individual existence. He gains this experience not through a meaningless comparison of lexical items, nor even through the interaction of associated commonplaces— not many readers will have experienced anything similar in their own lives—he gains it through what Ricardou terms 'la litteralité de la figure',[42] the figure understood as real. In this sequence metaphor transcends its own representation in writing.

The death of Phiphi de Pantin dramatises a linguistic impasse; the death of Arnim le Souabe underlines the value of imaginative fiction as a means of understanding unimaginable real-life events. By creating metaphorical meaning from an act of absolute violence, Tournier inspires genuine horror: the horror of war, the horror of Nazism, the horror of the camps. The revelation of the Ogre in his symbolic plenitude, which allows the reader to feel this horror, is also a culmination attested by many preceding events in the narrative. However, Tournier's pre-plotting is not simply a case of pre-figurative chains linking references, each of which are neutralised in the sense that none is accorded special significance. The narrator in *Le Roi des aulnes* is not impartial. The grisly fate of Lothar and the twins, destined to flesh out the ancient heraldic symbol of the Teutonic Order, is, of course prefigured by the cowardly roasting of Tiffauges' three prized pigeons. Indeed the cardinal events in the extended narrative recounting Tiffauges' life in Germany are all plotted in advance. 'Les Pigeons du Rhin' is an embedded narrative, an allegory of the whole, not merely a cleverly-encoded reference, but a complete, detachable story. Its relation to the narrative proper is one of scale. Just as the simple metaphor is the fictional narrative in minutiae, so the story of Tiffauges the *colombophile* is a miniature of the narrative in which it features. A narrative which moulds into one hefty chunk of text childhood fantasies of elks, forests and ogres, references to Greek ontology, German Romanticism, and twentieth-century phenomenology, Nazi propaganda, the events of the Second World War and the Holocaust, to mention but a few of the main themes—there are many more offshoots —needs just such a clearer focus.

Throughout his career as an hermeneutic philosopher Paul Ricoeur has sought to operate an entire metaphysical system that pivots on the metaphorical relation between language (structuralist/post-structuralist thinking) and event (phenomenology). In *Le Roi des aulnes* Tournier develops the ogrish, mythological essence of Tiffauges in counterpoint to the evidence of history. Analysis of discrete passages such as the death of Arnim reveals an author wrestling with the demands of a difficult text, trying to achieve a balance between the language he uses and the effect created. It is an equation which is replicated elsewhere in the text and which matches language against reference and structure against history. Still, a careful reading should help to clarify Tournier's primary message: that, in addition to the genocide of the Jews and other non-Aryan ethnic groups, Nazism was barbarous because it happily sent to the slaughter the young it purported to venerate. Tournier's ability to use fiction as a means of conveying this historical reality is fully demonstrated. However, the latent, underlying, and arguably most important theme of this text concerns the writer's struggle to do justice to the victims of Nazi oppression in the context of a fictional narrative which constantly lures its reader away into a very different world of fantasy and myth. In order to achieve this reconciliation, Tournier promotes the need for communication. This is why the double focalisation of the *Ecrits sinistres* with the third person narrative is important. *Le Roi des aulnes* enacts a dialogue, between character and observer, myth and history, past and present. This is also why the novel needs to be read as a narrative rather than as a bits-and-pieces collage. We communicate linearly, through time, by accumulating and then assessing the information we receive. Therefore, within the framework of the novel Tiffauges' encounter with Ephraïm assumes great significance. Some time has elapsed since the scruffy black pigeon escaped a roasting, and since the second diminutive form was unearthed from the peat bog. When he finally appears, not only does Ephraïm introduce a spiritual dimension to Tiffauges' world, he initiates communication, and what he has to communicate activates the allegorical potential lying dormant in the text, thereby disclosing the reality of Tiffauges' *destinée*. Ephraïm is a symbol of the Other, in the sense that the post-Holocaust philosopher Emmanuel Levinas uses the term; as meaning the one to whom we in our separate subjective identities are always a 'hostage', the Other which always comes before the self.

CHASING SHADOWS: *LES MÉTÉORES*

Les Météores is the third and most ambitious of Tournier's novels. It also marks a turning-point in his career, for not only are the metaphysical arguments evinced of a scope, depth and complexity unparalleled elsewhere in his work, they are towed along by a narrative in which material, earthly well-being comes to depend in the most absolute of senses on the resolution of abstract conflicts. In the guise of a story about a pair of identical twins it consists of a meditation on the temporal predicament of human existence encapsulated in the word *temps*, meaning both 'weather' and 'time', and traces a dialectical process of thought to its logical conclusion, the displacement of the mechanisms of recognition by which human identity itself is defined, a malfunction which is all too vividly inherent in the phenomenon of the identical twin. The metathesis is articulated through a plurality of voices that appear frozen in solipsistic reflection even when they are driving the narrative forward; in one notable instance the reader is treated to a lecture in theology via the reported dialogue between two intellectually sophisticated protagonists, Alexandre and Thomas Koussek (M, 143–61). The dialectic takes on a number of concrete manifestations; it also initiates an intricate play of ideas. If the pastiche of Jules Verne's *Le tour du monde en 80 jours* in the latter stages of the novel, when the dominant twin is pursued around the world by his recessive brother, signals the cross-cultural import of the thesis—Zen Buddhism will play a pivotal role in the attempt to resolve contradictions—the twins' globe-trotting is also a desperate game of catch-me-if-you-can. Here Tournier is wrestling with a set of universal, or universalist values. His reader thus risks the plight of Paul, the 'jumeau déparié'; should he lose sight of the target, the philosophical edifice over which Tournier's narrative of the twins is draped, then the search for truth is definitively over and the lurch into a relativist world assured. In *Les Météores* Tournier seems to be testing out what I take to be his own Enlightenment values, the sum of knowledge contained in the large book cabinet standing in his back room. He no longer consults his favourite philosophers as much as he once did, but, as he has said, 'ils veillent sur moi'.

In approaching a text like *Les Météores* Kant is as good a point of reference as any, given Tournier's remarks on the usefulness of Kant for literary critics. Moreover, Kant's description of what constitutes 'aesthetic judgement' seems particularly appropriate in the context of the philosophical enquiry that underpins this most difficult of novels; that it should also have resonances in Ricoeur's theory of metaphorical cognition (outlined in Chapter 1) is an additional bonus.

In 'Les Malheurs de Sophie', the final chapter of *Le Vent Paraclet*,

Tournier is in wistful mood. Novalis' requiem for the death of a 14-year-old girl chimes out the damage inflicted by the Romantics on the true ideals of philosophy. 'Qu'a-t-on fait de la sagesse?', Tournier demands, 'Sophia, sapientia, wisdom, Weisheit' (VP, 275). By *sagessse* he means the guiding principle of Spinoza's *Ethics*, the greatest of all the metaphysical treatises in Tournier's eyes, because here the fusion of true knowledge and just action acquires a geometrical coherence. But this principle, which makes the conduct of one's life the ultimate expression of philosophical truth, has fallen by the wayside. The 'soleil simple et nu de la sagesse' (VP, 281) has been definitively eclipsed, first by Rousseau and then by Kant. It is the discourse of the latter which, for Tournier at any rate, is coiled python-like around the *modus vivendi* of western civilisation. He writes:

> Nous vivons sous le terrorisme d'un savoir abstrait, mi-expérimental, mi-mathématique, et de règles de vie formelles définies par la morale. Tout cela, qui sent la caserne, peut à la rigueur faire une existence, certainement pas une vie. (VP, 275)

However, Tournier has also absorbed lessons from Hegel, who saw that the dialectic of one era is solved in the construction of the next. Thus the Kantian 'architechtonic' stands resolutely in the way of western Man's 'wasting' of his Cartesian heritage. Kant's noumenon/phenomenon distinction remains the singular *point de repère* for Derrida, likewise he is a constant reference in the deconstructionist writings of Paul de Man, and it is his influence that Foucault implicitly attempts to nullify in his description of the modern *épistème* in *Les Mots et les choses*. Kant's rigorous attempt to articulate the various forms of human knowledge—pure reason (epistemology), practical reason (ethics) and aesthetic judgement—is in itself a demonstration of the limits of understanding which many philosophers feel has been equalled only by Wittgenstein in the modern era. Tournier proposes Kant as a model for the philosophical interpretation of art, one branch of which is literary criticism.[43]

Initially, Tournier identifies what he perceives to be the simple foundation of Kantian philosophy: that any assertion subscribes to either an *a priori* or an *a posteriori* judgement. *A priori* judgements are governed by the faculties of Reason. These would include the earliest mathematical principles, such as Pythagoras' theorem, and the great intellectual achievements of this century—Einstein's Theory of Relativity, and the theory of quantum mechanics pioneered by Heisenberg, Schrödinger and Dirac—judgements that can be made in any context, and that require no empirical verification.[44] Conversely, *a posteriori* judgements are not universal judgements because they are not necessarily true. With the aid of a simple experiment we can show that water boils at 100 degrees. If the same experiment were conducted at an altitude of 3000 metres, it would yield a different result. Tournier argues that these same principles apply to literary criticism. *A priori* judgements concern the reader's expectations. They are in place before he reads the work. For example, we know that any given Racine play will respect the three unities of Greek classical tragedy. This formulation is anathema to Tournier, who promptly declares, 'Il y a nécessairement dans la novation créatrice une transgression des règles reçues' (VV, 53). But, even as he writes this sentence perhaps, Tournier is also aware that it is he who is delivering an *a priori* judgement by virtue of his instruction to budding artists that their work should break all pre-existing rules of the genre, an instruction that Tournier the novelist self-evidently disobeys. Similar paradoxes inhabit *a posteriori* criticism, which seeks to bring out the qualities of a finished work. It generally comprises a self-satisfied narrative, a sequence of references to the finer points of rhythm and more complex structures that the average reader may have missed. But the *a posteriori* judgement forwards no criteria for the recognition of the work in the first place. Hence it will lapse into meaningless subjectivity, and the fool can pronounce 'Shakespeare is a bore!' with impunity. Once *a posteriori* criticism issues a value judgement, it becomes *a priori*.

However, Tournier's assumptions about Kant's theory of aesthetic judgement are misplaced. Kantian logic does not permit the art or literary critic to make the sort of assertion about any given piece of art which Tournier evidently sees as the stuff of criticism, for, according to Kant, aesthetic perception—his term for the critical reception of Art or Literature—is distinguished from theoretical understanding by its not conforming to the cardinal rule that every intuition be brought under an adequate or corresponding concept. Thus, 'the concept of beautiful art does not permit the judgement upon the beauty of a product'.[45] Equally, Kantian-inspired literary criticism rules out the possibility of textual objectivity. The text cannot be the locus of aesthetic judgement; this can only occur at a reflective moment. The text occupies a continuum of space. It is the same at any given time. The reflective moment is a point in time, when the coincidence of reading is registered. Therefore, the text is, at most, what is reflected upon at the reflective moment.

In all three of Kant's *Critiques*, the aesthetic functions as a go-between, bridging the gap between otherwise disparate orders of knowledge. However, it is most prominent in the *Critique of Judgement*, where Kant famously isolates the Beautiful and the Sublime as the two main categories through which the critique of aesthetic judgement performs this work of reconciliation. Kant's description of the way in which art is 'received' anticipates Ricoeur's plotting of the different stages of metaphorical cognition. Kant argues that there is no such thing as objective beauty readily available to those who contemplate art. Nothing is essentially beautiful. However, the beautiful may be manifest in the response elicited by the work of art, the response in which the mind enjoys a uniquely heightened sense of its own cognitive powers. At these moments the powers of cognition exist in what Kant calls a state of 'free play', Ricoeur's moment of *épochè* when the usual procedures by which human beings apprehend the world are suspended. This is because, and I reiterate, the aesthetic signifier is, uniquely, not subject to any controlling concept. The appreciation of art in Kantian terms therefore involves a necessary detour through the form-giving powers of subjective response, and it is only then that the artwork takes on those 'harmonious' or 'purposive' attributes that make it an object of beauty. This comes about through Imagination's power to conjure up experiences 'as if' in accord with the way that Understanding normally works to bring intuitions under concepts. Although Ricoeur lays more stress on the 'as' of the 'as if' equation, this is essentially a pre-statement of his view that the metaphorical utterance adds a new twist to reality. The beautiful (work of art, or literary fiction) thus stands in a strictly analogical relation to that process of combined conceptual and intuitive grasp by which we gain knowledge of the world. Only, in Kant the truly temporal predicament of the human being is properly exposed.

Kant's four definitions of the beautiful—that it is a source of pleasure without prejudice, that it is both universal and subjective, that it pleases universally without requiring a concept, that it is constantly finite—display the temporal paradox inscribed in the act of aesthetic judgement.[46] This paradox in itself serves to accentuate a fact of life. Our behaviour is oriented in two different directions; we react to things that happen and we plan ahead according to our expectations of what will happen. Every day we live the temporal paradox of which our perception of art provides the concentrated expression. This paradox is not, therefore, immanent to artistic expression. It does not originate in the art-object, be it a literary narrative or a painting. It is we who, through our aesthetic judgement, bring the incommensurable nature of the artist's genius, that which in Kant's eyes sets it apart from science, theory, and the labours of Enlightenment critique (epistemology), into the orbit of time, into the doubly temporal condition of human life. Art, and literature in particular, throws into sharp relief the form in which our thoughts appear, a form which has long since been naturalised.

Kant's 'aesthetic judgement' reflects the temporal contradiction at the heart of human existence. And it was on account of this power to depict the true nature of this temporal condition that Kant accorded such a privileged position to the Aesthetic. However, in the modern era the illumination through art of important political and social currents in the western world has progressively dimmed. As a means of interpretation the Aesthetic has been side-lined. It may well be that philosophical debate has waned in the face of the logical positivism that underpins the theorems of modern science. Yet artistic representations in the wake of the Holocaust, Hiroshima, the Algerian War and other histories that have shaken people's belief systems to the core have continued to stir strong feelings, court controversy, evoke hostility. Re-reading Kant is to re-discover the value of art, and the formalisation of this value.

Although his 'Analytic of the Beautiful' is only one part of his theory of the Aesthetic, Kant's other aesthetic signifier, the Sublime, prohibits by virtue of his definition of the term much further discussion. In the case of beauty, the analogy holds between Imagination and Understanding. With the Sublime it points in a different direction, since here the mind is brought up against the limits of phenomenal cognition by its encounter with strange, overwhelming or mysterious kinds of experience, for which no adequate object can be found. Whereas the Beautiful exists in a state of harmonious balance, the Sublime forces us to acknowledge the limits placed on understanding by its need to represent experience in the form of intelligible concepts.[47] The Sublime marks, then, the limit to aesthetic perception. It is worth bearing in mind the significant number of Tournier fictions, conspicuous amongst which are three of the novels—*Le Roi des aulnes*, *Les Météores*, and *Gaspard, Melchior, et Balthazar*—that end on a note of the sublime, especially in the light of the problems of interpretation posed by these endings. It may well be that Tournier, by deliberately evoking a concept of the Sublime at the culmination of the action, draws the line at which interpretation, or rather the reader's literalisation of the fiction, should cease. A reminder of the fictive origin of the text, the Sublime (in Tournier's work at least) puts a restriction order on the creativity of the reader.

Kant's work is usually regarded as the epitome and apogée of Enlightenment thought; however, his place as the first modern philosopher of metaphor is somewhat less secure. The word 'metaphor' does not feature in any of his treatises, whereas the writing of contemporary poets and aesthetic theorists like Coleridge is steeped in references to the importance of the figure. The charge is answered retrospectively by Nietzsche, who, exploding the network of Cartesian principles and Kantian categories, glorified the aesthetic at the expense of the epistemological. In 1873 Nietzsche wrote:

> What therefore is truth? A mobile army of metaphors, metonymies, anthropomorphisms: in short a sum of human relations which become poetically and rhetorically intensified, metamorphosed, adorned, and after long usage seem to a nation fixed, canonic and binding; truths are illusions of which one has forgotten that they are illusions; worn-out metaphors which have become powerless to affect the senses...[48]

In Nietzsche's philosophical revolution, metaphor, in other words Kantian analogy, is taken to be the very condition of truth. Which is not to say that he necessarily contravenes Kant. Despite the radical tenor of his language, Nietzsche viewed his own work as a continuation of Kant's project. 'Since Kant', he wrote, 'all talk of art, beauty, knowledge and wisdom is sullied and made messy by the concept of disinterestedness ... Only as an aesthetic phenomenon is the world and the existence of man eternally justified.'[49] The difference is that whereas in Kant analogy or metaphor is put at the service of truth, in Nietzsche it is abrogated in favour of mythology.

In Tournier's *Les Météores* these dramas are played out in experiential modes. One of the more frequent vehicles for metaphysics in the novel is the notion of travel: 'Le voyage qui se présente de prime abord comme un déplacement dans l'espace est plus profondément une affaire de temps. Temps de l'horloge et temps des météores' (M, 497). Genuinely modern phenomena such as air travel serve to illuminate more clearly Tournier's metaphysical imperative. On a flight to Reykjavik from Paris, and then again over the North Pole to Tokyo, Paul, the 'jumeau déparié' of *Les Météores*, senses the possibility of the eternal. It is but an arm's length away: 'Ma main gauche est posée au bord du hublot ovale qui me découvre l'horizon occidental où justement le soleil demeure en suspens' (M, 497). Source of light, life and vision, the immobile sun could be, if we recall Derrida's reading of Hegel, the philosopher's supra-metaphor. However, Paul understands that this glimpse of the Hegelian Idea[50] is not the permanent setting of the sun in the West, it is not the end of history, but merely another demonstration of the vicissitudes of the *météores*. Real time is not affected. His wrist-watch, powered by the energy expended each time the tiniest muscle flexes in his body, keeps on ticking, and the aeroplane begins its descent towards Japan, the ancient Land of the Rising Sun, which of course became the modern site of the rising cloud.

Paul's in-flight speculations afford a glimpse of the dialectical structure of *Les Météores*. At the beginning of the text a specifically metaphysical self-consciousness is signalled. The author is figured, reclining on a Breton beach, as a gust of wind (the result of a build-up of pressure in the stratosphere that will interrupt the course of predicted events in the lives of a thousand others at that same moment) turns over eight pages, all at once, of his holiday read, Aristotle's *Météores*. The predicted linear sequence of his reading, the expression of time through language which is the pinnacle of human achievement, is broken by the 'intémperies' of the weather system, a brief disruption but one long enough to reveal a gap in his (and our) knowledge, or rather a dislocation of the cognitive faculties (equivalent to eight pages of Aristotle's *Météores*). This fracture is the metaphor of time, encapsulated in the French word *temps*, alluding to both the rhythmic tempo of ordered, humanised time represented by clock and calendar, and the chance nature of the meteorological event. The dichotomy has survived the march of technology. Advanced satellites are unable to relay climatic developments with decisive accuracy, even those that are about to happen. Major meteorological events in history—droughts, floods, storms, avalanches, volcanic eruptions, earthquakes, etc.—have been, almost without exception, natural catastrophes resulting in the destruction of things built from human labour, often on a massive scale. When these events occur now, they are still regarded as signs of the supernatural. The only philosophical alternative is to take on board the view enshrined poetically by Mallarmé, that each human life is but one more throw of the dice. Faced with the sheer scale of human destruction incurred by the 1755 Lisbon earthquake, Voltaire found himself unable to choose between a vengeful god and a godless world. The immutability of chance grounds the dialectical structure of *Les Météores*.

Kant argues, in the preface to the *Critique of Pure Reason*, that once all matter observed in any given object is subtracted, we are left with 'pure forms', and that there are only two such forms: Space and Time. External aspects of the world are governed by spatial relations, whereas what Kant terms 'our inner perceptions' are related in terms of time. Astronomists have now been able to map out the space of the universe with a degree of objectivity. However, time is still resolutely concerned with, and applied to, human observations. Our continued desire to master time says something vital, not only about the human mind, but about the inner, bio-rhythms of human life.

There need be no distinction made. For Franz, 'l'enfant-calendrier' of Saint-Brigitte, time and tempo together form the intrinsic whole of his existence. Franz's mind operates within a temporal structure, which is one of pure chronology. Thus, he is able to state with total accuracy the name of any weekday on which any given date in the future, or the past, will fall, or will have fallen. He dreads two things: the pure succession of time, or 'temps mort', which has no structure, and any irregular temporal sequence which he cannot make conform to some sort of pattern. 'La météorologie' above all, because it introduces the unpredictable into Franz's calendar—'une série sans raison—une histoire de fou' (M, 74)—may induce the severest of panic attacks. Consequently, Franz's life consists of the construction of various defence mechanisms to ward off these periods of blank time. By day he gravitates to the factory floor of Les Pierres Sonnantes, where the mechanical movements of the huge loom—'ce tic-tac nombreux mais rigoureusement concerté' (M, 77)—soothe his anxieties. By night, he focuses on the play of light on his bedroom ceiling, into which the intermittent reflections of the three revolving lighthouse beams introduce a welcome synchronicity. But, Franz knows that the beam of l'Etendrée, the biggest lighthouse on the coastline, should further add to this 'jeu de reflets', because he has calculated its range and compass. It doesn't. The beam is blocked off from his bedroom window by the headland. On one particularly dark night he is moved to take a boat out in order to circumnavigate the headland, so that he can fix on the alternating red, white and green beams of l'Etendrée. He and the other inmates of Saint-Brigitte who join him in the boat are drowned.

The fact that Franz is mentally handicapped should not inspire pity, for his condition accentuates a disjunction under which we all labour. His obsessive and necessary chronologising is merely a natural, logical process of the human mind taken as an absolute. The difference is that Franz cannot tolerate the illusions under which most of us plan and live our lives. Franz is Hegel and Marx and a whole host of other thinkers who claim to have solved the riddle of history. He cannot be blamed for it because he is 'innocent'; should they be? Possibly, we find out in the course of the long conversation between Alexandre and Thomas Koussek, because they ignored the invaluable contribution made to philosophy by the Christian theologians. Theology has always identified the temporal predicament of Man's existence as the core question to be answered by any philosophy, whether it be Christian or Pagan. In his *Confessions* Augustine embraced the conception of the three basic temporal states governing human existence—a past, a present and a future—each of which are recuperable only in present time. Hence, the idea was implanted in people's minds that their notions of the future and the past were imaginary projections of a present time, the nature of which could never be objectively ascertained. Therefore, any thought, however abstract or essential, belonged to an interminable, indeterminable present.

Koussek maintains that orthodox Christianity (not to be confused with either the Greek or Russian Orthodoxies) was derailed by its fixation with the figure of Christ as God. The significant present was somehow stabilised and given eternal, symbolic form through the figure of Christ on the Cross. The Christian faith then amounted to the worship of a death icon. It became concentrated into 'le christocentrisme ... fatalement une religion de la souffrance, de l'agonie et de la mort' (M, 154). However, Koussek argues, the death of Christ was not an end in itself; rather it paved the way for the coming of the Holy Spirit. Therefore the great Christian celebration ought to take place at Whitsuntide, which signifies the coming of the Pentecost and the beginning of the history of the Church. The refusal to accept this coming of the Holy Spirit precipitated the schism with the Orient. What Koussek terms 'christocentrisme', the elevation of the Christ figure, or rather the worship of Christ out of the context of the Trinity, has locked western Christianity into a sterile body/soul dichotomy whereby the physical suffering of Christ on the Cross is seen to redeem the mortal sins of all men. The result is that modern Christianity is now predominantly associated with death, and the end of civilisation as figured in Revelations; hence the recent and widespread growth of evangelism in the west. The idea of regeneration and life, qualities uniquely associated with the Holy Spirit, has been lost. What is more, the exclusion of the Holy Spirit from the sphere of worship has effectively severed contact with the Word of God.

In the Old Testament the Holy Spirit is carried on the breeze. The Hebrew term *ruah* equates to the tangible presence of the spirit manifest in the winds circulating around the globe. It is a median presence, a channel of communication between the starlit heavens of the Father and the earth below to which the Son descended, along which the very seed of life is transported: 'C'est une sphère vivante et bruissante qui enveloppe la terre comme un manchon plein d'humeurs et de tourbillons, et ce manchon est esprit, semence et parole' (M, 158). As well as being the seed of life, the sound of the wind rustling in the trees recalls the divine logos of the Apostles, who, by preaching the Gospel in a universal dialect, overcame the diversity of tongues in the world that had originally poured forth from the Tower of Babel. Hence the Holy Spirit is the repository of universal sense, the sign of the original language of Eden where the words are 'les choses en soi ... et non leur reflet plus ou moins partiel et menteur, comme le sont les mots du langage humain' (M, 159). The Fall of Man is thus signified by a linguistic rupture, the separation of sign from referent enforced by the post-Babel division of language into tongues, and the only redemption is through the Word of God. Meteorology, therefore, can never be an exact science: 'Ses prévisions sont constamment ridiculisées par les faits', says Koussek, 'parce qu'elles constituent une atteinte au libre arbitre de l'Esprit'. Weather forecasts are notoriously fickle. The 'troposphère orageuse', Koussek proclaims, 'est en vérité une logo-sphère' (M, 159). To compensate perhaps for the circular non-time of the weather systems, the human mind has evolved the concept of linear time. Our essence is chronology, and even though we can perceive that some things are not chronological, our sense of time is so deep-rooted that the notion of chaos, of events occurring entirely at random, is always perceived as negative. We know nothing outside time. Koussek sees the human projection of time on existence in the raw, the absurd existence recognised by Camus, as Man's supreme response to the builders' confusion at Babel. Our languages are metaphors which seek to represent the world as we perceive it. These representations exist within time. Christian societies especially are held to an eschatological mode of thought. Our attempts to heal by our metaphors the fracture dividing the logos are haunted by finitude.

In *Les Météores* the Hegelian dialectic, probably the strongest philosophical challenge to the temporal constraints imposed on knowledge by theology, is tested. A form of synthesis is eventually achieved at the end of the novel, but with many other episodes the thesis/anti-thesis conundrum is resolved negatively. Jean's attraction to Denise Malacanthe, the *de facto* shop steward for the *cardeuses* in the textile factory, presages the break up of the 'cellule gémellaire'. The opposition between the generally cheerful, extrovert *cardeuses*—whose job is to stretch out and separate the fibres on the *carde*—and the *ourdisseuses*—the stolid, respectful team of women who reconstitute the fibres on the *ourdissoir* in order to produce the cloth—is constantly replayed throughout the narrative. The murder of Crochemaure is motivated by the bitter rivalry between the *chiffonniers* and the *éboueurs*; the Philippine pearls are re-united, but only at the cost of Briffaut's ear. In *Les Météores* the ontological commitment of metaphor is shattered; by the realisation, firstly, that it can never rejoin the original oneness of being and language which Heidegger sensed in the thinking of the pre-Socratic Greeks and which Christian theologians accord to the logos of the Creation, and secondly by the realisation that metaphor, like Hegel's *Aufhebung*, is essentially a unit of gain and loss, remorselessly tracked at its every manifestation by the guiding figure of human existence—Time. Heterosexual copulation, the ultimate 'metaphorical' unison of two separate bodies, is deformed through the intervention of Alexandre's homosexual dog. The wily mongrel spies his chance and mounts the unsuspecting, copulating male dog, so as to form an unlikely threesome. The delighted Alexandre views it as a cynical solution to society's marginalisation of sexuality; 'cynic' derives from the Greek *kuon* (= dog).[51]

Les Météores is decidedly fin-de-siècle. Vaudeville characters like Alexandre and Fabienne are having a ball, whilst others teeter on a precipice. Ordinary relations, ties and conventions are put under extraordinary strain. This is a world fit for monsters. Tiffauges makes an appearance, back in his natural habitat. He has an affinity for the twins, themselves objects wondered at and commented upon by the public at large. At the *fête foraine* Jean-Paul is/are both fascinated and horrified by photographs of Siamese twins, sutured together at various points of the body, spectacular physical manifestations of the 'cellule gémellaire'. When Jean is threatened with possible injury in the barrel of the Rotor, he is saved by Tiffauges, who, resisting the immense centrifugal force, bears him to safety.[52] If I am correct in reading *Les Météores* as the portrayal of a world in disintegration, of an historical era in which old philosophical sureties are giving way to the pressure of modernism and its view of a chaotic world constituted by the random collision of atoms, then Paul's vision of Tiffauges' face in the Rotor, horribly distended by the centrifugal force, is aptly symbolic. In concordance with his ogrish essence, Tiffauges is impelled on the one hand to carry the child, and on the other to resist the fragmentation of a unitary perspective. But the strain is now immense. When the storm destroys Ralph and Deborah's garden on the Île des Lotophages, the process is complete. The garden, situated in the vast expanse of desert, signifies ordered, human life, 'cette maison, ce jardin à l'opposé du désert immobile et éternel qui les cerne—tiennent registre du temps, à leur manière, gardant trace de tout ce qui arrive et part' (M, 466). Its destruction leads to Deborah's death. Hers is the death of an ideal, or rather the idea that ideals are possible in a world in constant temporal flux. Arriving some two weeks later, Paul sees clearly through the illusions of his own situation and deciphers the meaning of the event: 'Toute cette désolation a un sens bien sûr. C'est qu'un couple sans-pareil, voué à la dialectique, ne peut sans imposture s'enfermer dans une cellule et défier le temps et la société' (M, 483).

The principal theme of twinship illustrates the major consequence of this sea-change, which is that it entails a loss of identity. In view of the huge preponderance of myths and legends recounting cases of reciprocal denomination (Jacob and the Angel, Oedipus and the Sphinx, Roland and Oliver, and many more), George Steiner rates the recognition of self against others as an achievement of formidable difficulty. Steiner suspects that our mechanisms of identity—'the enormously intricate procedures of recognition and delimitation which allow me to say that I am I, to experience myself, and which, con-comitantly, bar me from "experiencing you" except by imaginative projection, by an inferential fiction of similitude'[53]- evolved slowly, perhaps over millennia, before culminating in the Cartesian cogito. It is now a fact of language, which is emphatically denied by the twins' cryptophasia. The living reality of the identical twins puts this mechanism of identity under the tensional aspect of metaphor.

The twins are self-alienating, like the Venetian mirror. As Paul tracks his twin brother around the globe he is struck by the 'lueur aliénante' (M, 425) in the eyes of the people who recognise him as Jean. The expression on Hamida's face is testimony to the assault on both the faculties of reason and perception perpetrated by the figure of the identical twin: 'Je revoyais la mine incrédule et soudain hostile de Hamida, l'effort que lui avait coûté l'assimilation de cet énorme paradoxe: ce Jean qui n'était pas Jean' (M, 480). But Paul is desperate to retrieve this essence, and he begins to imagine himself as Jean. The three words 'Je suis Jean' soothe his anxieties. It is appropriate that this simple phrase, the clearest verbal pronunciation of a separate human identity, is the one form of the copula in the French language in which the divorce between the self and the conscious self (the awful splitting of the self into two or more separate identities that ruins the lives of so many people who have contact with schizophrenia) is also prevalent. Paul wants to be Jean, but in truth he is following Jean, on a madcap chase around the globe which ends as the tunnel under the Berlin Wall (former symbol of the east/west divide) caves in, and the entire left side of his body is crushed.

The one remaining, unified perspective on this world, torn asunder by a self-generating process of dialectical change, is held by the twins' uncle, Alexandre, the *dandy des gadoues*. When Alexandre inherits the family business from his despised elder brother, he realises that the management of refuse constitutes the 'prise de possession totale de toute une population, et cela par-derrière, sur un mode retourné, inversé, nocturne' (M, 36), the ultimate revenge of the homosexual marginalised by the 'heteros' in charge. Alexandre is crowned 'le roi de la SEDOMU' (M, 36). The six depots over which he presides are, then, a window on the world, or rather 'une grille de déchiffrement', the piles of rubbish in the tips a huge wealth of meaning, engaging both the visual and the olfactory: 'La gadoue n'est pas une puanteur massive ... globalement pénible. C'est un grimoire infiniment complexe que ma narine n'en finit pas de déchiffrer' (M, 98). Viewed as a totality, the *gadoues* constitute 'une archéologie du présent, ayant donc un lien de filiation immédiat avec la civilisation d'aujourd'hui. Une société se définit par ce qu'elle rejette—et qui devient un absolu—homosexuels et ordures ménagères notamment' (M, 236). Alexandre flaunts his victory over the disunified, heterosexual world by the wearing on his lapel of six medals, each encrusted with the dried, compacted specimen of *ordures* taken from each of the six towns whose waste products fall under his control. The medals represent a form of taxonomy, a classifying of knowledge which is conspicuously denied to other characters in the novel. However, Alexandre goes further in his ruminations. His reading of the refuse—'cette substance grise si riche d'abstractions que les livres y poussent comme des champignons'—informs an aesthetic, a kind of neo-Platonic, pseudo-modernist ideal developed originally by Diderot,[54] in which the essence of the phenomenon observed is released in the copy of its representation. When the Roanne refuse collectors go on strike, the town is transformed by the appearance of the rubbish on the streets, in all its degenerative vitality. Alexandre rejoices in this blossoming of the 'oms dans leur fraîcheur primesautière et naïve, déployant sans contrainte tous leurs falbalas' (M, 209). It augurs the rise of the marginals, a kind of revolution in which 'Les oms tiennent le haut du pavé' (M, 210). Alexandre looks forward to the collapse of the entire social and political framework, and subsequently to society's subjugation to 'l'ordre exécrable'.

As long as Alexandre is alive, the world portrayed in *Les Météores* retains a cohesive, perceptible shape: 'Tout se tient, tout conspire, tout est système' (M, 137). However, Alexandre's system is predicated on his homosexuality, which is vulnerable to feelings of love. 'Amour = sexe + coeur' (M, 106), desire and tenderness. In this domain also, Alexandre proclaims himself master, 'C'est que je suis tout d'une pièce moi, un homme entier!' (M, 108). However, although desire conforms to the 'Alexandrine' pattern—it is 'l'équivalent érotique de l'idée de l'idée, de la copie de la copie: la proie de la proie' (M, 109)—this model does not facilitate the combination of desire and tenderness, encapsulated for Alexandre in the slender frame of Daniel. Having left the Hôtel Terminus (!), Alexandre takes up solitary residence in a caravan situated in the middle of a huge rubbish site at Miramas. On his way to visit the dandy, Daniel is caught in the savage dialectic, 'le poil et la plume', that governs the world of the *gadoues*. He arrives at the wrong time, during the evening changeover when the rule of the gulls gives way to the rule of the rats, the rival 'gaspards' of the animal kingdom. Alexandre discovers Daniel's body a few hundred yards from the caravan. He must have stumbled and been unable to escape the mini-avalanche of rubbish triggered by the black mass making its way to the surface.

In the last chapter of *Les Météores*, 'L'Ame Déployée', the stricken Paul overcomes the pain-anaesthetic condition of his existence, and in so doing transcends the dialectic in which he has been gripped for so long. The 'jumeau déparié' is *dépassé*, as the subject passes into a state of 'hyperconnaissance', free from contingency: '*Je suis* un moi absolu, intemporel et sans situation. Je suis, c'est tout' (M, 605). He hears the clock strike three, with a simultaneous echo, and feels his amputated left hand begin to come to life. Gradually he is assimilated into the environment; his joints stiffen with the onset of the morning frost. The essence of Paul folds into the natural world, as the sunkissed layer of snow evaporates into the ether without leaving a trace of its thawing.

This ending, which is in itself a rather beautiful, unusually poetic piece of writing, has been prepared in the form of the instruction Paul has received from Shonin, the Japanese ascetic. Paul's injuries sustained beneath the Berlin Wall signify what Paul de Man has termed 'the wound of a fracture that lies hidden in all texts',[55] the image of loss and renunciation experienced by each of the major characters in *Les Météores* in their individual attempts to reconcile the dialectic that dominates their lives. Now, the dialectical principle in *Les Météores* is presented under the sign of two crucial oppositions: the random, unpredicted event is opposed to the structured, human time of the clock, and the objective world to our subjective perception of it, that is, the world expressed through language. The first term in each opposition is the alienating, non-human factor, and it is with these exteriors that the Japanese Zen garden enters into symbolic relation. Typically, the meteorological event would be distilled through a wet/dryness opposition—a dialectic is introduced into the dialectic. The disruptive element turns in on itself. Through the mediation of the garden, which promotes an infinitesimal number of exchanges with the natural world, a balance is restored between 'l'espace humain' and 'l'espace cosmique'.

Like a poem, the Zen garden asks to be read. The mood is one of absolute serenity. Its most important aspect is its size; the Zen is a miniature garden. And herein lies the key to a method, as the reader is informed in the didactic narrative style to which he has now become accustomed, 'La possession du monde commence par la concentration du sujet et finit par celle de l'objet' (M, 537). This is a complete inversion of the rationalist procedures by which western man has gained his knowledge of the world. Whereas the rationalist starts from the apparently secure position of the subject and focuses outwards, the Japanese sage starts from the object—the world as it is represented in the Zen garden—and focuses inwards. The relation of scale is proportional. Shonin says, 'Le jardin nain, plus il est petit, plus vaste est la partie du monde qu'il embrasse' (M, 540). Hence the most eminent sages own the smallest gardens. Alexandre possessed the world in his six medals. It is only when Paul sees his wounds as Japanese gardens that he begins to transcend his bodily pain and accede to the sublime.

It is ironic that Tournier's 'big' novel—he quotes Kant's definition of the sublime as 'ce qui est absolument grand' (VV, 62)—should eventually have recourse to an aesthetic which exerts a relentless pull in the other direction. It is, of course, a familiar pattern. *Vendredi* is characterised by an 'intrigue de prédestination' founded on the Tarot divination, *Le Roi des aulnes* on the prefigurative structures exemplified by the allegory of the pigeons. The structural and thematic parities between the apparently diverse narratives discussed to this point are instructive. In fact *Les Météores* marks a significant landmark in Tournier's career. In his two preceding novels alternative visions of the world are upheld and disproven, although in each case the drive towards a totality of thought, a metaphysical system, is assumed to be the natural mode of operation for the inquisitive human mind. In *Les Météores*, metaphysics is initially asserted, and then violently deconstructed, before its final, tentative refloating. As a novel it is a relative failure. The book loses interest for many readers when Alexandre meets his death, about two-thirds of the way through the narrative. This is a calculated risk according to Tournier, taken by any author who puts a flamboyant homosexual 'type' character of the Vautrin/Charlus ilk on centre stage.[56] The stakes rise sharply when he is the one 'rounded' character, the one character with a strikingly original point of view that the reader can easily identify, and he is killed off prematurely, or so it seems. For the reader at least, the confirmation via Shonin's discourse of what we suspected after *Le Roi des aulnes*, that Tournier's 'poupées-gigognes' formalism encodes a philosophical message, comes too late.

After *Les Météores*, Tournier's fiction undergoes a number of related transitions. He embarks on a quest for narrative concision, investigates the possibility of a child-centred metaphysics, and reins in the philosopher's discourse which is such a prominent feature of his first three novels. The Big Idea has lain dormant, only to resurface in 1996 with the publication of a short work of fiction which, unlike *Gilles et Jeanne*, has the confidence to describe itself as a novel. This is a Moses-inspired, biblical western entitled *Éléazar ou La source et le buisson*, in which Tournier confronts liberal theology. As we shall see later, *Éléazar* suggests a new departure, for it constitutes Tournier's most serious attempt yet to combine the intellectual sophistication of his earlier novels with the more populist aesthetic of writing which he has subsequently developed.

CHAPTER FOUR

The Kingdom of the Narrator

READING COMMUNITIES

Tournier is a prominent media figure in France. In addition to his fictional output he is an accomplished essayist and expert on photography, and has contributed numerous press articles on subjects ranging from food, to German history, to arms sales. Just as the thematic content of some of his fiction has provoked hostility, so views that he has expressed in articles or during interviews have proved controversial. Inevitably therefore we are invited not only to read his work in the company of other Tournier critics, but also to situate it within the matrix of contemporary society. Tournier is not an artist in the mould of Matisse—who made a virtue of isolation in his relentless pursuit of a personal aesthetic—however much the calculated imbrication of his fiction-writing with critical essays on literature and art, notwithstanding the extensive analyses of the self as writer that have evolved from *Le Vent Paraclet* through to *Des Clefs et des serrures* and *Le Vol du vampire*, may at times encourage us to think of him as a writer obsessed by his own work and its reception. In this section I want briefly to discuss the specialists' view before extrapolating on the relation of Tournier's fiction to contemporary culture.

The climax to *Les Météores* appears to betray a desire for some form of elemental unity, a pre-Socratic fusion of language and Being. Critics are agreed that this movement is common to most Tournier narratives. His fiction thus tends to chart two conflicting episteme or bodies of knowledge which must eventually be harnessed and yoked together to form 'l'impossible mariage des contraires inconciliables', to borrow Taor's summative assessment of his own life story in *Gaspard, Melchior et Balthazar* (212).[1] Different commentators identify different episteme; for Kirsty Fergusson, Tournier stages and restages the fight between metaphysical system and ironist subterfuge,[2] for Martin Roberts it is a Platonist aesthetic of representation versus the postmodernist veneration of the simulacrum.[3] At whatever level, the emphasis seems to be on opposition and struggle; for Michael Worton,

Tournier used to be guilty of authoritarianism, interfering wilfully with the libertarian nature of the intertext,[4] for Colin Davis, the author's self-readings still constitute an obstacle to interpretation.[5]

In 1994 Tournier published *Le Miroir des idées*, a book of short essays on binary terms which reads initially like a series of home truths. Each essay is characterised by a limpidity of style and capped with a witty or elegiac quotation. The subject-matter of Tournier's homely wisdom will have come as no surprise to *tourniérologues* familiar with his meditations on fire and water, salt and sugar, the bull and the horse, talent and genius, primary and secondary characters, and other such differential equations, which have been either the subject of narratorial speculation in his fictional texts or have appeared previously in non-fictional form. Likewise his habit of recycling ideas and representing them in a different order or with a change of emphasis is an integral part of his methodology. However, in the preface to *Le Miroir des idées* he does make a point which is often overlooked. The ethical frameworks within which much modern debate is conducted are still somewhat crude and unwieldy, dominated by good–bad, right–wrong valedictions. Judaeo-Christian eschatology has left its indelible print on the western psyche. We tend to forget that the Devil is a fallen angel. As Prelati, Gille de Rais' *de facto* advocate, states unequivocally at the trial, 'Satan est l'image de Dieu ... Il n'est rien de Satan qui ne se retrouve pas en Dieu' (GJ, 147). Thus, the temptation is always to see differentiated terms as antagonistic. Tournier, drawing on the wisdom of oriental religions, demonstrates via his elegant expositions of a series of paired concepts ranging from the particular to the universal, how the prevalent mode is reciprocal rather than conflictual, with the emphasis on balance and harmony rather than hierarchy and domination:

> Comme dans d'autres tables de catégories, ces concepts sont accouplés par contraires. Mais il faut bien voir qu'il ne s'agit pas d'oppositions contradictoires.
>
> A Dieu par exemple s'oppose le Diable, être parfaitement concret, et non pas l'absence de Dieu de l'athéisme. De même à l'Être s'oppose le Néant qu'illustrent des expériences vécues, et non pas le Non-Être. L'amitié est confrontée à l'amour, et non à l'indifférence, etc. (MI, 12)

Le Miroir des idées generates a number of fascinating arguments, or lines of inquiry, not least the compelling idea that the powerful human instinct to metaphorise, to imagine, to see the unknown, the intangible *as*, is dangerous because it obscures the real battle which should always take place at an abstract or theological level. For example, the main threat to Christianity in the west comes not from the 'Satanists' of Bible-belt rhetoric but from the creeping advances through the different and often divergent philosophies of the modern period of atheism. However, what is most interesting to *tourniérologues* is the extent to which *Le Miroir des idées* may be seen in terms both of its form and its content as an aesthetic manifesto. Tournier's espousal of a concrete binarism appears in many ways as a natural evolution. It is a brilliant reformulation of his stance as a writer, in which he acknowledges his debt to others in the form of the citations at the end of each piece thereby reasserting the value of scholarship. But it also gives a clearer insight into his preoccupations as a writer and thinker. The prose style is lucid and simple. His language is his instrument, more a vehicle for the accurate communication of ideas and less the site of poetic speculation. The world, according to Tournier, is a sensible, coherent entity. The real is sufficiently explained by abstract metaphysics so as to allow a cosmic order to prevail over the constantly shifting patterns generated by history and myth. However, the unsolved problem of consciousness causes reality to blend with fantasy, thus ensuring that our individual windows on the world are more likely to be opaque than transparent. Likewise, the certainty of death and the question mark over the existence of God ensures that rationalist thought remains susceptible.

Through *Le Miroir des idées* Tournier, not for the first time, redefines himself. The accent is put once again on Tournier the mystical naturalist, the writer who deals in the symbolic and the concrete, the metaphysician *conteur* and the chronicler of everyday lives. The image of the dusty bibliophile labouring over his research-heavy text is demoted. The educator is to the fore, the scholar withdraws from the limelight. Whereas in *Le Vent Paraclet* the creative process appeared so important, since *Le Vol du vampire* Tournier seems to want to stress the product, though like all other writers he is so immersed in the process that he cannot help but return to it from time to time. In terms of the critical reception of his work, *Le Miroir des idées* is the clearest sign yet that the received view of Tournier as a bringer of impossible solutions to intractable problems, though far from misconceived in the first instance, is in need of modification. Certainly it would seem that the oppositional tension germane to his first three novels—the planned series of contradictions and paradoxes which I have tried to feed into a metaphorical dynamic—has since dissipated. The debate has important literary and societal implications: for the nature of reading—how should we be reading not only Tournier but literature in general?—and for the identity of the reader—who exactly is the projected recipient of Tournier's and other literary narratives in the late twentieth century?

Martin Roberts' analysis of 'La Fugue du Petit Poucet', a modern fairy tale from the *Coq de bruyère* collection, provides an interesting case study.[6] Consistent with his view of Tournier as a champion 'bricoleur' constantly mixing and matching hugely diverse sources in the creation of his fiction, Roberts reads 'La Fugue' as a juxtaposition of two distinct strands of *bricolage*. The story is modelled on Perrault's *Le Petit Poucet*. As he did with *Vendredi* and *Robinson Crusoe*, Tournier transposes a number of the finer details from his source text, some of which are then modified. For example, the seven league boots that enable Perrault's ogre to travel great distances become 'bottes de rêve' (CB, 65) in Tournier's version, capable only of transporting the imagination. This is a more narrowly targeted form of *bricolage*; as Roberts points out, in reworking Perrault, Tournier plugs into a specifically French cultural consciousness. However, familiar processes of inversion and displacement are also at work in the Tournier text. Just as the roles of teacher and student are eventually swapped in *Vendredi*—in an act of literary heresy given the strict delineation of these character roles in Defoe's text—so Perrault's ogre becomes a gentle, dope-smoking, vegetarian hippy in Tournier's version and it is Poucet's father who is revealed as an urban ogre, profiteering from the timber business. Having clunked his customary two horse-powered engine of dualistic referencing into gear in 'La Fugue', Tournier is then free to introduce with a measure of subtlety several master theses; not merely the reinscription of the ogre motif with all that it recalls from his previous fictional output, but also the attack on conventional views of gender foregrounded in his habitual rewriting of the Cain and Abel story, and the challenge to Christian orthodoxy manifest in his numerous rewritings of the Creation myth and general sifting of Old Testament text.[7] Although probably all writers, whether consciously or not, re-use their own material to some extent, Roberts is nevertheless justified in emphasising Tournier's *auto-bricolage*, given that it is, as he demonstrates, such a systematic enterprise. Here he mulls over Tournier's play of doubles to show convincingly how a text which is ostensibly a mirror-image of its seventeenth-century model delivers a stinging rebuke to the technological metropolis of the late twentieth century.

However, Roberts' reading of 'La Fugue' does raise a number of interesting issues, principal amongst which is the obvious implication that in order to be able to gain very much at all from Tournier's short story, the reader must be well-acquainted with the Perrault original. Is it fair to suggest that, given his systematic manipulation of the source text, Tournier deliberately excludes those readers who have not read Perrault? The evidence points to the contrary. Unlike *Vendredi*, 'La Fugue du Petit Poucet' is a late twentieth-century folk tale containing a number of messages about contemporary society which are easily discernible without any knowledge of Perrault's story. Appropriate environmental, ecological concerns are given a harder edge by Tournier's lament at the gradual disappearance of traditional crafts and craftsmanship in the face of a technological onslaught. The narrative is filtered through the child's mind's eye in counterpoint to his father, thus privileging the superior wisdom of child over adult, a standard Tournierian theme to which we will return later. Logre is a modern stereotype of the 1960s hippy, therefore by the mid–1970s a thirty-something parent. It might be argued that in his use of stereotype Tournier is parodying not only the then fashionable ideas about the 'progressive society' but also his own obsessive revisiting of mythical archetypes. Perhaps all artists and writers are ogrish in their different ways. What is clear is that in his flagging of proper names—the Petit Poucet of the title, and the untranslatable Logre—Tournier encourages his readers to rediscover the world of Perrault rather than slating them for their ignorance, thus exhibiting a characteristic though frequently underestimated modesty.[8] Yet the argument does not finish here, for as Michael Worton has pointed out, it is precisely in his play with words and especially proper names that Tournier runs the risk of being seen not only as an élitist writer but a writer whose élitism runs contrary to one of his most frequent statements on the nature of his art: that he writes with a view to reaching the widest possible audience.

Worton depicts Tournier as the ultimate linguistic craftsman, a writer of poetic sensibilities for whom each and every semantic resonance demands to be recognised. At the same time, this writer for whom no words are innocent has frequently asserted that the pre-pubescent child, alert and inquisitive, is his ideal reader. In his excellent study of *La Goutte d'or*, which, it is recalled, Tournier intended 10-year-old children to be able to read as competently as adults, Worton suggests that the passivity of Idriss, the naïve protagonist who fails to read the signs, is offset by the active intervention of a more sophisticated reader, 'who will ensure the metamorphosis of Idriss from simpleton to hero'.[9] Given the dazzling referential infrastructure common to all of Tournier's fictions and especially evident in the linguistic motivation behind his choice of proper names, Worton cannot entertain the idea that Tournier's elevation of the naïve or immature reader should be taken seriously. He writes:

> Tournier is, no doubt, playfully disingenuous in his many novelistic and metacritical justifications of naïvety. His texts are so erudite and intertextually complex that alert readers cannot but recognise that their semantic functioning contests any global authorial statement and that all apparently episodic details need to be scrutinised for both their intratextual and their extratextual meanings.[10]

Worton's commentary on *La Goutte d'or* is exhaustive, a mine of information assembled with a mental agility which is not always a feature of the academic world. He tends to focus on the individual lexical unit (unlike Mireille Rosello, for example, who concentrates intensively on the power relationships between author, narrator and reader in her own work on Tournier) and is generally less interested in narrative structures. At times his own research appears to mirror Tournier's fascination with etymologies and semantics. However, as he teases out the multiple ramifications of the proper names in the final chapter of his study, Worton shows signs of concern. The names have a 'potent semantic force', he asserts, 'but often in a hidden, elitist way'.[11] His quest for meaning in the name of Zett Zobeida, an important figure who initiates and closes the narrative, takes him from the symbolism of the letter (z), to the meaning of her name in an Arabic dialect, to a namesake in the *Arabian Nights*, and on to a better informed comparison of her role in the text with that of another emblematic figure, Oum Kalsoum. Worton accepts that there is a place for such 'transcultural play', but he cautions against a whole category of names in *La Goutte d'or* which refer to Tournier's own friends. More ridiculously still, a majority of the tissue of quotations forming the calligram in the encrypted story, 'La Reine blonde' are attributed to two 'famous', though strangely unheard-of writers, one of whom rejoices in a Germanic-sounding name, Edward Reinroth. Edouard is Tournier's second Christian name, and Reinroth suspiciously close to an anagram of Tournier. Worton finds redemption in Tournier's mocking of the authority of texts, but in truth we have travelled a long way from the democratic notion that the pleasure of reading an imaginative work of fiction should be available to all in equal measure.

Worton highlights the dangers of an approach to reading Tournier which is exclusively rooted in semantics. He illustrates how the educated reader of *La Goutte d'or* risks being engulfed in the research text as surely as Ibrahim in the well, and Idriss in the alginate. Whereas in Philippe Sollers' 'experimental' novels of the late 1960s and early 1970s individual words are supposed to run wild, in Tournier's fiction they are circumscribed within a more immediately intelligible discourse, the function of which is to endow the imaginative fruit of Tournier's researches and observations with a structural coherence. The subterfuge of writing is an essential issue for Tournier's critics, but it remains in my view an ancillary part of his novelistic project. As in contemporary film studies, what is important is the reception of the work. Its value is determined by the effect it creates in the collective mind of its readership, a response which takes us back not to the genesis of the text but to the inspirational qualities of the writer's imagination which are manifest in it.[12]

Another critical consensus concerning the evolution of Tournier's art promotes the view that the publication of *Le Vol du vampire* in 1981 constitutes an important staging-post on the road to artistic maturity. In the title essay of the collection, Tournier, once described as a 'protective terrorist' on account of his apparent desire to establish author-sanctioned readings of his own work,[13] acquiesces fulsomely to the necessary contribution to the artistic process of his readers. This change of policy arrives in the form of a superb extended metaphor:

> Un livre n'a pas un auteur, mais un nombre indéfini d'auteurs ... Un livre écrit, mais non lu, n'existe pas pleinement. Il ne possède qu'une demi-existence ... L'écrivain le sait, et lorsqu'il publie un livre, il lâche dans la foule anonyme des hommes et des femmes une nuée d'oiseaux de papier, des vampires secs, assoiffés de sang, qui se répandent au hasard en quête de lecteurs. A peine un livre s'est-il abattu sur un lecteur qu'il se gonfle de sa chaleur et de ses rêves. Il fleurit, s'épanouit, devient enfin ce qu'il est: un monde imaginaire foisonnant, où se mêlent indistinctement—comme sur le visage d'un enfant les traits de son père et de sa mère—les intentions de l'écrivain et les fantasmes du lecteur. Ensuite, la lecture terminée, le livre épuisé, abandonné par le lecteur, attendra un autre vivant afin de féconder à son tour son imagination, et, s'il a la chance de réaliser sa vocation, il passera ainsi de main en main, comme un coq qui tamponne successivement un nombre indéfini de poules. (VV, 10–11)

The wonderfully dramatic book–vampire equation is supported by two carefully chosen similes. The blood of the reader flows into the book, mixing the machinations of his or her imagination with 'les intentions de l'écrivain', as seamlessly as the features of mother and father merge in the face of their child. Once the book is finished, it is recommended to another person, and then another, stopping at each site on a theoretically endless journey, like a cockerel inseminating vast numbers of hens. This development of the vampire metaphor is not merely a figurative animation of the critic's prose. Neither the 'genetic' nor 'virile cockerel' similes are especially meaningful in isolation; both conspire to accentuate important aspects of the dominant figure. All three images bear witness to the aggression of a writer anxious to convey his ideas. However, this aggression is balanced by the direction of flow. The input of the reader's blood embodies the necessarily creative, individuated autonomy of the reader. Most importantly, the 'genetic' simile affords an insight into what I take to be the central plank in Tournier's aesthetic of the novel. A successful work of fiction involves the creation of 'un monde imaginaire foisonnant', in which the vision of the artist-producer sparks or connects with the imagination of the consumer to form something new. The significance accorded by Tournier to this productive interaction between author and reader gives strong inducement to read each of his fictions, and indeed the literary text generally, as experiments in (the art of) metaphor.

The title essay of *Le Vol du vampire* is also a conscious attempt on behalf of the writer to restore the literary text to its rightful place in the world outside it. Stress is laid on the material existence of the process; less on the unseen writing of the text and more on its publication, dissemination and reception. Tournier's stylistic presentation conceals a point of blinding simplicity: namely that writing is one among many activities that most of us indulge in on most days, that it is also only one of the oldest among an ever increasing number of communicative techniques at our disposal and, therefore, we should not overstate the significance of the letter.[14] In three of Tournier's novels the act of writing features conspicuously as a narrative event, a physical process that consumes the energy of the character(s) involved. In *Vendredi*, Robinson painstakingly constructs viable writing materials, in *Le Roi des aulnes* Tiffauges' diaries are interrupted by the war, and in *La Goutte d'or* Idriss is shown the techniques required to perform the ancient art of calligraphy which, when revealed in its dual function of aesthetic object and interpretive code, supplies a latent, retrospective commentary on the preceding events of the novel. These novels demonstrate the language of literature in relation to a bigger, and infinitely variant world, as well as in relation to its own being. In *Le Vol du vampire* the author for the first time encodes the limits of this textuality.

The existence of writing agents within the narrative of fiction incites interpretation. It is as if by personifying the process of writing in his texts Tournier is trying to make of his readers less an abstract, theoretical concept and more a human presence whose participation in the production of meaning is evoked almost in terms of a spiritual communion. In his 'Christian' novel, *Gaspard, Melchior et Balthazar*, the narrative is commanded by the 'readings' of the three kings, whose interpretation of the blazing comet determines the direction they should take. However, the meaning of their respective journeys to Herod's court is also pre-determined by issues which are pertinent to each individual king. Each sophisticated comet-reading falls under the aegis of a personal history. Gaspard sees it as the head of the blonde woman who will forever spurn the advances of the black king, whereas Balthazar, art-collector and amateur entomologist, sees the reincarnation of his prized butterfly specimen which has been destroyed by the fanatical, image-hating priests at his court. The astronomical phenomenon has no objective authority whatsoever. Indeed Melchior, the pauper king, is so beset with his own personal difficulties that he does not even notice it. For a while this royal community of readers is disturbed by the feared authority of Herod, whose comprehensive intelligence network makes him privy to the exact details of each king's personal situation. It appears that the readers have been brought to kneel before the author-tyrant who is prepared to implement 'la terrible loi du pouvoir'; that is, until it is revealed that the ailing Herod, too, has been reading the comet, as 'l'oiseau de feu—qui détient le secret de ma succession' (GMB, 152). The comet (text or symbol) is to each king that which concerns him most.

The arrival on centre stage of the legendary fourth King, Taor, injects a stream of fantasy into the principal vein of the Nativity narrative.[15] Taor hails from distant shores. Like many other Tournier protagonists he is on a learning curve. Arriving too late for the Nativity, the naïve Prince treats the over-twos of Bethlehem to a sweets party on the hillside as the Massacre of the Innocents takes its ugly course in the valley below. He finds out too late. Elephants and entourage are lost and the sweet-toothed Taor accepts a 33-year imprisonment in the salt kingdom of the Sodomites. Finally, this 'perpétuel retardataire' misses the Last Supper, but is the first to take the Eucharist.

As Tournier indicates in a post scriptum to the novel, the narrative of *Gaspard, Melchior et Balthazar* feeds on the many entailments generated by the iconography of the magi. However, the Taor narration crystallises into a purposeful meditation on a theme to which Tournier returns often, the Old Testament distinction between 'image' and 'likeness'. Tournier's interpretation[16]—that the absolute identity between God and Man is conveyed through the verse in Genesis in which it is said 'God made Man in his image and after his likeness', the likeness but not the image being lost once Adam has fallen from Eden—is reiterated in the novel by Balthazar, who will go on to reveal himself as one of the first theologians:

> On ne saurait trop méditer les premières lignes de la Genèse, dit-il. Dieu fit l'homme à son image et à sa ressemblance. Pourquoi ces deux mots? Quelle différence y a-t-il entre l'image et la ressemblance? C'est sans doute que la ressemblance comprend tout l'être—corps et âme—tandis que l'image n'est qu'un masque superficiel et peut-être trompeur. (GMB, 47)

Whereas the fallen Adam represents Man divested of his likeness to God but retaining his superficial image, Christ figures the return to the totality of God and Man. Thus, Taor, the legendary or invented king, shadows Christ, but in the guise of Adam. The parallelism between Christ and Adam is established by Gaspard, who, with a surreptitious glance in the future direction of Darwin, sees the Christ-child in the manger as black: 'N'est-ce pas logique? Si Adam n'a blanchi qu'en commettant le péché, Jésus ne doit-il pas être noir comme notre ancêtre dans son état originel?' (GMB, 220).[17] Taor's real journey begins at this point. Precipitated by the birth of Christ, it is an inversion of the Fall from the Garden of Eden, a journey back to the oneness of God and Man and a journey forward to the propagation and widespread acceptance of Christianity. Taor's symbolic role complements his supratextual function as a prototype of the ideal Tournier reader. His naïvety, which is stressed in the earlier sections of his narration, is redressed by a contemplative nature that yields greater insight. If experience can be substituted for scholasticism, then Taor's quest is that of the Tournier reader, and his grail the sacred communion by which he will graduate to a superior reading status. However, lest biblical scholars get carried away, Tournier issues his customary warning. In this instance his spokesman is Gaspard, speaking in the tones of a tourist who has been on one guided tour too many:

> Nous devions nous retrouver le lendemain dans la grotte de Macpela qui abrite les tombes d'Adam, d'Eve, d'Abraham, de Sara, d'Isaac, de Rebecca, de Lia et de Jacob, bref un véritable caveau de famille biblique, auquel il ne manque que les cendres de Yahvé lui-même pour être complet. Si je parle légèrement et de façon irrévérencieuse de ces choses pourtant vénérables, c'est

sans doute que je les trouve très loin de moi. Les légendes vivent de notre substance. Elles ne tiennent leur vérité que de la complicité de nos coeurs. Dès lors que nous n'y reconnaissons pas notre propre histoire, elles ne sont que bois mort et paille sèche. (GMB, 46)

Gaspard, Melchior et Balthazar was published in 1980, *Le Vol du vampire* in 1981. The coincidence is interesting. Whereas Tournier with his multi-faceted collection of reader-characters exalts the pleasure of reading in its essential diversity in the first text, the direct address to the reader in the second raises the question of who Tournier is actually talking to; or rather it presupposes that we already know, roughly, the make-up of his bloodthirsty horde. And yet although Tournier values most highly the inspiration he receives from this loyal multitude of amateur readers, much of what we know of reactions to his work are the opinions of the 'professionals': reviewers and career academics.

Over the past thirty years some leading intellectuals, including George Steiner, Alain Finkielkraut and Marc Fumaroli, have moved that the literate, literature-loving public coveted by novelists like Tournier is in sharp decline. Steiner cites research published as long ago as 1970 which assesses the literacy of more than half the adult population of the USA at a twelve-year-old level.[18] In classical lettrist mode he argues that the promotion of science is coeval with a comprehensive decline in traditional ideals of literate speech, with the result that many people now living in the west are unable to penetrate syntax to any but the shallowest reach. The link is not a direct one. What he proposes is that the explosion of imagistic technological devices, a development we can easily gauge by the proliferation of screens over the twenty years since Steiner's book first appeared on the shelves, has entailed a diminution of our reliance on language as a primary means of cognition. Thus we live in what Steiner calls a 'post-culture'; our mass technocracies are characterised by a semi-literacy. The argument is familiar to those who have followed the cultural debates that have taken place in France throughout the 1980s and early 1990s, and especially to those acquainted with Alain Finkielkraut's attack on 'la culture du zapping' contained in his book, *La Défaite de la pensée*. Finkielkraut is in the vanguard of an anti-postmodern movement which promotes the cultural pre-eminence of Enlightenment values. Eighteenth-century concepts of truth, justice, reason, and a belief in progress are seen as inviolable because they constitute the bedrock of the French nation-state. Via a negative critique of contemporary society in which he emphasises the banality of a relativist culture, Finkielkraut defends the universalist principles enshrined in the *Déclaration des droits de l'homme* which are manifest in cultural terms through the necessary provision of a classical education for all and by the recognition afforded by the unwritten rules of society to those who acquire knowledge and appreciate the *beaux-arts*.

Neither thesis seems tenable. In particular Steiner's assertion that too many people nowadays are unable to read long sentences and, by logical extension, have lost the capacity to formulate thoughts and link them syntactically, is bogus. Even those environmental linguists who are diametrically opposed to the Chomskyan axiom that Man is fundamentally a grammatical animal would concede that only the few unfortunates who suffer from genetic impediments are unable to communicate at an extraordinarily advanced, 'syntactic' level. In which case, the debate pivots on the question of education. More pertinently, if there is a literacy problem or indeed a general lack of aptitude for reading, then attention should be focused on education in the primary sector rather than on the supposedly pernicious influence of mass culture.[19]

At the root of this cultural backlash is a paternalistic concern for the well-being of the written sign. Over a long period of time, some 5,500 years since the first 'script' was developed among the Sumerians of Mesopotamia, the western consciousness has 'interiorised' writing. What was once a science has been naturalised; nowadays we seldom make a conscious effort to differentiate between writing and speaking, unless our children are palpably deficient in one or the other aspect. Both are assumed to be immanent to language. However, it was not always thus. Eric A. Havelock has argued that Plato's exclusion of poets from his Republic was in fact a rejection of the pristine, aggregative, paratactic, oral-style thinking perpetuated in Homer, in favour of the keen analysis and dissection of the world and of thought itself, made possible by the interiorisation of the alphabet in the Greek psyche.[20] Writing has its own history, its special rites of passage stretching from the Greeks' introduction of vowels into the alphabet (to which Havelock attributes the ascendency of Greek analytic thought)[21] via Caxton's first printing press, to the numerous self-verifying tricks built in to the modern word-processor. This history has involved a restructuring of human consciousness, the shaping of a mind accustomed to the sophisticated, mnemonic formulas of an oral culture, into one in which the referential incision of the written sign could be accommodated. The manifold relations of Man to his environment that form the context for all philosophical and scientific debate were opened up by this fixing of knowledge through the possibility of temporal stasis to be achieved through writing. In a scintillating piece of scholarship Walter Ong marks the various stages in this conflictual transition from oral to literate based cultures. Language, Ong reminds us, is over-whelmingly oral. Of the many thousands of languages that have existed, we know of only 106 that have ever been committed to writing to a degree sufficient to have produced literature. And, of the 3,000 or so languages spoken today, only some 78 have a literature. Therefore, Ong affirms, 'The basic orality of language is permanent'.[22] Whereas writing has been interiorised into the western psyche, speech is inseparable from our consciousness.

Ong is inspired by the example of the American classicist, Milman Parry, who transformed the nature of research into the Greek epos. Parry discovered that virtually every distinctive feature of Homeric poetry is due to the economy forced on it by oral methods of compo-sition, methods that can be reconstructed by careful study of the verse itself, once the scholar puts aside assumptions about expression and thought processes engrained in the psyche by generations of literate culture. For example, Parry noted that Homeric epithets used for 'wine' are all metrically different, and that the use of a given epithet was determined not by its precise meaning so much as by the metrical needs of the passage in which it turned up.[23] This sort of poetic feature in itself does not provide enough evidence to support the grand design of Parry's thesis; however, as other intrepid classicists took up the slack, it became gradually apparent that only a tiny fraction of the words in the *Iliad* and the *Odyssey* were not parts of repeated formulas, and (to a degree) devastatingly predictable formulas. Whether Homer was one or several persons, it appears that he (or they) had had, as Ong puts it, 'some kind of phrase book in his head'.[24]

The wider implications of this constant reformulation in the Homer epics of old set phrases are clearly perceptible. The Homeric Greeks must have valued such clichés because not only the structure of the poems but the general organisation of thought in an oral world, a situation which is for the most part unimaginable to all literate peoples, relied upon a continually rehearsed formulaic constitution. Parry's work and the work of those influenced by him has cleared up some of the puzzles in Homeric studies, concerning the lack of depth in the characterisation and the non-cohesiveness of the plots. To assure weight and memorability, heroic or villainous figures are presented as types: wise Nestor, furious Achilles, clever Odysseus. This same mnemonic economy can be seen at work in the figures populating children's fairy-tales—the very innocent Little Red Riding Hood, or Jack's incredibly tall beanstalk—narratives which are themselves the residue of an oral culture. Parry's early insistence on the structural importance to the narrative of Homer's 'memory-banked' prosody elucidates a difference in form between oral and literary narrative. In his *Ars Poetica*, Horace writes that the epic poet 'hastens into the action and precipitates the hearer into the middle of things'.[25] There is no semblance in Homer of a plotted narrative, even though after centuries of telling (and, more importantly, summarising in writing) the *Iliad* has compacted into a 'good yarn'. In Homer's day the events would have had a singular importance, rather like the individual scenes in a good play, but they would not have been crafted together. It would require a remarkable feat of memory for an epic poet to retain anything other than the simplest of plot structures in only the briefest of narrations. However, although the sequential, ordered nature of written discourse may be lacking, this should not necessarily be viewed as a deficiency of oral discourse; rather the latter should be evaluated in accordance with a different set of conventions, the bare bones of which are adumbrated by Ong:

> The oral song (or other narrative) is the result of interaction between the singer, the present audience, and the singer's memories of songs sung. In working with this interaction, the bard is original and creative on rather different grounds from those of the writer.[26]

Ong stresses the fact that the acoustic sign is power-driven. Oral peoples consider words to have a magical potency, and it is easy, Ong argues, to understand why this is. A hunter can see a buffalo, smell, taste, and touch a buffalo when the buffalo is completely inert, even dead, but if he hears a buffalo he had better start running. Unlike the classicists, Ong does not attempt to recover the aesthetic beauty of a lost oral age, for he knows that the essence of oral culture, which depends so much on the performance of its arts, is irretrievable. The technology of writing has driven a wedge between oral and literate societies. It has taught us to perceive language in ways—as a structure, vehicle for thought, instrument of propaganda—which were simply 'not thought' before writing. However, Ong's analysis is valuable because it alerts us to the continued influence of oral structures over present-day realities. He notes the prevalence of oral modes of thought in non- or anti-western cultures, and particularly in those Islamic countries which retain much of what constituted 'primary orality', such as the ritual prayer recitations and the political power of vatic addresses. He also reveals the surprising extent to which orally-based patterns of thought still motivate social behaviour in advanced western societies. With telephone, radio, television and various kinds of sound tape, electronic and digital technology has brought us into an age of 'secondary orality'.

Technology equates to an ever-increasing speed of communication, which in itself is in inverse proportion to the pruning of our attention span. As we all know, we live in the 'three minute' culture, in which meaning, as in the totality of meaning, is synonymous with the message imparted instantly, via the still image of the advertisement hoarding or the moving image of the television or cinema screen. This connotes, in one sense, an intellectual return to the immediacy of oral communication, to the impulsive action-speak of 'ordinary language' conversations. Radio and television have brought major political figures to a larger public than was ever possible in the pre-electronic era. However, these discourses are stage-managed. They are constructed, plotted, edited and controlled by people who do not actually participate in them. Ultimately, discursive exchanges over modern media are subject to the clock. The invisible television producers are the invisible authors of yesteryear. By way of contrast Ong takes us back a mere 130 years into American history and to the 1858 Lincoln/Douglas presidential debates, in which the combatants (for this is what Ong says they 'clearly and truly' were) faced one another in the scorching Illinois summer sun outdoors, before hugely animated crowds of 12,000 or more.[27] The speakers were on their feet for at least three hours, speaking at length, and at the end of each bout they were hoarse and physically exhausted. In these conditions of heated rhetorical exchange, argument really is war, or, specifically in this case, a boxing match. Since then, there has been a shifting of focus, from the flashpoints of the antagonistic debate to the representative value of the image. Seeing is believing. Video-recorded evidence has become a common feature of our law courts.

It may be that Tournier's reader, the addressee of 'Le Vol du vampire', is constructed within this dichotomy of image and (linguistic) sign, that he is intimately and pleasurably involved in the interaction between a written discourse which has recovered some of the vitality and immediacy of past oral traditions and the primacy of imagistic communication in a post-industrial society. It could be seen as ironic that, in this age of 'secondary orality', we seem prepared to sacrifice the depth and intellectual clarity of the written text on the altar of a predominantly pictorial representation of the world. But this is in itself a false dichotomy. Michael Worton has shown that in spite of the commitment to a clearer, more immediate, concretist narration in *La Goutte d'or*, the subtleties and ambiguities of Tournier's writing craft lie just beneath the surface crust. There is no call for sacrifices. Tournier has always protested the need for a simplicity of expression which is inextricably linked to the evocation of bold, well-defined images. Ostensibly *La Goutte d'or* privileges the opposition of the corrupting, image-dominated society of the west against the ancient cultural practices of the Middle East where meaning and understanding are channelled through an Islamic conception of the sign. The other interface explored in *La Goutte d'or* is the more fertile ground shared by image and sound. The main character, Idriss, literally travels from a state of 'primary' to 'secondary' orality.

SOUND AND VISION: *LA GOUTTE D'OR* AND AFTER

La Goutte d'or tells the story of a young Saharan goatherd's journey to Paris in search of his photograph. The reader is plunged *in medias res*. Idriss is introduced within the temporal horizon of his existence—'la veille', 'l'avant-veille', 'la semaine précédente' (GD, 9). He is 15 years old, lonely and bored, but reluctant to leave his oasis in search of adventure. The narrative refers to the atavistic pull of the warning stories his mother used to tell him when he was a child, 'en vertu sans doute d'une tradition orale remontant à l'époque où les nomades razziaient les populations paysannes des oasis' (GD, 9). The themes of narration and the active, functional role of story-telling are thus introduced at an early stage in the narrative.

Idriss's story begins with the first momentous event of his life, the chance meeting in the desert with the Parisian couple in the Land Rover. The blonde woman takes his photograph, and promises to send it to him once it has been developed. The encounter is described as a confrontation between two different worlds, in which the inhabitants are looking at each other. It is given from Idriss's point of view, but, as he looks on, he perceives himself to be 'visiblement ... l'objet d'une discussion entre l'homme et la femme' (GD, 13). A hierarchy is immediately established. Idriss admires the Land Rover. The owners of such a splendid mechanised camel, he thinks, must be 'des seigneurs'. In addition, the white couple brandish their camera, an instrument of power because it allows one person/people to represent another. The unauthorised taking of someone's photograph is the appropriation of their image. It is to dispossess them of something that is rightfully theirs. It is, therefore, as Idriss will come to realise, an oppressive act. However, at this early stage of the narrative the young oasian thinks only of the prestige attached to the one existing photograph in his oasis, the one depicting his uncle, Mogadem, in full military regalia.

This opening scene leaves an overwhelming impression, especially on the western reader, of cultural difference. In the pages immediately following, difference is reinforced positively, as the narrator describes the various cultural traditions that frame and occasionally enliven Idriss's monotonous life at Tabelbala. The narrative dwells on the uninhibited sexuality of his nomadic friend, Ibrahim (GD, 19), on the elaborate hairdressing rituals of the women, and on the imminent tazou, or wedding feast for the opening night of a ten-day-long marriage celebration joining Tabelbala and a neighbouring community (GD, 28). Importance is placed on the aesthetic aspects of the event. The relaying of sumptuous gifts between the two families contrasts with the grinding poverty of life in the Sahara. However, the most concerted emphasis is on the performing arts; on the hypnotic rhythms of the almost entirely percussive music, and on the dancing of Zett Zobeida, which now has a special significance for Idriss. The raven-haired dancer and her 'goutte d'or', the golden necklace she wears, are juxtaposed with the blonde woman in the desert wearing the camera around her neck: 'Que Zett Zobeida et sa goutte d'or soient l'émana-tion d'un monde sans image, l'antithèse et peut-être l'antidote de la femme platinée à l'appareil de photo' (GD, 31). The evening celebra-tions culminate in the narration of a story, 'Barberousse ou Le portrait du roi', performed by a professional storyteller, in which it is shown how the unchanging image of the king's red beard is revealed as a sign when it is transposed from one culture to another.

This physical, sensual world of sound and rhythm may appear, to the European reader, somewhat alien to the pastoral world of the Saharan oasis. Yet it is immanent to it. In the desert there is no change of landscape to excite the visual sense, neither is there fragrance in sand, nor variety in texture. Therefore, sound and movement indicate life. Perhaps this is why, the narrator tells us, the Muslim Berbers dread the image (GD, 15). Idriss's mother chides him for not keeping the photograph, predicting that he will fall ill (GD, 22). Even worldly-wise Mogadem, the old sage, is gloomy about his prospects: 'Non tu vois, les photos, faut les garder. Faut pas les laisser courir!' (GD, 56). The point has already been made through another storytelling episode, in which is revealed the fate of the two soldiers pictured with the young Mogadem who, unlike him, were destined never to see the photograph of themselves (GD, 55).

On Idriss's journey north in search of his photograph he encounters successive representations of himself, his people, and the life he has left behind. The nearer he gets to France, the less authentic these representations become. At first Idriss is inspired by Salih Brahim's eulogy of the west: 'Trois mots pourtant avaient éclaté dans sa tête avec une séduction irrésistible: cinéma, télévision, bal' (GD, 63). He is also thrilled by the 'discours' of the guide in the Sahara museum at Béni Abbès. However, the superstitious *contresens* of the image, regarded as having 'un pouvoir maléfique' by the Berbers, remains with Idriss. In particular it is reflected in the 'mauvais oeil' of Lala Ramirez, who leads him to the grave marked by a photograph of her son, and insists on foisting her dead son's name, Ismaïl, on the hapless oasian. He also learns from his acquaintance with the goldsmith on the Mediterranean ferry that, just as the fascination with image may lead him to slavery, so the coveting of gold will bring similar misfortune, 'l'or porte malheur' (GD, 105). Signs change their meaning in the journey from one culture to another. On disembarking at Marseilles, Idriss is disappointed that the feelings of 'dépaysement' he anticipated do not materialise. It is only on the train to Paris that he becomes aware of the real nature of his estrangement from this image-led society. What he perceives at this point is the gulf that exists between the imagistic representations of the culture he personifies and his own conception of self. This reflection is triggered by a conversation with the young Frenchman sitting next to him on the train. Philippe's ethnocentrism, corroborated by the album of family photographs he carries with him (particularly the photo of his sweetheart), inculcates a sober truth:

> Tout ce que le jeune français lui avait dit sur lui-même, sa famille, leur maison, son pays, tout ce qui le distinguait d'Idriss venait de se concrétiser dans l'image de cette femme. Philippe appartenait à la race de blondes voleuses de photo et de goutte d'or. (GA, 116)

At this point in the narrative the stage would seem set. Idriss is about to drift into a life of manual labour and relative poverty, and will become one more of the many thousands of North African French immigrants who fall victim to exploitation and institutionalised prejudice. For a while (much of the rest of the novel) he escapes. It is not that the issue is avoided in the text. Idriss's cousin, Achour, in conjunction with Isodore, the gnarled old *pied-noir* in the HLM, provide an ample social history. At one point Achour exclaims, 'La France moderne, c'est nous, les bougnoles, qui l'ont faite' (GD, 123). However, Idriss initially profits from this work. He drifts almost effortlessly into what might be described as a state of 'secondary orality', in which there is a clearly-felt harmony with his own cultural roots.

La Goutte d'or is narrated entirely in the third person. Since the plurality of narrators found in other Tournier novels is absent here, there is no tension between competing points of view other than that of Idriss and the mimetic artists in various guises whom he meets en route. We are left with a concept of narration *en soi*, symbolically represented by the numerous storytelling episodes which are assimilated into the main body of the text. Idriss's story is narrated in the vernacular. It comprises essentially short sentences, active verbs predominantly in the past historic tense, and dialogue. Throughout the narrative he is witness to a series of 'orientalist' representations that take themselves to be true.

'Orientalism' is the term coined by Edward Said in his book of the same name. It denotes a historical process beginning effectively with the Crusades, though Said traces it back further, in the anti-Islamic development of Christianity. Said argues that in the course of this long history the west has mapped out the Orient in terms of its own ethnocentric, conceptual schemas. The word 'Orient' is a canonical term used by writers such as Chaucer, Mandeville, Shakespeare, Dryden, Pope and Byron to denote anything of North African, Middle or Far Eastern character. It is also a geographical entity, adjacent to Europe; the place of Europe's greatest and richest and oldest colonies, the source of its civilisations and languages, its cultural contestant, and one of its deepest and most recurring images of the Other. Orientalism is thus defined by Said as a 'Western style for dominating, restructuring and having authority over the Orient'.[28] A typical example of orientalist practice would be Napoleon's invasion of Egypt in 1798, which he describes as 'the very model of a truly scientific appropriation of one culture by another, apparently stronger one'.[29] However, orientalism is primarily evinced by a vast corpus of literature, loosely grouped under the heading of 'Oriental Studies', although fictional representations of the Orient (in Flaubert or Lamartine) also come under its umbrella. It

ranges from the blatantly xenophobic (in Prideaux and Kipling) to
subtle condescension (Gibb and Massignon).[30]

Said emphasises the extent to which western literate societies are
consumed, transfixed even, by the need to interpret the world through
the act of writing, making the further important point that this writing
is essentially taxonomic. In the context of orientalism, Idriss's quest for
his photograph reads as a precocious inversion of western incursions
into the Orient. The narrative, in keeping with the oasian's orally-based
cultural heritage, adopts an epic mode. The journey to Paris is punc-
tuated by a series of encounters with episodic characters, each of whom
contribute to the hero's understanding of the world he is destined to
reach before falling by the wayside. Once in Paris, Idriss meets the
unlikely aristocrat Sigisbert de Beaufond, who regales him with a desert
drama of Lawrentian proportions (GD, 130–36). More epic scenes
follow. Le Grand Zob takes on the pinball machine (GD, 137) and
Idriss is employed as an actor in an orange juice commercial, involving
a desert backdrop and a real camel. We learn of the affinity between
Idriss and the film director, Achille Mage, who, like the young Saharan,
does not recognise himself as he is portrayed by others, in particular by
the troop of adolescent gamins he pays in return for sexual services: 'Je
vois dans les yeux des garçons l'image d'une grosse tante sentimentale,
bigleuse et bourrée d'argent. Je n'arrive pas à me persuader que c'est
moi' (GD, 145).

The making of the advertisement bears the hallmarks of an oral
narration, accelerated almost beyond recognition. In order to get the
thing off the ground, Achille Mage, the director, must perform. By
assuming the roles of each member of the team, he brings their characters to life. The narrative is rehearsed time and time again. After
fifteen takes the commercial is finished. However, for Idriss the drama
has only just begun. The filming is over, but nobody knows what to do
with the camel. Mage is unexpectedly—'sa réflexion dérapait dans un
sens imprévu' (GD, 151)—seized with a desire to identify the camel. Is
this unfortunate, single-humped beast a 'chameau', as he maintains, or
a 'dromadaire', the alternative choice defended with equal vigour by
the cameraman? Interestingly, both advocates resort to etymology in
order to prove their cases. Idriss, the expert, has no idea. For him
language has an expressive, rather than a denotative function. They
resort to the telephone directory, in order to find the address of the
nearest knackers' yard.[31] This flurry of linguistic activity heralds
Idriss's finest hour, as he leads the cauliflower-munching camel on an

impromptu 'Paris Baille-Naîte', from the cemetery at Montmartre to the gare Saint-Lazare, past la tour Eiffel and on, to the doors of the abattoir where the prospect of 'biftèques au chameau' is not welcomed. By now morning has broken. Tired and weary, Idriss and the camel head for the trees, and stumble on the Jardin d'acclimatation. The camel greets a tethered confrère, and Idriss's problem is solved. As he heads back, the relocated camel ambles past, 'pomponné ... avec sur le dos une grappe de petites filles hurlant de joyeux saisissement' (GD, 159).

However, as his epic journey progresses, Idriss runs into more and more substantial orientalist representations. Milan's aesthetic of the mannequin is mitigated by Bonami's 'Je n'ai pas le type maghrébin'. Idriss is offered the job as model for the wax effigy. It is a painful process. As the trapeze pulls him out of the mould, it is as if he is being born again: 'La masse alginate laissait émerger le corps nu en produisant de terribles bruits de pet, de succion et de déglutition' (GD, 188). The modelling of Idriss at the Glypto engenders the concrete representation of the Orient by the west, the Orientalist's Oriental to be exposed in the vitrines of the capital. It is a metaphor for the typecasting that has already taken place in centuries of European writing about the Orient. In *La Goutte d'or* this suppression is offset only once, with the unforgettable image of Idriss's and the camel's nocturnal trek across Paris, 'La silhouette ridicule et navrée surgissant dans l'aube grise et pluvieuse de Paris ébahissait les passants et agaçait les sergents de ville' (GD, 153), the perfect inversion of the epic European forages across the desert, from the Crusades to the Paris–Dakar.

Idriss's honeymoon period in Paris is soon over, and he withdraws into the North African community. There he rediscovers his cultural identity through the 'sombre et exaltante beauté des discours politiques diffusés quotidiennement par La Voix des Arabes' (GD, 192), and the singing voice of Oum Kalsoum, 'l'âme d'Egypte et de tout le monde arabe' (GD, 193). And he also discovers for the first time the one form of representation, in which the essence of these exquisite verbal performances is consecrated, the art of calligraphy.

Many commentators have read *La Goutte d'or* as an attack on the hegemonic superficiality of the image in western society. Worton and Salkin-Sbiroli have both drawn attention to the fact that the majority of Idriss's mentors are in some way optically deficient. Ibrahim is one-eyed, Mustapha, the artist-photographer 'très myope' (GD, 82), Lala Ramirez stares at him with her 'yeux sans cils' (GD, 89) and others warn enigmatically of her 'mauvais oeil' (GD, 90), Philippe on the train looks at Idriss 'sans le voir' (GD, 113), and Achille Mage has a squint. As Salkin-Sbiroli points out, this constellation of optical malaises tends to demean the perceptions of these counsellors, a deficit which is gloriously recouped at the end of the novel by the story of the old, blind man who was so moved by the power of Oum Kalsoum's singing that his national singer appeared to him in beatific green.[32] Interestingly Amouzine, the rapporteur in this instance, is unsure as to whether Idriss has understood the message of his story, 'que la parole soit assez puissante pour faire voir un aveugle' (GD, 196).

Worton draws on Tournier's other work, especially the warning treatise on photography contained in 'Les Suaires de Véronique', a short story from the *Coq de bruyère* collection, and on the anti-spectaclist stance of Situationist Guy Debord, co-founder of *the* intellectual cult in France of the 1960s, in order to illustrate the extent of the anti-imagist critique in *La Goutte d'or*. Thus, Idriss is presented as a character who cannot see beyond the surface reality of the images that surround him, a situation which naturally impoverishes his intellectual and spiritual capacities. This impoverishment is seen furthermore as a reflection of the trough in which western culture currently wallows:

> Idriss, the child of an anti-image culture, is seduced by the apparent identity between representation and reality. He therefore functions as a paradigm of contemporary Western man who believes (in) the surface of visual representations rather than seeking for their epistemological and/or ontological meanings.[33]

Some of the stories in *Le Coq de bruyère* appear to indicate that the cultural and intellectual poverty associated with the society of the spectacle is a persistent theme in Tournier's writing. Here, a striking number of characters beat a retreat from the world of vision. Lucien, 'le nain rouge', spends his time indoors, away from the gaze of others, and Martin, 'le fétichiste', recoils from the sight of his new wife's stark nudity, though he cherishes the sensuous warmth of her underwear. However, in spite of this dread of the image, radical anti-image action is definitely not prescribed. The wife of the eponymous 'coq de bruyère' cannot bear the public admiration of others aroused by the spectacle of her flamboyant husband. Likewise, she is repulsed by his collection of erotic photographs, though, having found them, she cannot resist a peek. She closes her eyes too often to her husband's indiscretions. When he leaves her for a younger woman, she shuts herself off completely from the world of vision. 'Fermer les yeux', turning a blind eye, induces a psychosomatic form of blindness and a lonely old age.

Although Tournier insists on the fundamental opposition of image and sign, he does not explore it in a confrontational sense through his own writing. Indeed Tournier rarely if ever engages in any form of challenging, formal experimentation in his fiction. His style implies the acceptance of a conventional reading pattern, of an unproblematic relationship between word and image. Thus he sees the relationship as contiguous. The opposition in *La Goutte d'or* is exclusively theological, for it is concerned with the prohibition of images under Islamic law. Moreover, Martin Roberts has shown how the narrative of *La Goutte d'or* undermines the explicitly anti-image discourse contained in the novel. Roberts dissects Tournier's 'ode' to calligraphy contained in 'La Reine blonde', the encrypted story which is supposed 'to solve' the problem of the image. In order to break the spell of the queen's portrait, the calligrapher Riad writes down a series of aphorisms. The meaning of each aphorism is secondary to the meaning created by the disposition of the hieroglyphs when the transluscent sheets are stacked on top of one another and the scripts superimposed to reveal the image of the queen's face. As Roberts points out, 'the antidote to the image consists not in *ekphrasis* (a written description of the image); instead, writing is used to reconstruct the image into another image ... The antidote to the image, in short, is ... the image.'[34] Roberts also indicates that, for all the narratorial pontification about the danger posed by an image-dominated culture in *La Goutte d'or*, Tournier's own powers of observation and his (aesthetically motivated) fascination with detail remain in good order. Nowhere is this more prevalent, Roberts argues, than in the description of the moulding of Idriss, where 'the violence implicit in the fabrication of images is made most blatantly apparent'.[35]

It would seem that Tournier's fabled oppositions, including the image–sign opposition in *La Goutte d'or*, tend to be played out at a metadiegetic level. Although he has fun with language, and insists always on the precise meaning of words,[36] the ability of language to summon forth ideas, images, to articulate a vision of the world, is never called into question. If, at times, he stresses unduly the importance of the other, non-visual, senses, this is not because he sees the image as necessarily flat and deceitful; rather he is wont to alert his readers to its deeper significance. An integral part of Riad's training as a calligrapher is his initiation into the world of the 'figure', which connotes the woman's face but also the numerous 'figures of speech'. With such a huge rhetorical arsenal at his disposal, Riad can read properly. He now has access to the infinitely richer, imagistic world of the poet's imagination.[37]

Tournier's fiction is first and foremost a hymn to the reader's imagination. Viewed from this perspective, the bulk of his creative writing since *Les Météores*, short stories and novels alike, testifies to an intriguing aesthetic evolution. The debate now seems to revolve around the redefinition of Tournier's imaging powers through a more sound-based universe. In *Gaspard*, *La Goutte d'or*, and especially in *Le Médianoche amoureux*, he seems preoccupied with the literal telling of the story, with notions of performance and performativity. This is not to say that the written sign has been eclipsed but that Tournier's later writing practice is more consonant with a view of the fictional text as an organic whole. In this context the image–sign opposition which author and critics have identified as the axis around which the circular narrative of Idriss's quest turns in *La Goutte d'or* is something of a red herring. As we have seen, this image–sign conundrum is effectively undercut by an image–sound reciprocity. The oral and the visual intersect in a more dramatic way in 'Tristan Vox', a short story from the *Coq de bruyère* collection.

This story about a late night disc jockey with unwarranted sex appeal is inspired by Tournier's experience in the 1950s working in the publicity department of a radio station. There, he was evidently struck by the immense power concentrated in the 'micro', a power gleaned from the possibility of vocal radio contact with a mass audience, a whole people even, 'je prenais conscience de la vaste rumeur qui bruissait à mes oreilles comme le souffle de l'océan … cette âme collective de tous nos contemporains que l'on peut appeler l'opinion, la masse, le peuple' (VP, 163). For Tournier this power is quasi-mythical: he compares radio communication with the oracles of the ancient gods. And indeed 'Tristan Vox' is the myth of Tristan and Isolde replayed over the radio, through the lovers' discourse between the late night 'spiqueur' and his entirely female, lonely hearts audience, with two female characters, Mlle Flavie and Tristan's wife Amélie, playing the roles of the imitation and the real Isolde respectively. However, the underlying theme in the text concerns the 'imaging' quality of sound.

The words disseminated over the airwaves each night by the 'spiqueur' have no meaningful content. They are essentially formulaic. However, the extraordinary timbre of Tristan's voice, caused by chronic laryngitis and a wobbly double chin that vibrates as sound is emitted, is sufficient to summon up a striking image of the voice-

producer in the imaginations of his devoted listeners. This image—
'd'un homme dans sa seconde jeunesse, grand, mince, souple avec une
masse de cheveux châtains indomptés ... masque noblement tour-
menté, aux pommettes un peu hautes ... grands yeux mélancoliques'—
contrasts spectacularly with reality. Tristan's real name is Félix Robinet
and he is 60 years old, short, fat and bald. In the world of radio,
however, the gulf between fiction and reality is mediated through
sound. Events spin out of control, and Félix is obliged to take a break
from the waves; he must 'fermer le robinet'. Shortly after his temporary
retirement, he returns from the local café one evening and surprises his
wife Amélie and a neighbour huddled over the radio, listening to the
soft, husky voice of ... Tristan Vox. Félix's retirement suddenly
becomes permanent.

Up to this sting in the tale, the sequence of events narrated has been
just plausible. At the end, however, the fiction intervenes to affirm a
specific message: that the invention of the TSF marked a divorce
between the medium of communication and the agent of communication, and that this piece of scientific wizardry inaugurated the propaganda age, the inception of the modern myths that now dominate our
lives. At the same time—and here Tournier in common with many
French intellectuals would disagree with Ong—the era of the wireless
was a golden age for sound. In this sound universe the human voice is
absurdly privileged as a means of communication.

The phenomenon of the single voice holding sway over millions of
attentive listeners is a fantastic magnification of the situation that
occurs in so-called 'primitive' societies whenever the storyteller arrives
in the village. Stories like 'Tristan Vox' affirm Tournier's close affinity
to a predominantly sound-based world. Indeed his radio days have had
perhaps a more important influence on his subsequent literary career
than many people realise. His exposure to the power of sound may
have helped shape his ideas on literature and especially his progression
towards the less cluttered, more economical and resolutely concrete
mode of storytelling which he has coveted ever since the first 'rewrite'
of *Vendredi*. His attempts to recast the vitality of 'live' narrations in
written form have also thrown into relief his use of language. Tournier
has always assumed—some would say naïvely—the existence of a unity
between language and object, thought and action, born out of a belief
in the effective use of language as the primary means of communicating
ideas. In Tournier's prose, words paint pictures and drive the action.
His is a sense-oriented, intuitive narrative discourse that looks out on

to the world rather than in on the process of writing. In terms of a philosophy of language he is, unwittingly, closer to Lakoff and Johnson than to Saussure or Lacan. The metaphorical unison between sign and object wrought by Lakoff and Johnson, when resituated in a narrative context, translates readily to the symbiotic relationship created between the oral storyteller and his audience. Similarly, Tournier's view of language as essentially expressive, rather than subversive (in a poetic sense) predisposes him to classical storytelling. At the same time, as Worton and others have testified, Tournier is acutely sensitive to linguistic connotation. Indeed language games still form an important area of study in his later work, but as the furious desire to achieve a simpler, more lucid form of expression continues unabated, his writing remains driven by an illocutionary force.

LE MÉDIANOCHE AMOUREUX: A THEORETICAL FINESSE

Many of the discussion-points on the most effective forms of creative writing raised in the context of Tournier's work coalesce in the immaculate design of *Le Médianoche amoureux*, a work which, I suspect, comes close to Tournier's literary ideal. First published in 1989, *Le Médianoche* is a collection of nineteen short stories, some of which, such as 'Pierrot ou Les secrets de la nuit' and 'La Légende des parfums', had already been published independently. The volume is launched by a narrativised dialogue, 'Les Amants taciturnes', the function of which is to incorporate each subsequent 'short' into a 'live', oral context. At stake is the marriage of Yves and Nadège, the silent lovers of the title, who no longer have anything to say to each other, 'ils ne s'entendent plus' (MA, 45). They decide to announce their separation on the occasion of 'un médianoche d'amour et de mer' (MA, 45), a seafood meal they intend to give, at which each of the guests will be invited to say their piece on love and marriage, 'ce sera la grande palabre sur le couple et l'amour' (MA, 45). The guests' contributions are, of course, the stories that fill out the volume. And, lo and behold, this table-top narration operates a remarkable transformation in the fortunes of Yves and Nadège. The ritualistic exchange of stories over the course of the meal, a veritable narrative communion, succeeds in revitalising the marriage through the creation of 'une maison de mots' (MA, 48). Noise and food act as a glue, binding the couple together in common recognition of the regenerative and evocative power of ritual.

Nadège pronounces Yves, 'le grand prêtre de mes cuisines et le conservateur des rites culinaires et manducatoires qui confèrent au repas sa dimension spirituelle' (MA, 49). Form mirrors content, for in the final sentence of the final story in the collection, 'Les deux banquets ou La commémoration', the caliph repeats Nadège's invocation, using identical words, as he addresses the victor of his cooking competition.[38] The winning dish is an exact replica of the other contender's; however, since it is served a day later, it acquires, in the mind of the caliph, an added commemorative dimension. Repetition is thus valued above innovation; it is a commonplace in the oral tradition that the story should gain from each successive performance.

Le Médianoche amoureux is Tournier's most explicit statement to date on the value of literature to society. To a degree it smacks of nostalgia and whimsy. He seems to want to cling to the romantic notion that there was a time before the devouring march of technology when literature was considered a necessary part of life, when it really did function as a means of social bonding. At the same time Tournier delivers a more progressive message. What we now think of as literature should be seen as an ingredient in a wider form of cultural and social interaction which may have its roots in a pre-technological, oral tradition but can also be seen as a viable antidote to the computer-generated solipsism and nuclear family organisation of modern life. Getting on with people is about relating anecdotes, telling stories, enjoying a meal, whether clustered around the family table or at the weekly diners' club meetings of the Académie Goncourt. Thus, the literary cleverness of *Le Médianoche* masks a genuine concern for the future survival of an ideal which many sociologists see, given the demise of the established churches, as teetering on the precipice. This ideal relates to the need, in what is to all intents and purposes an agnostic society, to extend strong social ties beyond the confines of the family. It is what politicians blithely describe as a 'sense of community'.

Through its design—Tournier draws on the examples of Boccacio's *Decameron*, Marguerite de Navarre's *Heptaméron*, and the *Mille et une nuits*—and through the didacticism of chief interlocutors Yves and Nadège, *Le Médianoche* privileges the act of narration. The contrast between 'live' narrative and the verbal edifice of a more 'writerly' kind is filtered metaphorically through the eulogy of Patricio Lagos' ephemeral sand-sculptures in 'Les Amants taciturnes'. Lagos works on the beach, moulding beautifully-detailed human forms out of sand. The figures then lie prone on the shore waiting for the tide to dismantle them limb by limb until they are entombed forever in a watery grave. Lagos' sand-sculptures have a life-span, unlike the dead, eternal monuments of orthodox sculpture. As he says, 'Mes sculptures de sable vivent ... et la preuve en est qu'elles meurent' (MA, 30).

It would be unwise to draw too many inferences from the example of the sculptures, for eternal value is restored soon after the death of the work via the series of photographs taken of each exhibit at various stages of its disintegration. However, Tournier clearly finds an extraordinary potency both in the sand-sculptures as artefacts and in the process by which they are created and destroyed. Just as Lagos' work is animated by the constant rumble of the ocean, so Tournier in *Le Médianoche* pushes his meditation on noise to witty extremes. Driven to desperation by noise deprivation, Nadège resorts to the tape-recording of Yves' snores. She finds common cause with young wives everywhere who are imprisoned by their husbands' taciturnity and sketches out a (suspiciously writerly) 'philosophie ronchologique' in order to explain their situation. (Tournier drily outlines the biological process leading to the production of the snore.[39]) Genuine dialogue has been shut down by Yves and Nadège's profanation of marriage. The comedy of the snore reflects on the spontaneity and intimacy of oral communication, in which we may glimpse once again the proximity of literature to myth, thus allowing Tournier to articulate with renewed vigour his relish for sacred stories. In a modern context the endless repetition of a 'party piece' is rightly seen as boring. This is because our storytelling, our own myth-making, has become divested of its ritualistic, regenerative dimension. In *Le Médianoche* Tournier reminds us that the mythical topoi which are the marrow of our cultural bones are by and large initiation stories, narratives which were once fundamentally linked to human action.

Le Médianoche amoureux foregrounds the sociological implications of the literary process. The stories are enveloped in a common context, reminding the lonely reader that written texts are dynamic; originating in a world populated by real men and women, they are apt to engender repercussions in a world outside the text. Literature does make contact with the lives of readers. Thus, in relation to the sequencing of the stories, the well-being of the guests is paramount. Tournier must ensure that they leave happy, so the feast culminates in recitations of folk-tales or 'contes', which, according to the taxonomy of the short story bequeathed by Charles Perrault,[40] usually end on a note of reconciliation, communion and celebration. Conversely, recitations of earlier stories in the volume are likely to promote despondency, as the guests experience 'le goût âpre des choses réelles' (MA, 255).

The generic distinction that Tournier makes between *nouvelle* and *conte* hinges on the notion of 'vraisemblance'. The bitter realism of the *nouvelle* will often bring it into the sphere of history, whereas the *conte* is less localised. With the *conte* the reader is more likely to be re-acquainted with the transcendent arena of myth. A hardy researcher, Tournier enjoys spotlighting unexpected shades of the 'sad, brown world' that we all know, but the intuitive, mythical side to his personality leads him to value more highly the 'instruction cachée' of the *conte*, and preferably 'les contes que nos aïeux ont inventés pour leurs enfants' (VV, 35) beloved of Perrault. As his career has continued to flourish, Tournier has become better known as a short story writer. This is less the result of a generic shift away from the novel, a move that, with the recent publication of a new Tournier novel, *Éléazar ou La source et le buisson*, seems to have been halted, than of his constant quest for a purer narrative style. The technical problems posed by this apparent need to carve out diamantine narratives goes hand in glove with the issue which has flummoxed Tournier critics, namely his persistent veneration of the child-reader. To use one of his own metaphors, Tournier's interest in the world of children, and in parti-cular his long-held desire to engage the imagination of the child through his work, may hold the *key* to his entire literary enterprise.

CHAPTER FIVE

The Empire of the Child

THE *FAUX-NAÏF*

Few critics have addressed seriously the role of the child in Tournier's fiction. However, in his recent monograph David Gascoigne devotes an entire chapter to this, the most contentious issue in Tournier criticism. Gascoigne alights on a personal anecdote recorded at the start of *Le Vent Paraclet* in which Tournier relates the story of his grandfather who, as a six-year-old child at the time of the Prussian invasion of 1871, was made to hold up a heavy volume of music for the conductor of the German military band. The story seems to justify the placement of a typical Tournier epigraph—'un enfant en larmes caché par l'oeuvre qu'il porte'—to which Gascoigne accords special importance. He argues suggestively that not only *Le Vent Paraclet* but 'the whole of Tournier's oeuvre is ... sustained by the figure of the suffering child'.[1] Referring to *Vendredi* and *Le Roi des aulnes*, Gascoigne shows how Tournier asks his readers to juggle with metaphor in order better to appreciate his novelistic presentation of 'two of the uglier products of civilisation, colonial violence and mechanised warfare, as expressions of child-adult conflict'.[2]

Gascoigne's reading is consonant with Tournier's dislike of an all-pervasive bourgeois morality, which the latter often parodies in the invective of his own celebrated 'provocations', both literary and non-literary.[3] Tournier argues that a peculiarly nineteenth-century morality—'La pudibonderie qui ne triompha nulle part autant que dans l'Angleterre victorienne' (VP, 61)—has brought about a large-scale sanitisation of the modern educational programme in most western countries. Historically, the eighteenth century was the point of transition, the point at which Diderot, Voltaire and the other 'moderns' argued vociferously for a new system of education which should focus on learning about the philosophy, literature, and social and political structures of the modern world, rather than on gaining knowledge of the Classics. These critical interventions, which were intended to produce the active citizen rather than the passive 'clerc', have resulted, according to Tournier, in the marginalisation of what he calls 'une éducation morale', the idea associated with the Jesuit colleges that education should be about the formation of the whole person, that any system of education should attend to the spiritual and moral development of the child as well as to his or her intellectual and social needs. The commonplace view that such an education involves the clothing of the child in an unnatural, moral straitjacket is dismissed by Tournier as a misconception; it is the morality of the Victorians in all its prissiness rather than the morality of the Catholic church which informs both the secular and denominational sectors of the education system. Indeed Tournier's personal experience appears to vitiate the contract between sexual morality and the Catholic church:

> Fastueuse, subtile, érotique, telle est l'Eglise initiatrice dont je rêve quand il m'arrive de refaire mon enfance. Je remercie le sort que celle qui m'a élevé n'ait trahi qu'en partie cet idéal. (VP, 62)

The modern attenuation of 'l'éducation morale' has removed what Tournier considers to be a vital ingredient in the early stages of the educative process, which is the passage of the child from the bosom of the family into the wider society outside it, what he terms 'initiation'.[4] Various ramifications of the child's initiation into society are explored in 'Lucie ou La femme sans ombre', a short story from *Le Médianoche amoureux* which is discussed below. Though, as we shall see, far from unproblematic, Tournier's insistence on the importance of initiation is based on a solid anthropological foundation. However, his view that as a reader of literature the child is, at least, the equal of the adult has proved enduringly controversial. In *Le Vent Paraclet* he chastises those who deride the poetry of the Parnassian school, on the grounds that for the 11-year-old Tournier the Parnassians were the essence of poetry. He still admires and respects their work, '...non par un attachement gâteux au passé, mais parce qu'en l'occurrence, c'est le petit qui a raison (...) En vérité, le petit a toujours raison' (VP, 53). This kind of remark has continued to frustrate Tournier readers unable to reconcile the complexity of his fiction with the inevitable limitations imposed by the pre-adolescent's underdeveloped intellect and paltry experience of life. But, on this issue more than any other, Tournier demands to be taken seriously. Once again his target is bourgeois morality, which is naturally shot through with *mauvaise foi*. Tournier's critique of the bourgeois, however, becomes the springboard for his unusual argument in favour of the literary consciousness of the child.

Adult *embourgeoisement* is contrasted with the innocence of the child. The corollary of the child's innocence is the learning instinct, which, on account of the child's inevitable lack of knowledge or experience, is diffused into the world of the imagination. Thus, Tournier's 'child' lives in a state of imaginative innocence which finds its expression in the imaginary, magical world of children's literature. The evocative power of this literature will start to wane as the child first learns more of the adult world, then begins physically to change into an adult and lurches into adolescence, a period which Tournier seems to regard as the Dark Ages of the human life-cycle. Tournier's sensitivity to the importance of the child's imagination, however, is not misplaced, as we shall see from the following example which foregrounds questions surrounding the 'modernisation' of traditional children's literature. Two passages are cited below. The first is the concluding paragraph of Beatrix Potter's *Peter Rabbit*, which is every inch a children's book; Potter's literary miniatures were expressly designed for small hands to hold. The second is a version of the same paragraph taken from David Hately's modern adaptation of the Potter classic:

> I am sorry to say that Peter was not very well during the evening. [Paragraph] His mother put him to bed, and made some camomile tea; and she gave a dose of it to Peter! 'One table-spoonful to be taken at bed-time.' [Page] But Flopsy, Mopsy and Cotton-tail had bread and blackberries for supper.[5]

> Then Mrs. Rabbit took a closer look at Peter. 'Dear me!' she said to herself. 'His whiskers are drooping! He doesn't look very well!' So Mrs. Rabbit decided to give Peter something to make him feel better. She got out her camomile tea and waited for the water to boil. Peter groaned when he saw the tea. He knew that it tasted horrible. Peter was put straight to bed and Mrs Rabbit gave him some tea. 'One tablespoonful to be taken at bedtime,' she said as she tucked him up. But Flopsy, Mopsy and Cotton-tail had fresh bread, milk and blackberries for supper. They had Peter's share, too, and they enjoyed every single bit of it.[6]

The evocative power of Potter's limpid prose style is lost in the modern rewriting which is so preoccupied with the idea of the book as an educative tool that it allows for an arguably gratuitous expansion of the original text. In Potter's narrative there is a fine line drawn between Peter's curiosity and adventurous spirit and the consequences of his disobedience; in the modern version his naughtiness is hammered home. It is not that the rewriting is bad—drooping whiskers, the groaning Peter, and the triumphant sisters are all supplementary images broadly in keeping with the mood of the original—but that the modernised version is so self-consciously educational that it becomes an adult 'reading' of what was a children's story. In its desire to provide a moral framework for Potter's laconic text, to flesh out meaning that Potter was content to leave the reader to deduce (often in the gap of the turn of the page), the modern narrative smothers the child's imagination with a blanket of adult anxieties and preoccupations.

As we shall see, Tournier, like Potter, writes to recapture the lost islands of our childish imaginings. However, the idea that he is 'deeply interested in the relationship of children to the society around them'[7] is less persuasive than it might at first appear. The author's 'Romantic' vision of the child as the innocent Ideal of Rousseau's *Emile*, yet to be inculcated into the vicious ways of adult society, is a somewhat static perspective that impedes rather than fosters an understanding of the situation of the modern child. One story from *Le Médianoche amoureux* collection, 'Lucie ou La femme sans ombre', brings Tournier's idealistic conception of the child into contact with contemporary society.

Tournier's provocative scenario involves the child protagonist being 'bedded' by his schoolmistress, Lucie, who, the narrator insists, fulfils the role of substitute mother. The Oedipal schema underpinning the narrative is highlighted, because in the course of remembering (this event in particular) the narrator starts to indulge in some myth-making of his own. The first person narrative tells the story of a ten-year-old boy who returns from school one day to find that his mother has left the family home. Now under the sole charge of a cold and distant father, he absconds that same evening to Lucie's house. The sensuous image of the teacher as she greets him, silhouetted in the door-frame, emphasises the contrast between adult sexuality and childish innocence:

> Lucie était là, debout dans la pénombre où sa chemise de nuit formait une grande tache claire. Un détail me frappa aussitôt et me parut d'une importance merveilleuse: sa natte était dénouée, et un flot de cheveux sombres couvrait ses épaules. Ne sachant que faire, ni que dire, je lui tendais ma pomme qu'elle accepta. Je prononçai: 'Maman est partie'. Elle dit: 'Viens!' et elle m'entraîna à l'intérieur de la maison. (MA, 158)

This description of Lucie is endowed with significant detail and therefore with a vividness that gives the illusion of a temporal *rapprochement*. In fact, the narrative is generated through an identity of place; the narrator has returned to the area of his childhood as a young man and walked once again down the disused railway track to the old signalman's house, long since vacated by Lucie and her family. His destination in this case serves as the beginning of a quest to recover the meaning of the specific childhood events surrounding the memory of his seduction by Lucie. In the course of this research, the truth of these eidetic images is first disputed and then reaffirmed. When he tracks down Lucie, he finds in her a transformation. The 'âme généreuse' of his *sixième* has been superseded by the image, 'parfaite, impeccable, stylée' of the *directrice de lycée*. Lucie is no longer attractive to him. However, correspondence with her now estranged husband, Nicolas, reveals that her personality has fundamentally altered following a long bout of clinical depression. The narrator is reassured, for it is Lucie who has changed; his recollection of her is validated, and her reality is now a function of his memory. These revelations also instil within him the writer's confidence to proceed with committing the unadulterated story to paper. In narratological terms this confidence translates to a situation where the narrator enjoys complete mastery of both narrative and story time. His is the undisputed point of view on the event, which he is able to reconstruct as if it were yesterday. 'Donc j'avais dix ans et j'aimais ma maîtresse', he surmises on the second page of *his* narrative. This supremacy remains unchallenged throughout much of the narrative.

However, we are not told exactly what happened that fateful night on which Lucie's family conveniently stopped over at Grandma's. Certainly the narrator spends it in his teacher's bed, where he enjoys what is described as a 'lait nocturne'. Moreover their liaison is motivated sexually by the narrative, which extends its punning on the French word *maîtresse*. This superfluous drawing out of connotational meanings brings unforeseen consequences:

> Il est en effet bien remarquable que le français emploie le même mot pour désigner l'amante d'un homme marié, sa seconde femme en somme, et l'enseignante qui se charge des écoliers les plus jeunes ... La première femme d'un enfant, c'est évidemment sa mère. L'enseignante ... c'est la seconde femme de sa vie, sa maîtresse, et il n'est pas rare que par advertance il l'appelle maman. (MA, 152)

It is a careless *divagation* on the part of the narrator, for it changes crucially the terms of reference. No longer can we say that this is the story of a young boy's first sexual experience at the hands of an older woman, since the convergence of the roles of mother and infant schoolteacher encourages us to read it as the narration of an act of 'secondary' incest.

The nexus outlined by Otto Rank in his classic study of the phenomenon associates incest strongly with notions of doubling and death.[8] Once this connection is made, the unduly symbolic emphasis which is placed on Lucie's doll, 'sa poupée-fétiche', and unsatisfactorily explained in Nicolas' concluding letter, receives instant clarification. The doll represents another Lucie, who died as a child and bequeathed to her as yet unborn sister her name. Lucie's essence and therefore her function in the narrative is double, as the image both of the dead child and the absent mother. She comes into existence the moment she buries the doll, in a ritual signifying the creation of a separate identity that comes with the dissolution of the Oedipus complex. However, this interpretation does not conform to the point of view presented in the narrative. The event is reported in Nicolas' letter to the narrator which completes the latter's investigation of the past. Reproduced in italics at the end of the story, the letter stands out. Its revelatory contents make of it a classic device of narrative closure. We are reminded of the narrator's identity as a character in the fiction—*Cher Ambroise*. This naming substitutes for a loss of identity, that of the 'real' Lucie whose memory is treasured by Nicolas and the narrator alike. This image of the past is consecrated, etched in writing into the page. However, Nicolas cannot bring himself to describe the new, 'shadowless' woman: '*Il est inutile que je te décrive la nouvelle Lucie que je voyais de semaine en semaine se composer sous mes yeux*' (MA, 172).

In the course of the dialogue preceding the act of narration, Ambroise embroiders on the medieval myth of the shadowless, or desexed, woman. The woman, he intones, is the shadow of the man, and he, the man, lives in this shadow, from which emanates warmth and colour. Thus, bereft of her shadow the woman loses the essence of her being. The theory may be a paltry one but nonetheless the narrator fails to underscore the specific nature of the sexual relationship implied by the shadow, which is the figure *par excellence* of the double. The shadow is an extension of the self, a physical projection that evokes immediate comparison with the myth of Narcissus. In one version of the myth, Narcissus is rendered inconsolable by the death of his identical twin sister, and when he sees himself reflected in the water he transfers to his own image the love that he felt for his dead twin. There is an interesting gradation here, from pure narcissism to a love relationship with another self, which entails the desire for incest.[9]

The narrator's experience is supposed fully to explain the myth of the shadowless woman. By the end of the narrative he has filled the lacunae in his own memory, solved the contradictions in his own mind and thereby preserved a coherent, unified view of his world. Once it is all set down on paper, the subject is closed. He writes in the final paragraph:

Tourner la page. Laisser derrière nous l'ombre sainte où nous avons cheminé. Cette ombre, je l'ai enfermée pour toujours dans mon coeur … (MA, 181)

This cosy ending is concerned almost entirely with the will-to-power that characterises male sexuality. In old-fashioned feminist terms, the injustices of the patriarchal society are paraded in an optimistic light and without apparent shame. Prospective son and prospective father connive to produce and uphold a world-order which excludes the voice, or rather the character of the Other, the woman. In the course of the narrative the real mother emerges, but there is no room for her in this world. She is discarded in favour of an idealised image of the past. In the prologue the narrator associates her name with the verb *élucider*, and therefore with a kind of educative perceptiveness. It also recalls Lucie, the Patron Saint of Light and Clear-sightedness, who gouged out her own beautiful eyes in order to deflect the lust of unconverted Romans. Little wonder that the lusty narrator is in a hurry to leave this 'ombre sainte' behind. He is thus spared the fate of Oedipus, but how much more interesting his story would have been had he found the modern-day Lucie as alluring as the one of eighteen years previously. Then, the morning after his sexual initiation he went out to play with Lucie's two sons. The three boys embarked on an adventure that almost ended in disaster. They found themselves trapped far down a disused railway tunnel on the wrong side of a curtain of fire, only to escape in the nick of time. They were followed out of the inferno by a large, white owl. This magical post-suite to the drama commemorates the event in the mind of the narrator:

Nous eûmes le temps de voir sa face plate et ses yeux arrondis tournés vers nous. Ainsi, par notre faute, l'oiseau de Minerve, au lieu de prendre son vol au crépuscule, selon le mot du philosophe, arraché à ses douces ténèbres familières, fuyait éperdument dans le soleil de midi. (MA, 169)

The image of the owl triggers a reflective commentary on changing trends in the field of education, which addresses the issue of the impact on education of the post-war technological boom in the west. The narrator argues that increasing use of visual aids at primary level teaching has privileged the stimulation of the child's optical sense to the detriment of tactile perception, to such a degree that the educational environment has become dangerously de-personalised. Just as the scorched owl emerges suddenly from the dark shadows of the tunnel into the blinding light of the midday sun, the young child is catapulted from the human warmth of the kindergarten into a world of screens, and thereby misses out much of what the narrator terms 'sa vocation d'enfant'. At the very end of the narrative, the flapping wings of the disorientated owl are recalled, in place, as it were, of the image of the lost mother. We, the readers, are prodded at this point into the realisation that the narrative of 'Lucie' oscillates continually between sensory poles: the eye of the portrait-painter[10] translates to the contact of the narrator with Lucie; Lucie's attachment to the doll feeds into the pristine image of the new Lucie; and the narrator's brush with the owl in the tunnel precedes directly the latter's exit into the world of absolute vision. The doll, the owl and the woman's shadow are presented as important in the narrative because it is principally through the evocation of these figures that a timid reconciliation of the two senses, sight and touch, is performed. Tournier does not underestimate the unique role of tactile perception as a means to apprehend reality,[11] but the cardinal link is provided by Freud who reminds us that seeing is 'an activity that is ultimately derived from touching'.[12] Moreover, Freud maintained that education plays an important role in the repression of the sexual instincts of the infant. Acting like a dam, a formal education will filter these sexual forces through the child's latency period and on into adolescence and sexual maturation. Whether elements in the child's early life—environmental factors, parental intervention, and education—act as sluice-gates, or as repressive buffers, storing up sexual energy and consequently distorting it, Tournier's thesis, promoting a more gradual absorption of the child into society than exists at present, is consistent with the findings of Freudian psychoanalysis.

'Lucie ou La femme sans ombre' thus ends on an appropriately double note of disconfirmation and concordance. In the principal matter of the narrator's exploration of a formative event in his past it presents the results of his investigation as true, and yet the narrative supports a view of the Woman as an idealised object-image, which most modern readers know to be false. This falsely-imagined experience then yields a new idea, which, the narrator senses at the end of the story, will be the more valid in the eyes of the community.

Suspicions that a latent misogyny and an inappropriate veneration of tradition for the sake of tradition may obscure Tournier's interesting ideas on education are deepened by another story from *Le Médianoche*, 'Blandine ou La visite du Père', in which Woman is described as the 'gardienne du foyer' whose presence as wife in the home deprives the husband of the friends he once had as a bachelor, 'un ami qui se marie est un ami perdu'. In spite of a sting in the tail, 'Blandine' is a poor story. It tells of the blandishments of a middle-aged single male writer—the narrator—who relishes the company of the young schoolgirl, Blandine, on the frequent occasions when she interrupts her journey home from school with a visit to his house. There are echoes of *Lolita*, 'Blandine était à l'âge délicieusement troublé où la tendresse se confond avec le désir et la bourrade amicale avec l'étreinte amoureuse' (MA, 133–34), and Lewis Carroll's habit of photographing girls exclusively under the age of twelve is cited approvingly in the text. 'Blandine' is typical of Tournier's writing on the theme of the child, in the sense that the narrator's superimposed commentary does not seek to further the reader's general understanding of children. Tournier supplies nothing of interest about the behaviour or activities of the child. Nor does he seek to investigate the attitudes of children or the exclusive nature of a child-centred society. There is nothing of what has come to be known as 'Youth Culture' in his work. Ironically, in view of the blueprint for education set out in 'Lucie', Tournier adopts more often than not a peculiarly Victorian notion of the child, which is seen exclusively in terms of its relation to the adult world. It would seem that at times this literary champion of the child divulges a curious uninterestedness in one of his favourite subjects.

Gascoigne does not see Tournier's vision of the child in quite the same way, drawing our attention to the pivotal structural and thematic role played by the child-prophet, Nestor, in *Le Roi des aulnes*. However, this in itself does not equate to the contention that we, in the adult world, should, in Tournier's eyes, defer to the dictate of the child, especially since the passages of metaphysical speculation accorded to Nestor in *Le Roi des aulnes* constitute precisely the 'fatras' which Tournier hopes to excise one day when he writes a new, child-friendly version of his second novel. It is probably safer to resituate Tournier's relationship with the child within a wider educational context. Thus, the epigraph which 'covers' the beginning of *Le Vent Paraclet*—'un enfant en larmes caché par l'oeuvre qu'il porte'—foreshadows the image with which Tournier's much discussed intellectual autobiography ends:

> Les vies les meilleures ne connaissent pas de phase adulte. L'homme s'enrichit de chacun de ses avatars successifs ... Un enfant émerveillé reste caché jusque sous le masque du vieillard. (VP, 282–83)

The sad child hidden by the book with which he is burdened may be transformed into the astonished, marvelling child hiding behind the mask of the old man. In this second image, however, the notion of the child is no longer an obvious fact of existence; it represents a quality, in Gascoigne's words, 'an Ideal of Becoming rather than just Being'.[13] The closing words of *Le Vent Paraclet* conclude a meditation on the value of wisdom, a cherished Tournier theme. Gascoigne's close analysis lights up a path which takes us from the standard adult-to-child injunction, 'd'être bien sage', to a New Testament definition of 'sagesse' seen as a 'capacity for growth and change'.[14] Gascoigne goes further, arguing that Tournier's fiction is predicated on 'a kind of immaturity ... a refusal to accept all the codes of adult, "civilised" behaviour'.[15] Thus, the 'dynamic of discovery, conquest and metamorphosis' that drives 'all of Tournier's heroes out of the rut of predictably ordered lives'[16] is sparked by a childish contestation, tantrums that the adult onlooker should perhaps take with more than a pinch of salt. Notwithstanding a degree of overstatement and the liberties he takes in bending some of Tournier's fictions into this tight interpretive shape, Gascoigne here scents the essence of Tournier's writing.

Reading *Vendredi* and *La Goutte d'or* through the grid of Voltaire's *Candide*, Lynn Salkin-Sbiroli has also shown how the 'young' protagonists of his novels, who are metaphorically young if not literally so, set off down this road to wisdom in a state of 'epistemological immaturity'. If they are to reach their goal, Salkin-Sbiroli argues, they must first undergo 'a process of unlearning'. In the course of her analysis Salkin-Sbiroli arrives at some interesting conclusions regarding the form of Tournier's narrative. Initially she remarks that *La Goutte d'or* is not a novel but a 'tale which uses all the tonalities characteristic of a rural storyteller'.[17] Later, the art of the storyteller is extended to cover the entire Tournier oeuvre:

> If realism, which took hold after the Enlightenment, has been put into question by the contemporary 'crisis of Reason', Tournier's counter proposal is not the empty formal experiments of the nouveau roman, but the subversive return to a more 'primitive' and archaic form of symbolic story telling which, through its magical unreality, teaches us a great deal about what is real.[18]

There are two conclusions that may be drawn at this stage regarding Tournier's empowerment of the child. Firstly, the child, if educated properly (in Tournier's terms), will afford a fleeting glimpse, roughly around the age of twelve, of a lost ideal of *sagesse*. Secondly, as Tournier's career has progressed, he has become ever more focused on the desire to recover through his own writing the essence of this childish wisdom. Such an evolution in the nature of any writing project necessarily entails a reassessment of its form and of the manner in which these newer fictions are received. However, before Tournier's case is discussed in isolation, it is worth briefly considering the separate genre of children's fiction, which has developed its own forceful critical and theoretical voice.

In a startling book, the self-styled 'experimental' children's story-teller Peter Hunt marshalls a number of declarations elicited from various sources which, taken as a composite, sweep away many of the received ideas about critical and theoretical practice under which 'academic' readers have become accustomed to labour. His analysis privileges the activity of reading, and specifically the reading experience of the child. Hunt attacks conventional critical practice, rejecting a bits-and-pieces view of the text in favour of an holistic approach. Any book, though on the one hand a real, concrete, money-spinning artefact, is, on the other, a rather more fluid conceptual entity. It can provide no objective justification for anything that is read into it, because the very practice of reading involves an interaction between reader and text so complex and individuated as to throw up an infinite number of vari-ables. Just as there is no clear interface between language and the mind, so there can be no lines drawn in literary criticism or theory between the reader's general consciousness and his or her consciousness of any given text at any given moment. Thus, Hunt declares that:

> ... it is artificial to make any distinction between the things that we perceive and the things that we respond to in a text. We do not distinguish the medium from the message, any more than we distinguish our own input from the text's.[19]

Many readers may experience some difficulty in reconciling them-selves to such an apparently nihilistic outlook. When Hunt advises that we should refrain from distinguishing between various aspects of the text—character, plot, imagery, and so on and so forth—lest this detract from our enjoyment, the temptation is to start sniffing for rats. However, he is careful to rebuff the charge of anti-intellectualism. The problem, he explains, is one of speed. What happens as we read a text happens 'in microseconds', thus rendering the examination of literary meaning 'endlessly cumbersome', but nonetheless 'endlessly fasci-nating'.[20] For Hunt this process starts and ends with the connections made between adult-narrator and child-reader through a written text, often read aloud by another adult to his or her young audience. If a reading is to be successful, then the transmission of a specific world-view, or the enunciation of a particular handle on the world, must occur, and successful transmission relies on a number of textual features which, Hunt argues, derive from an oral culture and are found nowadays uniquely in the world of children's fiction. Features such as the use of 'strings' rather than patterned groups, apparently random analepsis and prolepsis, limited cataphoric reference, and opening *in medias res* are not, therefore, simple mnemonic devices, or, in Hunt's words 'proto-written' strategies; instead, they relate to a 'distinctive world-view'.[21]

At times Hunt's commentary degenerates into a diatribe against 'adultist' misconceptions about literature, and more particularly children's literature. But his zeal does not prevent him from making a compelling case for the serious study of children's fiction. Not only do children's books exert a huge social and educational influence, but they are important politically and commercially.[22] Also, children's literature crosses established generic, historical, academic and linguistic boundaries. Most interestingly, Hunt ventures, the study of children's literature may change fundamentally the ways in which we approach all literature.

Hunt cites experts in the field who point out that good children's fiction refers in greater measure to concrete things and actions, so as to facilitate comprehension. The corollary of this prerequisite is that these concrete narratives, like the original version of *Peter Rabbit*, have tended to the elliptical, and thus offer themselves to a diversity of response or interpretation. Hence it has been argued that the child-oriented narrative is also intrinsically poetic. Jill Paton Walsh reconciles these apparently contradictory principles by contending that, in children's fiction, this *a priori* 'need for comprehension' imposes 'an emotional obliqueness, an indirection of approach, which like elision and partial statement in poetry is often a source of aesthetic power'.[23] Neil Philip takes Paton Walsh's argument one step further, and in so doing slays another sacred cow. He argues that writing in general reflects:

> ... the complex and ambiguous nature of human thought. It suggests rather than states. The further a writer progresses along this road, the more nearly his effects approach those of the oral poet or storyteller...[24]

Observations such as these fly in the face of academic tradition, according to which reading poetry is understood as a difficult exercise requiring the undivided attention of a fully-developed, well-trained adult mind engaged with a written text. Huge questions concerning the history and philosophy of language are at issue. The study of language, or linguistics, has inevitably resulted in its classification, in the breaking down of language into discrete, analysable units. As we have seen, one of the clearest separations is that of dialect or the spoken tongue from the written sign. Philip's premise would be that, however common-sensical this separation may appear, it constitutes a manufactured and unnatural schism. He advocates the educationalist's position whereby speaking and writing are conceived as an indissoluble whole, as two halves of the same coin. According to this view, any narrative fiction is a legitimate site for the coalescence of written and oral forms of communication. However, perhaps because it communicates in a more direct fashion than sophisticated adult prose or because pre-teenage children are generally more comfortable reading a written narrative than actually producing it themselves, for these and a myriad of other possible reasons, good children's fiction is a perfect vehicle for a 'whole language' approach to reading. This view receives oblique support from Michael Halliday, one of the most respected of contemporary linguists. Although Halliday insists absolutely on the requirement that we discriminate between the spoken and the written language, he stresses even more the need for our educators to understand how the spoken language works. He writes in conclusion to his study on the differences between written and spoken forms that, 'If we persist in treating speech as a caricature of itself, while putting writing (like an inscription) on a pedestal, then there is no way we will ever come to understand how it is that a human child is able to learn'.[25] What Halliday actually says about these differences in the course of his book supports what was referred to above as a 'whole language' approach to reading. In particular he demonstrates that spoken language activates a more complex system of linking phrases and other linguistic connectors than its written counterpart. Therefore, he adduces, it possesses a grammar which is more intricate than the grammar of written language.[26] (Conversely, written language uses the space which is filled in the spoken language by grammatical functions to extend and increase its lexical reference.) An oral text will, therefore, constantly signal the elements within it which are designed to knit the constituent parts together. The main aim of any speaker is to achieve coherence. The same procedure applies to written discourse, the singular difference being that coherence is easier to achieve when the words are written down. Thus the written language has the potential to go further in its investigation into the communication of meaning, in some cases so far as to challenge or manipulate the conventional notions of coherence on which all acts of communication are predicated.

The theories of Hunt and other enthusiasts for children's fiction are not always consistent. Hunt may write with aplomb of narratological anarchy in children's texts, but he will also concur with the conventional idea that children demand narrative closure. Also, it is an easy thing to appeal to the 'poetry' of children's fiction without describing what this 'poetry' is—in relation to, let us say, our 'adultist' preconceptions about poetry—or, how it functions. And Hunt can have no answer to the charge that not only is he a practitioner of children's fiction, and therefore earns his living by it, but that he is disadvantaged by his own adult status, in the sense that he is likely to find intellectual value in something which is not necessarily intended to impart intellectual ideas. Adults will always read children's books as adults. On the other hand, his achievement is to identify the reading situation of the child as an archetypal reading situation, and from this starting-point he is able to develop a literary theory which is applicable to all literatures, and which, moreover, chimes harmoniously with many of the principal traits of Tournier's writing. The crux of the matter is linguistic. Underpinning Hunt's insight is the assumption that the primary feature of any language is its syntax. Were he a linguist, he would be a Chomskyan, for whom the twin towers of Generative and Transformative Grammar contain the secret of the child's linguistic evolution. In the less arcane world of children's literature, we can deduce from Hunt's work that the same succession of ideas may be transmitted equally effectively via oral or written discourse. This is not to say that lexical choices or variations, or even deviances, are unimportant, nor that either mode is richer in its semantic stock, though this is precisely the line which Halliday takes. The point is that the vast majority of narrations will seek to communicate something much greater than the sum of its constituent parts. What happens in literature is that the addressee—reader or audience—is allowed prolonged access to the imagination of someone else. A writer like Tournier is fascinated by narrative fiction, literature rather than film, on account of the way that language mediates in the transmission of images, in the journey between two sites, the writer's and the reader's imagination. Thus, his career to date has assumed the character of a search for the most effective way to get his 'vision' across.[27]

Tournier's infamous practice of rewriting two of his novels,

Vendredi ou les limbes du Pacifique and *Gaspard, Melchior et Balthazar*, ostensibly, though he has always vehemently denied this, in order to break into the lucrative market of children's literature, is a decisive landmark in the evolution of his literary aesthetic. In the context of education, privileged access to another's imagination is, as Geoffrey Summerfield explains, an extremely important part of the overall educative process:

> In animating the imagination, literature is vital and indispensable. It is a notorious but ill-acknowledged fact that, as we grow older, our language tends to become tired and jaded, more approximate and generalised, less intimately responsive to experience, less individual, less vivid. The signs we wish to make conform more and more to a set pattern, become rational and mechanical; so our idioms become more conventional and more stereotyped ... Too often we impose our wearied, neutralised language on our pupils; if we are not careful, we begin to expunge from our pupils' usage anything that is vivid, startling, incisive, edgy, adventurous, or vulgar.[28]

It may be that Tournier felt compelled to 'redo' *Vendredi* and *Gaspard* in order to sharpen up his language, and that his own genius allowed him to see that this could only occur in the context of a 'childist'-oriented audience. As we know, critics such as Genette and Koster have argued that Tournier's self-censorship in the rewritings of *Vendredi* and *Gaspard* is unjustifiable. In *Gaspard*, for example, a series of false beginnings—the quests of the traditional three kings of the Christian legend—devolve towards a long ending which builds into a crescendo with the fantastic evocation of the city of Sodom and its underground salt-mines. Like the juxtaposition of the massacre of the Innocents with the fourth King's Indian sweets party for the over-twos on the hillside above Bethlehem, these details are absent from *Les Rois Mages*. Interestingly, one notable defender of the *Rois Mages* enterprise, Michael Worton, argues that the rewriting is indeed an improvement because the congregation of narrators in *Gaspard* is dispersed to allow for a unification of narrative voice in *Les Rois Mages*, an important modification which accentuates the parabolesque structure germane to the first novel. In the rewritten version, the performative aspect to the text is therefore highlighted through a more direct mode of narration, intimating the presence of a single storyteller, whereas in *Gaspard* it was, to some degree, dissipated among the different narrative voices.[29]

It is debatable whether the recasting of *Vendredi* and *Gaspard* justifies Tournier's pruning of 'unsuitable' episodes. Equally, assertions to the effect that children are blessed with an intuitive literariness which disappears at puberty should be treated with some scepticism. There are areas of human endeavour where children compete on an equal footing with adults, including mathematics, music, chess, painting even, but with these activities the prodigal child is always in the role of performer, or creator. On a different tack, Tournier may still argue, in the vein of J. D. Salinger, that his re-narrations respond to a need to chase truths that are too often concealed by 'phony' adult discourse. After all, Raymond Queneau's Zazie receives all kinds of verbal and non-verbal replies to her awkward question 'Qu'est-ce un hormo-sessuel?' other than the correct one. This may be true, but it avoids the real issue, which is concerned with how we, as children and adults, read; hence the importance of contributions from interested parties whose primary concern is with the education of children. Peter Hunt's contention—that children's fiction elucidates in a manner unique to its genre qualities common to all fiction which often pass unrecognised—brokers an interesting solution to the impasse in which Tournier critics have found themselves.

It is worth recalling that the *table ronde* discussion of children's literature in the context of Tournier's work which took place at the Cérisy Conference was enlivened by an intervention from Michael Worton who challenged the grounds on which his fellow participants were debating, by questioning whether the child is, in effect, a cate-gorisable entity. Childhood is a state of rapid evolution towards adulthood; therefore, to talk of 'the child' is meaningless. In reality, the 'child' will always be a figurative design, a figment, or projection of the adult's imagination, relating to what the adult thinks children are like or, more probably, to what the adult thinks he or she remembers about being a child. Over a long period of time, Tournier has taken the trouble of touring the *collèges* and *écoles primaires* of the Ile-de-France in order to give 'live' renditions of his latest creations. It is as if by performing the stories before his favourite audience, he is testing the product. Tournier's perception of children is coloured by their parti-cipation as readers in the realisation of his work. In his eyes, the child represents the ideal reader, or is at least an example to follow for adults, who, if they are to enjoy fully Tournier's fiction, should take a fresh, 'childist' look at his work without remaindering their adult culture.

If Tournier's idealisation of the child suggests the coveting of a certain kind of reader, then it is possible to draw a tentative list of the 'childist' qualities this imaginary reader should possess. This list would contain, *ipso facto*, central criteria on which to base our evaluation of

Tournier's work. The private reader of Tournier should then strain his or her ears to catch the echo of an oral context for the work in hand. Tournier's reader participates—often without realising quite how much—in the construction of meaning; he is involved in an interactive milieu in which the performance value of the story is stressed. Tournier places undue faith perhaps in the 'natural', learning curiosity of the child, and thus solicits on behalf of all his readers the willingness to question what they are being told. The absence of an ontological or epistemological framework of thought—already in place and operational in the developed mind of the adult, and therefore extremely difficult to dislodge—is another factor which predisposes Tournier to a children's audience, or at least to a 'childist' approach; in shorthand, the child's response to what he or she hears or reads is not predetermined by too many *idées reçues*. The child is also sensitive to narrative devices; children value repetition, suspense,[30] and closure, the stock-in-trade of the *conteur*. Lastly, children need to believe in what they read. Even if the story deals in monsters and fairies, the sequence of events must be plausible, for without *vraisemblance*, or narrative verisimilitude, the storyteller loses his hypnotic hold over his audience.

THE LIMITS OF *VRAISEMBLANCE*

Tournier writes neither for reviewers nor academics. Indeed he cares less than he might for what they think of him. But the near-telepathic relationship he enjoys with his non-professional readership is a talisman, a form of magic which is rooted in an assiduous writing practice, for whenever Tournier writes, he enters into a fundamental engagement with the Other. This Other will of course be a projected perception, but Tournier works hard at it, since he knows that in each instance, with each published text, his fictional world must make contact with the real worlds of other people. His enterprise thus presupposes some sort of shared reality.

Kirsty Fergusson characterises Tournier as an 'ironist metaphysician' who presents a dissected reality in his fictions: 'perceptual reality', which emerges in 'stories redolent with the smell of burning wood, Autumn mushrooms and wet fur', and 'conceptual reality'—'such sublime metaphysical inventions as Descartes' cogito, Spinoza's three types of knowledge, Leibniz' monadology'.[31] In Tournier's earlier fictions this fundamental distinction is often all too apparent, in the form of heavy-handed, barely-disguised narrative *divagations*. However, as Tournier has refined his technique, as the performative aspects of his texts have become more pronounced, the prose style more contracted and the images more evocative, this gap between body and mind has rapidly closed. Now, he is more than ever conscious of the need to use language in such a way that it conveys the sensory nature of reality. As Fergusson says, when we read Tournier, we should still feel the 'rock of the absolute shaken by the drumbeat of fate' beneath the 'leafy green canopy and brown furrows', but, for the writer himself, perfection is when the absolute is immanent to the concrete world of things. Tournier is a communicator who creates symbolic worlds, whose fiction is read as metaphor. But its effectiveness as metaphor depends on the presumption that it recounts a shared experience, that, to paraphrase Lakoff and Johnson, by reading Tournier's fictions we better understand our own experience of the world. Thus, the somewhat old-fashioned concept of fictional *vraisemblance* is integral to Tournier's narrative art, and he usually manages it with great skill.

The name of the chief protagonist in 'Que ma joie demeure' is Raphaël Bidoche, a combination of elegant artist and clumsy hod carrier which neatly encapsulates the central theme of the story: how an artistic vocation dips into mediocrity, but is never entirely abandoned. Raphaël, a promising young pianist, marries early and, in need of money, takes a job in cabaret, accompanying a singer called Bodruche. As Raphaël descends the cultural escalator, the financial rewards increase. He lands a further job as a solo pianist, but faces instant degradation. On the first night he follows an act in which a dwarf dances a tango with a fat woman and finds that his very presence on stage is intended to create a humorous effect, as the deadpan seriousness of the young pianist contrasts with the grotesque farce that has just played itself out seconds before. The situation is exacerbated for Raphaël, who has now very much assumed his identity as Bidoche, as he accidentally falls off the stool and gropes on the floor for his glasses. He is greeted as a comic *tour de force*, the new Buster Keaton, and congratulated by the manager who heaps praise on his 'dons d'improvisation comiques'. Thus Bidoche earns a handsome living as a 'clown blanc', playing his piano deliberately badly. Employed by a travelling circus he develops the act, sabotaging the piano so that, at the touch of an appropriate key, outrageous special effects—jets of water, plumes of smoke, loud farts—keep the audience entertained. At the grand finale Bidoche's piano is supposed to explode, showering the audience with sausages, cream tarts, and black puddings. However, one night the calm is not followed by the storm. Instead, the 'divine mélodie' of Bach's famous cantata rises from the old circus piano into the ether of the big top and the audience is spellbound: 'Après l'enfer des ricanements, c'était l'hilarité du ciel, tendre et spirituelle, qui planait sur une foule en communion' (CB, 98). The piano lid yawns open to trigger the explosion, but instead, 'il laissa fuir un bel archange aux ailes de lumière, l'archange Raphaël, celui qui depuis toujours veillait sur lui et le gardait de devenir tout à fait Bidoche' (CB, 99).

'Que ma joie demeure' exemplifies the transition in Tournier's work from the abstract to the concrete, the prolix to the concise. Ostensibly a paen to Bach,[32] it also speaks of a child's ambition and parental expectations, as well as of the performing arts. At the same time it activates one of Tournier's more subtle binary oppositions, that of the red and white clown, and the pre-eminence of the latter's ironic 'rire blanc'. However, the story works not on the conflict of two forms of humour but on their interaction. The opposition is no longer, and indeed never was contradictory. In 'Que ma joie demeure' it allows Tournier to display his wondrous feel for the transcendental. The nearest analogy is with Harpo Marx who could still the slapstick comedy of the brothers and the verbal virtuosity of Groucho with the commanding beauty of his harp-playing. A story such as 'Que ma joie demeure' that sets its stall on a particular opposition is transcended by the fictional possibilities enshrined in the narrative. Tournier strikes a sublime note precisely through the rooting of his fiction in a familiar world of disappointment and crushed hopes.

Tournier displays his realist cards whenever the question arises of the treatment of his sources. The more outlandish, far-flung, or fantastic the fictional situation with which the reader is confronted, the more likely it is to be rooted in the existence of some bizarre historical or natural phenomenon. *Le Roi des aulnes* is especially fertile territory for this form of literary research. I have already argued that, in the context of Tiffauges' ogrish vocation, the description of Arnim's death and Tiffauges' simultaneous shower of blood is far from gratuitous. For Arlette Bouloumié this incident triggers a number of valuable references to the cult of Mithra. Mithraism was an early religion which became established in Germany in the first century AD and spread throughout the Roman Empire, where it competed for recognition with Christianity. The showering of blood, Bouloumié writes, 'evokes Mithraic blood baptisms'.[33] Reactivated through the metamorphosis of the

Ogre, this appeal to the cult of Mithra substantiates the numerous epistemological quests for origins that have been used as intellectual props for Nazi ideology, most prominent among which are Nietzsche's Dionysian will to power and Heidegger's Germanic *Dasein*. Interestingly, Bouloumié's research into Mithraism and its underlying relevance to *Le Roi des aulnes* also calls attention once again to the role of Ephraïm. She establishes parallels between the cap worn by the Erl-King's entombed companion and the phrygian cap worn by Mithra, and between Tiffauges' black pigeon and the crow, symbolic messenger of Mithra. Further evidence suggesting that Tournier drew (extensively) on features of this ancient mythology is provided by the purple cloak, worn by Tiffauges in the novel but originally by the followers of Mithra, the prominence of hunting feasts in Germanic representations of Mithra, and the iconography depicting the god standing between two children carrying torches, which recalls the triad of Haro, Haïo and Lothar.

Some of the more fantastic elements of life as it is described in the fiefdom of Hermann Göring, Hitler's second-in-command, are authentic. Göring was, of course, a real person who was accustomed to travelling in the company of his pet lion, or rather a lion cub which would be replaced by another as soon as it reached unmanageable proportions. More incredibly still, the narrator refers to a prehistoric herd of cattle called 'aurochs' which graze in the hunting grounds of Göring's *Jägerhof*. These shaggy black beasts with huge bison-like heads and ferocious tendencies—the narrator tells of one who trampled the bicycles of a hunting patrol into the ground and went off parading a trophy of tangled metal on its horns—are the result, we are also told, of a back-breeding programme achieved through a judicious mixing of bull stock from Spain, Corsica and the Camargue. This experiment in genetic engineering takes its place in the prefigurative structure of the narrative, in anticipation of the thinly-veiled reference to Mengele's abominations represented in *Le Roi des aulnes* by the 'anthropological' discourse of Professor Doktor Blättchen. However, the extraordinary fact is that surviving members of just such a herd can be seen today grazing the pastures of the Parc naturel régional d'Armorique in Brittany.[34]

The difficulties associated with this sort of research are well illustrated by Michael Worton's discussion of the episode in *La Goutte d'or* in which the character Sigisbert de Beaufond recounts to Idriss an extraordinary story about the survivors of a plane crash who, stranded in the desert having run out of food and water, decide to slit their wrists. This turns out to be a futile means of suicide because they are so dehydrated that the veins will not bleed, and indeed will only start bleeding four days later when they have been rescued and sufficiently rehydrated. The story was originally relayed to Beaufond by the surviving pilot, one Alexandre Bernard. However, Sigisbert identifies himself so closely with Bernard's heroism that he holds his wrists out to Idriss in order to show him the scars, which, of course, the latter cannot see. This ludicrous inconsistency persuades Worton that Sigisbert's narration should be read as a parable of the naïve reader who is incapable of distinguishing fiction from reality.[35] In his post scriptum to the novel, Tournier mentions that Sigisbert is a 'mythomane', and then proceeds to give the truth, recalling his own encounter with an elderly Colonel Alexandre Bernard and the visible evidence of the scars. Why then does this make of the fictional Sigisbert a naïve reader? It would seem that Sigisbert is, in the first instance, an attentive listener and consequently a skilled storyteller, able to relate all manner of preliminary details concerning exact dates and distances, the names of places and destinations, the speed and flying heights of the 1920s aircraft, etc. He provides a detailed historical context to the story, strong characterisation in the person of the General Laperrine, and recounts the key events in a dramatic, suspenseful way. It is not therefore that odd that he should act out Bernard's authenticating gesture, nor is it unusual for oral storytellers to use more elaborate gestures like mime to enhance their performances. It would seem in this case that Sigisbert's self-mythologisation guarantees the quality of his narration, that the primary objective therefore of all narrators is to entrance their audience, to prevent them from being able, or even from desiring, to distinguish reality from fiction. Given that, in my version of Tournier's career, *La Goutte d'or* is a pivotal text operating the switch in Barthesian terms from a 'writerly' universe to a more 'readerly' and indeed reader-friendly environment, that it is a novel written in a more direct (for some didactic) style, that it pointedly reifies the tradition of oral storytelling, and that at the time of composition Tournier had an audience of attentive ten-year-olds in mind, Sigisbert's contribution should not be underestimated.

Paul Ricoeur thought 'vraisemblance' crucial to all rhetorical discourse. Tournier, however, is prepared to push 'vraisemblance' to the limits of credulity, especially in those of his fictional works which evidently have something to say about the world outside the text. One of the best examples of this kind of provocation is 'Les Suaires de Véronique', a warning story about the potential for exploitation in the intimate relationship between artist and model. In this case, the art-form is photography.

The fictional narrative is prefaced by a mini-thesis on photography. For Tournier, the best photographers are of two types: the roving cameraman who is constantly alert to the surprising, novel image and the 'stagers' who painstakingly construct the image, spending hours calculating angles, waiting for optimum light conditions, etc. The first look to consecrate the moment, the second search for eternal value. Neither, however, have much to do with Tournier's story, which is about portrait photography. The female photographer, Véronique, is presented as an ogress,[36] who progressively saps the strength of her model by over-photographing him. As he gets thinner, he becomes strangely beautiful. A number of indications in the narrative combine to suggest that Véronique—*vera icon*, or truth in the image—is prepared to go further in her quest for the ultimate aesthetic of portraiture. At one point Véronique proffers a maxim which is accredited to Valéry: *La vérité est nue, mais sous le nu, il y a l'écorché* (CB, 160). The literal sense of the epithet is not only substantiated by the seemingly implausible narrative recounting the model Hector's fate, but historicised via a lengthy digression on the activities of Vesalius, the father of modern anatomy who gave the first public demonstrations of the value to medicine of dissection. Hector winds up in hospital having been subjected to a series of 'photographies directes'. This process involved his skin being treated with chemicals and his body then being pressed against large sheets of photographic paper to create an effect similar to that of the Hiroshima shadows, the mortal remains of those caught in the blast of the atomic bomb. When the narrator does eventually meet with Véronique again, she talks enthusiastically of a museum of 'dermographie' where numerous canvasses of different body imprints hang from the ceiling, 'On songeait à une série de peaux humaines arrachées, puis étalées là comme autant de trophées bizarres...' (CB, 171). At the end we are led to believe that Véronique has taken the final step, and that Hector has been reduced to a selection of assorted 'suaires'.

The discourse on photography in 'Véronique' pushes *vraisemblance* to an absolute limit. The narrative is harnessed to a movement which conveys the reader towards a full exposition of Ricardou's 'litteralité de la figure'. Véronique will literally 'have the skin' of Hector; 'avoir la peau de quelqu'un' is an idiom meaning normally 'to give someone a wigging', or 'to carpet someone'. In 'Véronique' the narrator hears 'l'expression même employée dans sa lettre'. Sewn into the narrative is a referential strip of flayed skin. Valéry's unsubstantiated quotation brings to mind the image of the Baron Charlus 'enchaîné sur son lit comme Promethée sur son rocher' in Proust's *Le Temps retrouvé*,[37] the raw-skinned sodomites in Tournier's own *Gaspard, Melchior et Balthazar*, and the lampshades made of the skin of Jewish inmates belonging to the Kommandeur's wife in Jorge Semprun's *Le Grand Voyage*. Film-goers will be reminded of Anthony Hopkins' portrayal of serial killer, Hannibal Lektor, in *The Silence of the Lambs*. Although Véronique's shrouds bear a remarkable resemblance to Yves Klein's *Anthropométries* (1958–61), which Klein produced by imprinting bodies daubed in blue paint on to sheets of paper,[38] this writerly skin-grafting is supposed to be read metaphorically. Can we really believe in such a ludicrous plot? Of course not, in which case the reader's attention is diverted to the metafictional discussion on photography and Tournier's attitude towards the image which is also foregrounded in the narrative.[39] However, there are references to flayed skin that can be tied down to a specific historical period.

Executing a deft pirouette, Tournier's narrator overturns a commonplace assumption, arguing that the plague-ridden Middle Ages were in fact much healthier in body and soul than the glittering Renaissance, an age when morbid obsessions with death and suffering ate into the social fabric of the major European nations. A number of mostly artistic references, not all convincing, are cited in support of this statement, but the pivotal figure in this theatre of the macabre is Vesalius. The narrator writes a letter to Véronique in which he details the results of his research into the life of Vesalius. He recounts how Vesalius not only practised dissection, but also experimented with vivisection. In the dead of the night he would arrange for the release of certain prisoners, dope them with opium and then cut up their bodies. When he moved from Brussels to Madrid, dark rumours began to circulate, and Vesalius was hauled before the Inquisition and sentenced to death. Thanks to the intervention of Philip II, the sentence was commuted to one of 'enforced' pilgrimage. Some years later, in the course of his travels, Vesalius was reported to have been shipwrecked and washed up on a Greek island where he died of starvation.

Fascinatingly, the result of Tournier's research into Vesalius turns out to be a finely-judged mixture of fact and invention. There is indeed a mystery surrounding Vesalius' departure on a pilgrimage from Venice in 1564, and a lack of information concerning his whereabouts after this date. Accusations of bodysnatching and human vivisection are not taken seriously, but there are numerous reports of an incident in which the exposed heart of a corpse started to beat during a dissection performed by Vesalius in Spain. Medical scholars are sceptical about the possibility that Vesalius of all people could have made such an elementary error as mistaking a living person for a corpse, in public and with the Inquisition breathing down his neck. It is generally believed that he fell victim to a conspiracy of either religious fanatics, jealous Spanish physicians, or a powerful alliance of both these injured parties. Still, the story of the beating heart and the disappearance of one of the world's great early scientists has never been satisfactorily explained.[40]

Tournier homes in unerringly on such half-truths, on these stories which slip off the face of history into the realms of legend and myth. In the case of Vesalius he manipulates his source material adroitly, highlighting the sensational aspects whilst steering clear of the incredible. It is an important and delicate task, for Vesalius is to act as an historical guarantor for precisely the most implausible, outrageous elements of Tournier's own story about a fanatical photographer and her involvement in the series of events which literalises the metaphorical intent of Valéry's quotation. For the reader who takes Tournier's story at its metaphorical face-value and reads it as an essay on photography and the corrupting power of the image, the Vesalius story casts a shadow of doubt.

'Véronique' thus turns out to be more of a fable than either a classic *conte* or indeed a *nouvelle*. In practice Tournier's measured typology of short fiction is often shown to be fluid. For example, 'Que ma joie demeure' neatly escapes his own classification system. It is described as a 'conte': a tale of universal import and appeal, which appears to impart a message or moral, though that message may not always be easily discerned. In this instance Tournier sets out with one of his universal oppositions, exploring the relationship between the red and white clown, thus privileging the theme of humour. Moreover the story is wrapped up by another pairing, in which the subtle differences between talent and genius are evidenced. Raphaël has talent. He can earn a living through playing the piano, but he is not blessed with genius. In between, in the meat of the text, the impact of Raphaël's ordinary status is felt in the familiar, bitter world of the *nouvelle*. As we know, for Tournier the *nouvelle* tends to be revelatory of truths—

historical or moralistic—and the mood is invariably pessimistic. At the same time this infiltration of literature into the real can be uplifting. When, in *La Goutte d'or*, Bonami's mannequins are inserted into the natural landscape, they are not absorbed into it. Rather the mannequins 'jettent le doute sur le paysage' (GD, 181). The landscape is enhanced by this intrusion of the ideal, or the fake, just as the humdrum facts of daily existence can suddenly appear novel and exciting in the world of fiction. A quiet voice can be heard in the sublime finale of 'Que ma joie demeure' saying that there may be some truth in this made-up story about a non-existent person, that we, like Raphaël, could also rise for a fleeting moment above the mediocrity of our routine existences.

Even in the most beautifully-judged of short stories, like 'Que ma joie demeure', Tournier cannot disguise the fact that he has something to say. The lectern donated to the narrator of 'Ecrire debout'[41] allows him to write 'standing up'. It represents the writer's need to 'speak out'. Whatever the genre, Tournier's fiction is instructive. Indeed, his much-publicised commitment to the education of the young is reflected in the educative slant which is a common element to all his fictional works. This personnage of the educator, or the sage, steps out of two of the very best pieces from *Le Médianoche*.

BRILLIANT SHORTS: 'PYROTECHNIE OU LA COMMÉMORATION'; 'PIERROT OU LES SECRETS DE LA NUIT'

José Luis Borges, arguably the most famous, latter-day exponent of the short story, has refined a genre which now, more often than not, tells of its own coming-into-being. In 'Pyrotechnie' the self-conscious character of the short story is privileged, but in terms which are softly caricatured. The narrator is a Parisian writer, who has been exiled on the command of an impatient publisher to the small town of Monteux, near Carpentras, in order to get on with his next book away from the bright lights of the big city. He already has a provisional title for it ('Elle se mange froide'), a situation (the closed provincial community), and the genesis of a plot (a classic tale of revenge in which suspense will be created by the characters' expectancy of the retributive act). At the end of 'Pyrotechnie' he duly starts writing, 'cette histoire de vengeance étirée sur toute une vie dans le cadre d'une petite ville de province où tout se sait' (MA, 96). This self-reflexivity clearly circumscribes the text but its function is *not* to annihilate (gradually) the possibility of thematic interpretations, as it would be in a Borgesian narrative. Tournier is interested in the material fact of writing, in the reality of the writer's life. It is no accident therefore that in 'Pyrotechnie' his narrator is bothered about relations with his publisher. Will he be able sufficiently to dress up the 'mince canevas' of his story so as not to jeopardise his advance? Thus, the narrative flows *à rebours*, from the act of writing back into the world of the writer. What starts out as a self-conscious narrative becomes less rather than more conscious of itself. Moreover, the fiction is seemingly authenticated as the narrator is himself embroiled in the process of learning.

Familiar Tournier themes are prevalent in the early sections of the text. The proposed subject-matter for the narrator's book is, of course, a wink in the direction of Maupassant. Care should be taken, however, not to misinterpret the comic touch of the prospective title. Tournier's narrator emphasises a need to recreate the 'eyes everywhere' community that typifies the gritty realism of Maupassant's short stories by reiterating the fact that the vendetta should be public knowledge: 'de notoriété publique. Tout le monde le savait. Tout le monde attendait' (MA, 97). At this early stage his romanesque musings are already assuming an urgency that transcends the supposed fictional medium. This expository setting of the scene is significant. Tournier knows that the effects of any given crime are maximised when the crime occurs within a sedentary society; the people of Monteux are described as 'des sédentaires absolus' (MA, 96). Now the distinction between sedentary and nomadic peoples is a key dialectic in Tournier's thinking. The biblical story of Cain and Abel is the prototype for a dozen other narratives, including the portrayal of the outcast, Abel Tiffauges, in *Le Roi des aulnes*, the gradual dissolution of the 'cellule gémellaire' in *Les Météores*, and Idriss's quest in *La Goutte d'or*. Reifying this fundamental myth in 'Pyrotechnie', Tournier takes a leaf out of Balzac's *modus operandi*. Consider the way in which the explosion at the factory is described.

Tournier handles the description of this one big event with a typical flourish. The narrator is busy thinking socio-cultural thoughts at the local *boulodrome*, as the final player of the group prepares to launch his one remaining projectile, intended to disperse the cluster around the *cochonnet* in all directions. At the precise moment of impact there is a thunderous noise, and the scattering of the boules is reproduced in macrocosm by the sight of 'un feu d'artifice, mais chaotique' (MA,

106), illuminating the sky. Seconds later people are running towards the factory. Accustomed to the sequential configurations of pyrotechnics, the townsfolk react instinctively to the psychedelic orderlessness above their heads. This account, however, is written some time after the event. As an outsider ignorant of the possible consequences of the explosion, the narrator cannot react in the same way as the townsfolk. While everyone else dashes about, he can only watch, and would only have made sense of what he had seen at a later time. Balzac, who saw his art as the ability to achieve the coincidence of 'l'observation' and 'l'expression', is a singular inspiration. Tournier's narrator is there, with the people at the *boulodrome*, yet able to stand back at the vital moment.

If there is some doubt as to whether Tournier is angling for a Balzacian acuity of observation in his depiction of the reactions of the Monteux townspeople, then we ought perhaps to revert to that traditional stamping-ground of realist writing, namely characterisation, in this case the characterisation of the factory-manager:

> M. Capolini m'accueillit avec l'empressement d'un professionnel flatté qu'un ignorant de marque vienne de Paris s'instruire auprès de lui. Au demeurant il parlait si bien et si brillamment des feux d'artifice qu'il paraissait par moments devenir lui-même un feu d'artifice. J'ai rencontré plus d'une fois cette sorte de contamination totale d'un homme par sa profession, charcutière sculptée dans du saindoux, paysan pétri de terre et de fumier, banquier semblable à un coffre-fort, cavalier au rire henissant. Les mains de Capolini devenaient à tout moment fusées, bouquets, fontaines de feu ou soleils tournoyants. Ses yeux paraissaient sans cesse éblouis par quelque déploiement féerique. (MA, 99–100)

This kind of picture-portrait is reminiscent of the way in which Balzac tended to stigmatise his characters. The personification of spinsterhood through the character of Sophie Gamard in *Le Curé de Tours* shows how such blanket representations may be construed as prejudicial. Meticulously observed details of her physical appearance are conjugated so as to support Balzac's one overriding contention, that 'en restant fille, une créature du sexe féminin n'est plus qu'un non-sens: égoïste et froide, elle fait horreur'.[42] And, in describing the effect of this condition on Sophie Gamard, he pulls no punches, hinting that the dark rings under her eyes betray long hours of masturbatory activity, 'accusait les longs combats de sa vie solitaire'.[43] Balzac's discourse establishes a causal link between spinsterhood and sexual frustration; Sophie's petty attitudes and spiteful behaviour are explained by the lack of a good man in her life! Although the description of M. Capolini shows Tournier indulging his Balzacian tendencies, here it is more a case of playful stereotyping; one is reminded of the oft-heard remark about dog-owners coming with time to look more and more like their four-legged friends. However it has a very different, underlying purpose. The effect is impressionistic. Each dash of paint—the lardy butcher, the earthy peasant, the impassable banker, the laughing cavalier, not forgetting the effusive M. Capolini—imparts the sort of crisp definition which is necessary to bring characters to life in children's fiction. Moreover, Tournier puts his reader in contact with the symbolic functioning of the human mind, highlighting in this instance the figure of metonymy. The rich symbolism of the firework, through its metonymic definition of M. Capolini, comes to displace the character. M. Capolini's verbal dexterity is such that the symbol quickly eclipses the human actor.

Initially the firework signifies the intrusion of the fantastic, the irruption of the *conte* within the *nouvelle*. On the night of his arrival in Monteux the narrator witnesses from the window of his lodgings a marvellous firework display. Spectacular but odd, for he cannot understand why anyone should want to commemorate 25 July, St Anne's Day. He soon discovers that it was merely a routine product-testing operation. However, his curiosity is aroused by this 'manu-facture pittoresque', and even more so by the fact that a firework display, usually symbolic of important historical or political events, should form part of the daily routine, that it should not interrupt for a second the rhythm of the townspeople's lives. This lovely equation of the 'plus beau feu d'artifice' with ordinary life teases out a modest philosophical reflection on the nature of the phenomenon. Tournier shows through the reaction of his narrator how human perception and understanding of reality is conditional on factors of culture and environment, and therefore on the mythologies of specific cultures. The effect in 'Pyrotechnie' is to undermine the stable, symbolic value of the firework, its commemorative function. The narrator's experience of the staged firework display that commemorates nothing will turn out to be a prophesy. The next display witnessed turns out to be a tragic accident which *is* commemorative.

'Pyrotechnie' is the story of the narrator's investigation of the accident at the factory in which two men are killed. He is able to confirm that the incident was a case of simultaneous murder and suicide. The victim, Gilles, had an heroic reputation that dated back to the Resistance; the perpetrator of the deed, a young boy at the time of the war, held Gilles responsible for the public humiliation of his mother during the *épuration*. The explosion at the factory is eventually explained as the culmination of a vendetta which had been pursued commemoratively, the last in a series of unfortunate accidents that had befallen Gilles, usually on 11 August of any given calendar year. The key figure in the narrator's research is a retired journalist, 'un maniaque de la documentation' (MA, 114), for whom modern-day life is meaningless due to the absence of important historical events. His recollections of Gilles' former role as leader of the local Resistance group and account of the days following the liberation of the town in 1945 change entirely the perspective within which we read the narrative. As we come to understand how the apparently inexplicable occurred, why the explosion at the factory was an act of simultaneous murder and suicide, we also learn of unpleasant details concerning the liberation of the town in 1945—a story of scapegoats, of cruelty towards innocent people, of the rule of the mob. Suddenly there is a message in the text, introduced as it were through the back door, which says that the official view of the Resistance and the Liberation, the acceptable side to French history, is both glamorised and superficial.

This, then, is the twist in the tale of the firework factory, for the story is really about the art of the novelist. It presents him as if by accident 'sur le terrain' and we read of the sparking of his imagination and subsequently of his painstaking research. And yet as the narrative unfolds, the novelist becomes historian, and the historian, in the shape of the retired journalist, becomes novelist. For the latter history is a mere succession of names; the rest is fiction, as when he talks about the Great War: 'J'ai tant entendu parler de Verdun et du chemin des Dames, que je finis par croire que j'y étais' (MA, 115). This curious *va-et-vient* gives a fascinating insight into the change in preoccupations of European novelists in the aftermath of the Holocaust, and more particularly in France, in the aftermath of the Occupation. French literature since 1945 is speckled with important works relating to the Occupation. The *témoignages* of Vailland, de Beauvoir and Vercors preceded the semi-contemporaneous, allegorical account in Camus' *La Peste* (1947), which was itself a forerunner to the fully fictional representations contained in novels such as Modiano's *La Place de l'étoile* (1968), Tournier's own *Le Roi des aulnes*, and especially in the *oeuvre* of Jorge Semprun. In French cinema there has been a real sea-change. The end of the Gaullist interregnum saw a proliferation of important films, notably Louis Malle's *Lacombe, Lucien* (1973) and Marcel Ophuls' *Le Chagrin et la pitié* (first screened in 1971), which subject French society during the Occupation to uncomfortable scrutiny. These investigations into the national mythology of the French were 'fathered' by Alan Resnais' path-breaking 1959 film *Hiroshima mon amour*, in which the need to make better sense of historical experience is asserted. Above all, these texts, especially *Hiroshima*, ask awkward questions. Is it possible to make sense of history if it is unlived, and do those who have lived it use memory to recover or distort sense? Tournier reveals in *Le Roi des aulnes*, and here in 'Pyrotechnie', that he is aware of the difficulties encountered by the modern novelist who will inevitably find him/herself at some stage 'facing history'.[44] He may be criticised for not helping, for not proposing solutions, but as a novel as complex as *Le Roi des aulnes* shows, he should not be rebuked for not endeavouring to understand. Like Vercors, Tournier realises that understanding is possible only on a limited human scale, in the self-imposed dumbness of the girl refusing to connive with, to console even, the German officer in *Le Silence de la mer*, and in the image of the wretched, semi-illiterate Ange Crevet, the avenging angel in 'Pyrotechnie', standing each year in silent commemoration at the graveside of 'la crevette', his humiliated mother.

If we agree with Tournier that the good novelist is as much historian as writer of fictions, and that the creativity of the latter is predicated upon the research of the former, then we should also accept the truth contained in his depiction of the retired journalist, who has imagined himself so successfully as 'ancien combattant' that he has come to believe that this is what he now is, that the construction of the historian's narrative is a considerable feat of the imagination. Many historiographers, including Paul Veyne, Hayden White and Paul Ricoeur, concede that any attempted return to a past state is a huge reconstructive task based on the flimsiest of empirical evidence, and that the primary agent for these reconstructions is the imagination of the author. Ricoeur has written extensively on the areas of congruence in modern analyses of historical and literary narrative. In one collaborative collection of essays he stakes out the field for investigation, declaring that, 'l'enjeu commun à la théorie de l'histoire et à la théorie du récit fictif est la connexion entre figure et séquence, configuration et succession'.[45] Ricoeur conceives the figure or symbol as, in one sense, the beginning or the *déclencheur*, as that which gives rise to narrative. Figures inspire tropes which can act in turn like keys; they may open the doors to a greater understanding. In 'Pyrotechnie' there is one master figure; the secret of narrative lies in the firework.

The animated conversation of M. Capolini suggests that he is not only the manager of a firework factory, but also an enthusiastic *aficionado* of contemporary literary theory: 'toute la pyrotechnie', he explains, 'se ramène à une lutte contre le hic et nunc' (MA, 100). At the moment of detonation, of maximum presence therefore, the firework deploys both a spatial and a temporal configuration, a double property that it shares with narrative. The firework manufacturer, like the writer of narrative, must be master in each domain in order to achieve the desired effect: 'cette explosion', pontificates M. Capolini in the style of the modern *rhétoriqueur*, 'nous nous en rendons maîtres pour la déplacer dans l'espace et la différer dans le temps' (ibid). Irresistibly, it would appear, we are drawn back to this essential function of the firework, 'à différer dans le temps et à déployer dans l'espace'. But historiography and literary theory only provide half-answers. When, in 'Pyrotechnie', the factory manager is explaining the technical side to his business, he lets the narrator into a real secret. For the detonation of the firework to occur, there needs to be a conical space hollowed out of its centre, 'un vide ménagé en son centre et ayant la forme d'un tronc de cône' (MA, 103). Without it there would be no firework, but nobody knows why. M. Capolini describes this phenomenon of the pyrotechnic function resistant to human conceptualisation in suitably lyrical fashion. 'Sachez-le bien', he exudes, 'comme les femmes et comme les violons, la fusée possède une âme' (ibid). This figure, already three or four times significant (cf. Chagall's *The Cellist*, 'le violon d'Ingrès'), is philosophically exciting, because it seems to defy empirical verification. Interviewing Tournier in April 1990, the 'firework question' was on the tip of my tongue, intrigued as I was to find out whether this was one of those mysteries of science that comes along occasionally to befuddle the methodology of empiricist lore. Was it true? Tournier smiled as he shook his head. His job was done. The important thing was that I had begun to half-believe the fiction. It could have been true. And I, like the child who craves the instant gratification of a desire, needed to know the truth.

My reactions to 'Pyrotechnie' neatly demonstrate the theory developed by Frege in his famous essay, 'On Sense and Reference', in which he maintains that the action of the human mind is governed by an imperceptible and irresistible movement that takes us from the sense of the object to its reference.[46] The sense of 'Pyrotechnie' lies in the resolution of the crime, which is wrapped up in the organic evolution of the narrative and manifested through a series of temporal coincidences.

What is important here is the clarity, or perceptibility, of this structure, and not whether the events described are believable or not. Paradoxically, it is the inherent aspect to the firework which takes us outside the text. The manager's words, seeking as they do to impose human qualities on a machine, simulate the convergence of the most fundamental antithesis—that of living and inert matter—and lead us once again to the crossroads of Culture and Nature, that we technologically motivated creatures insist on reliving. (Witness our fascination with robots, daleks and the like.) This is the moment of metaphor, when the *as if* of the fictional narrative is dropped in favour of the *is* of the radical copula, when fiction impinges on and starts to redefine our conception of reality. It is only when we have finished reading that the writer's imagination makes its impact; it is only then that we begin to wonder about those fireworks.

This schema is diametrically opposed to the model proposed by Gérard Genette in his discourse on language and space. Genette considers that modern man is oriented primarily by spatial rather than temporal relations: 'L'homme préfère l'espace au temps'. Literary discourse in particular, he writes, 'ne se dit plus qu'en termes de distance, d'horizon, d'univers, de paysage, de lieu, de site, de chemin et de demeure: figures naïves, mais caractéristiques, figures par excellence, où le langage s'espace afin que l'espace, en lui, devenu langage, se parle et s'écrive.'[47] More than literature even, the cinema would seem to exemplify Genette's description of a 'spatialised' culture. In Wim Wenders' 1984 film, *Paris, Texas*, Harry Dean Stanton stares out into the vast expanse of the Arizona desert and starts walking, apparently into infinity. But this journey into space (the sheer scale of the panorama on the big screen is breathtaking) has a destination; it ends in the big city. In one of the finest scenes of contemporary cinema, the Stanton character confronts his estranged wife, played by Natassia Kinski, through a one-way perspex glass pane, as she begins to perform her ritual sex act for the paying customer. He stops her, they talk, and gradually she recognises who he is. At the end of his journey through space, the human identity of the characters involved is reaffirmed and the past relived, albeit through a perspex glass pane. A temporal framework is back in place.

Tournier's 'Pyrotechnie' leads the reader gently, inexorably away from literary questions about narrative to a world of elementary philosophy and story-telling. In his excellent book, *The Sense of an Ending*, Frank Kermode poses the question as to what basic human set founds the various paradigms of our existence. Kermode argues that our verbalisation of time as the tick-tock of the clock is the essential paradigm upon which we base our perception of reality. As he puts it, '*tick* is our word for a beginning, *tock* our word for an end. We say they differ. What enables them to be different is a special kind of middle.'[48] What Kermode is saying here is that we can perceive duration only when it is organised. The fact that we call the second of the two related sounds arbitrarily conferred on what would otherwise be pure chronicity *tock* is evidence that we use fictions to enable the end to confer organisation and form on temporal structure. The clock's *tick-tock* then becomes the model of what we call a plot, an organisation that humanises time by giving it form; and the interval between *tick* and *tock* represents purely successive, disorganised time of the sort we need to humanise. The function of the storyteller is to fill this emptiness, to endow it with 'significant season'. Within this organisation, what was conceived as simply successive becomes charged with past and future: what was *chronos* becomes *kairos*. This is the time of the novelist, a transformation of mere successiveness which E. M. Forster once likened to the experience of love, the erotic consciousness that makes 'divine sense out of a commonplace person'.

Kermode gives numerous examples in different contexts of the enormously complex fictions that we invent in order to give significance to our lives. They may be institutionalised, like those pertaining in the world of equity and law, or personal; we all live out our lives under the aegis of a series of false endings and beginnings. This is why stories are so satisfying; because reading them allows us to behave as young children do when they think of all the past as yesterday. In the words of journalist Michael Ignatieff, 'short stories assuage, within a miniature world of their own, our own anguish and uncertainty about what will happen next in our lives'.[49]

The soul at the centre of Tournier's rocket is an indication of the humanisation of time that occurs within the paradigm of his fiction, and it therefore signifies our need to go beyond the text and project its structure of beginnings and endings on the formlessness of our own existence. It did not take me long to reassert the 'truth' of Tournier's fiction. The theoretical physicist Stephen Hawking reminds us that when we throw a stone into a pond, the ripples spread out as a circle that gets bigger as time goes on. Hawking proposes that we think of a three-dimensional model consisting of the two-dimensional surface of the pond (space measured on the horizontal axis), and the one dimension of time (measured on the vertical axis). The expanding circle of ripples will, he says, mark out a cone whose tip is at the place and time at which the stone hit the water. This is the simple model for what Hawking terms the 'future (and past) light cone of an event',[50] which he uses to demonstrate how we ought to conceive of space and time in terms of the distance travelled by light-waves propagated from a certain indefinable point; not unlike the mysterious soul of the firework, whose secret resides in the hollow cone at its centre. The metaphor lives; and like the child for whom the story at bedtime is a prerequisite for sleep, its resurrection puts the critic's mind temporarily at rest.

The mind, however, should not remain inactive for long. The enduring image of 'Pyrotechnie' is of two silent men sitting either side of a table at the heart of the factory, composing Rockets and Catherine Wheels from brightly coloured powders contained in a series of vials. It suggests the medieval magic of alchemy, rather than the modern-day certainties of science. If the firework with its weird chemistry harbours the secret of narrative, then perhaps the symbol of the firework, like the Figure in Henry James' carpet, takes us beyond narrative and into a timeless, mythical zone. Perhaps this journey into the realms of our own imagination is what Tournier really means when he talks of myth as 'une histoire que tout le monde connaît déjà' (VP, 184). This journey is essentially regressive, a journey back into our own memories, into childhood.

As I stated in my introductory section, Tournier identifies Hans Christian Andersen's *The Snow Queen* as the story he would most like to have written. It is, of course, a classic fairy-tale. A fragment of the Devil's Mirror pierces little Kay's heart, his moral view of the world is inverted, and he is kidnapped by the Snow Queen. Plucky Gerda sets off in pursuit and, after a series of interesting encounters, succeeds in rescuing Kay from the Ice Kingdom north of Lapland. On their return to Gerda's grandmother's house everything seems much the same, 'the clock still said "Tick tock!" and the hands still marked the hours'.[51] The difference is in themselves, for they are now grown-up people. The end of childhood coincides with the end of the story. The splinter of glass has long since been displaced from Kay's heart, but their adventures are somehow eternised in memory, representing another life which we all believe we once lived. In fact, this other world is tangible; it is the world of children's fairy tales, a world in which those adults who become parents have the opportunity to relive.

Daniel Pennac contrasts the pain of the solitary adolescent who cannot get past page 49 of *Madame Bovary* with the infectious pleasure of the toddler for whom any number of reading sessions is never enough:

> Son plaisir nous inspirait. Son bonheur nous donnait du souffle. Pour lui, nous avons multiplié les personnages, enchaîné les épisodes, raffiné les chausse-trapes ... Comme le vieux Tolkien à ses petits-enfants, nous lui avons inventé un monde. À la frontière du jour et de la nuit, nous sommes devenus son romancier.[52]

Pennac sees no reason why this excitement over reading should not be extended through the school years, why books should not compete on an equal footing with television and video for the attention of the teenager, just as they do for the pre-school child. The key to achieving this regeneration of the subversive, thrilling quality to literature which used to entrance adolescent readers in bygone, more censorious eras, is in the slowing-down of the transition from a communal, oral reading situation to the solitary engagement with the text. Thus, though the child may have reached the point at which he or she can read unaided, the parent should continue to read aloud to his offspring until such a time as the child can not only spot the sections that have been skipped, but is able to fill them in without having recourse to the text. For Pennac, all literature should be infused with the fantastic, other-worldliness which Tolkien invented for his grandchildren. The dynamism of the spoken word must emanate from the written text; the oral must be encapsulated within the scriptural.

Tournier's 'Pierrot ou Les secrets de la nuit' is situated plumb at the crossroads of the oral and the written. With 'Pierrot', Tournier assumes his status as the Napoleon of contemporary French literature and gives the signal for his dragoons of young readers to invade the staid company of their 'elders and betters'. Predictably, when it was first published as an independent volume in 1979 'Pierrot' was largely ignored, in spite of Tournier's imprecations that it was the best thing he had ever written.[53] My discussion of it should be read in counterpoint to the reading of Ricardou's *Les lieux-dits* given in Chapter 1, for 'Pierrot' foregrounds the holistic experience often associated with the oral narrative in contrast to *Les lieux-dits*, which focuses on the differential problematic of the written sign. 'Pierrot' carries Tournier's bet on the ontological necessity of a language which speaks the world, which connects instantly with the experience of the Other. On the one hand it is a supreme piece of literary craftsmanship, on the other it reinvents the world through a child's mind's eye. Roberts treats it as one of the most multi-layered of Tournier's self-referential narratives. He concludes that the Pierrot/Arlequin opposition presents a clear bifurcation leading either to the classical, Platonic view of art or to the postmodern preoccupation with the simulacrum.[54]

We are immediately alerted to the possibility that Tournier is attempting to reconcile a huge disparity, between the superficial style of the *faux-naïf* and the underlying complexity of the metaphysical argument. If the effortlessness of the *rapprochement* in 'Pierrot' is surprising, it is because the distance covered is much shorter than that evoked by the 'union des contraires impossibles' which Roberts and others see as the guiding principle of Tournier's fictional project. The ontological argument here is not one of postmodernist versus platonist. (I think this is a mistaken reading). Rather 'Pierrot' tells of the origin of metaphysics, of the value of knowledge and wisdom as tools to penetrate the veneer of instant cognition. It is a fundamentally educational story, which follows a building-block pattern. The sequencing is minutely orchestrated. Anaphora and cataphora are used extensively. The narrative regularly refers back to remind the reader of important characteristics, to reinforce truths even, and it refers ahead so that the story gains a structural coherence. The text is literally knitted together as we read it. The context is ahistorical, and the characters are stock archetypes, taken from the *commedia dell'arte*. This second factor is unimportant in so far as our understanding of the story is concerned; we are given an explanation of the origin of Colombine's name in the first paragraph. But the *commedia dell'arte* does of course place a premium on the value of performance, on physicality, on entertainment—slapstick and farce—of a sort that would appeal to children. It is also essentially rural. More importantly, Tournier's narrative is generated from a number of fundamental associations that have their origins in popular mythology and folklore and are familiar conceits in a variety of children's stories. Some of these can of course be traced back to classical mythology.

The spinal column of what will emerge as a 'whole body' perception of literature is the eternal opposition of night and day. This is the first of many dualities highlighted in the text, and it immediately gives rise to another, that of work and rest. Pierrot, the baker's boy, embodies the night. He is fully a part of the night, he works when others rest. He is, therefore, a figure of the Other, often misunderstood, even feared. Naturally, it follows that he and the night are associated with scary things, such as wolves and bats. Colombine is associated with the day, or the everyday. The association is less strong than with Pierrot, but it is nonetheless represented by the concrete symbols of birds and flowers. The importance of work is reaffirmed. It takes Pierrot to two other 'obscurités encore plus inquiétantes': the cellar and the oven. The convergence of darkness and danger is reinforced by two rhetorical questions, the first of which introduces the rat: 'Qui sait s'il n'y avait pas des rats dans sa cave?' (MA, 259). Taboo creature and carrier of disease, the rat is the dread figure of Orwell, Camus, even David Attenborough. It is often found in cellars and is also, of course, associated with the dark. The second question—'Et ne dit-on pas: "noir comme un four"?' (MA, 259)—establishes a proverbial link with the oven and darkness, thereby suggesting the importance of language in developing our conceptual awareness of the environment. Rhetorical questions are a frequent occurrence in this text. Usually positioned at the end of paragraphs, they drive the narrative forward at crucial points and predispose the reader to the idea that this is a story written to be performed. Its self-affirmation is a clue to its educative function.

Throughout the narrative the reader is confronted with the physical and the concrete, with the tangible manifestations of nature. Although Pierrot comes to represent a form of spirituality, his temperament is first manifested through his physique. He is pale, with big eyes, and wears the baggy, white overalls of the baker. His look is that of the ubiquitous owl, nocturnal creature *par excellence*, and symbol, of course, of wisdom. The emphasis on clothes reminds us of the owl in 'Lucie ou La femme sans ombre', brushing past the children as it emerges from the disused tunnel. Also, it is suggested that Pierrot and Colombine may meet in the twilight zone, the hour of Minerva's owl. We are subtly reminded that wisdom could be defined as either the impulse or the capacity to react analytically to the vicissitudes of the world.

Pierrot is fundamentally lunar and owl-like. These two physical aspects externalise character traits. Pierrot is shy, quiet, loyal, discrete. He prefers solitude to the company of others, and writing—a solitary activity—to talking, which he finds painful and difficult. This is essentially cataphoric, because the character portrait of Pierrot refers ahead not to future encounters with Colombine but to the antithetical figure of Arlequin whom we have yet to encounter. At the same time the narrator instils in the sedentary Pierrot the capacity to change, to develop. His path leads him to Colombine. Theirs is not a promising start in life. The other villagers have always thought of them 'as an item', but the exigencies of their respective occupations enforces a schism which is hardened in Colombine's mind by the negative associations of popular myth and prejudice that prey on her at night as she hides beneath the blankets. Thus she is blinded to the most important aspect of Pierrot's character, namely that he represents knowledge.

What Pierrot knows is predicated on the two determining signs of his character, the natural phenomena with which he, unlike others, is in most contact: the night and the moon. Thus, two consecutive paragraphs each begin, 'Pierrot connaît la nuit...', and 'Pierrot connaît la lune...' (MA, 260). Pierrot knows that the absence of sunlight accentuates the stimulus to the full range of the human senses, including the optical. The river twinkles, the undergrowth rustles, and the smells of sea, mountains and forest are carried on the breeze. Sensory inspiration is in inverse proportion to the 'exhalaisons du jour, imprégnées par le travail des hommes' (MA, 260). From his moon-gazing Pierrot has learned the value of perspective, of the need to appreciate surface and depth, of the three dimensions integral to obtaining information by touch, but equally important in terms of optics.[55] But Pierrot is neither happy nor content in his world, because he loves Colombine, who inhabits a different and inimical world. What Pierrot does not know therefore he has to imagine, and his imagination is dominated by the figure of Colombine. On his dawn wanderings he imagines her 'soupirant et rêvant' in the 'moite blancheur' of her double bed (MA, 261). The roundness of a cheek or a breast or a buttock is transmuted through the eternal, abiding figure of the moon.

Through Pierrot the narrative has initiated its readers/audience into the twin values of wisdom and knowledge, but the world of love is still beyond reach. The problematics of desire lead Pierrot to an imaginary world. He is at an impasse, an impasse which is broken by the arrival of Arlequin. Arlequin signifies narrative, the fracture of the status quo. Naturally he arrives out of the blue, on a 'beau matin d'été ... enluminé de fleurs et d'oiseaux' (MA, 261). Flowers are heliotropic, they turn towards the sun, which is Arlequin's sign, and the joint flower–bird motif is anaphoric, referring back to the initial characterisation of Colombine. Arlequin disturbs Pierrot in the middle of the day. Having been rudely awakend the latter appears more owl-like than ever, 'tout-blanc, ébouriffé, yeux les clignotant à la lumière impitoyable de l'été' (MA, 262). Their essential difference is channelled through bird analogies; their fundamental, as yet undisclosed commonality, will be emphasised in the fusion of their linguistic skills. The mutual laughter of Arlequin and Colombine signals an immediate and apparently naturalistic rapport. Pierrot is left out, 'seul et triste dans sa défroque lunaire en face de ces deux enfants du soleil que rapprochait leur commune gaîté' (MA, 263). He is jealous, jealousy being a primal emotion *par excellence*, the first manifestation of a child's emotional being, the point at which the infant child starts to free itself from the shackles of babyhood and the point at which he is most sensitive to the existence of his physical environment, and therefore the point at which his cognitive skills are most intensively employed. Arlequin woos Colombine by colouring her in. Like a child armed with crayons before a blank sheet of paper, he decorates the white façade of her house. Perched on the scaffolding, he contrasts ornithologically with the owlish Pierrot, 'avec son collant multicolore et sa crête de cheveux rouges, il ressemble à un oiseau exotique' (MA, 264). In the space of a day the building is transformed from *blanchisserie* to *teinturie*, complete with a full-length portrait of Colombine dressed in the Arlequin costume. The next morning Colombine herself has duly metamorphosed and become 'une Arlequine'. The mortified Pierrot transfers his thoughts on to paper and pins a letter to Colombine on his rival's scaffold.

The reflective, sedentary Pierrot is categorised according to Tournier's own *caractérologie* as 'un personnage secondaire'.[56] On the contrary the flighty, nomadic Arlequin exudes 'primarité', and therefore will never stay in one place for long. Indeed he lives out a Tournierian ideal, that of the perpetual traveller who takes his own home with him, 'le vagabond immobile'. The scaffold collapses into what is described as his 'drôle de véhicule', which it is, literally and metaphorically speaking: Arlequin's mode of transport, a sort of mobile home *avant la lettre*, converts into the scaffold he needs in order to indulge in his grandiose painting projects. It is an image of totality, a symbol of existential and aesthetic plenitude. He lives on it, 'comme l'oiseau sur la branche. Il n'est pas question pour lui de s'attarder' (MA, 267). Neither should Colombine dither any longer. This is because their love is destined to be seasonal. It can only last 'le temps d'un beau temps': the Colombine and Arlequin couple fall victim to Tournier's most enduring of binary oppositions, contained in the pun on the word 'temps'. The autumn rains cause their bright colours to run and fade, and the leaves turn brown and fall. As they wake one morning, they are confronted with the immobilising effect of Winter in the guise of the first covering of snow, 'le grand triomphe du blanc, le triomphe de

Pierrot' (MA, 269). The narrator describes this first snowfall of the Winter as 'un coup de théâtre'; with his baggy white robes and slow, trance-like movements Pierrot is associated with Classical theatre, especially Tragedy, self-evidently contrasting with the gaudy costume of the dancing Arlequin, who represents the tradition of Provincial Farce. That night the crowning moment of this 'revanche du mitron' arrives in the shape of an enormous silver moon floating over the icy landscape.

The ever-more nostalgic, winsome Colombine discovers Pierrot's note and thereby the secrets of the night, or rather its sensuous colours; the deep blue skies and the golden ovens, 'des couleurs vraies qui se respirent et qui se mangent' (MA, 270). Colombine returns inspired by the 'essaim de mots en f' that she associates with Pierrot, manifesting an affinity with the symbol of the written letter which he is seen to represent, again in contrast to Arlequin, 'le beau parleur'. Significantly, the stirring of Colombine's imagination is a matter of language, and in the first instance one of sounds. Riveted by the prospect and actuality of her flight, the word 'fuite' re-enters her consciousness in the onomatopoeic description of her feet as she pads across the blanket of snow: 'Elle fuit dans la neige qui fait un doux frou-frou froissé sous ses pieds et frôle ses oreilles: fuite-frou-fuite-frou-fuite-frou...' (MA, 271). The sequence evokes a child's delight in the combination of like-sounding words. However, the emphasis shifts from phonetics to semantics, where the duality that seems carved into her existence once again plays itself out, firstly in the number of 'mots féroces', beginning with (f), which she now associates with Arlequin, and then in the congregation of 'mots fraternels' which confirms her decision to return to Pierrot.

Pierrot's note has engineered a crucial transition. Colombine can now see things differently. She is privy to another world that neither abolishes nor replaces her Arlequin-shaded existence but is somehow endowed with a subtler, deeper significance. She has learned like Idriss that 'true sight is a question of insight',[57] that the world is revealed through metaphor: 'Parce qu'elle s'est rapprochée de Pierrot, Colombine a maintenant des yeux pour voir' (MA, 271). Transfixed by the vision of Colombine bathed in the golden glow emanating from his oven, Pierrot decides to consecrate the magical moment. Whereas Arlequin reproduced her image in the form of a flat, two-dimensional, mimetic portrait, he will sculpt her out of dough. The story ends with an orgiastic, life-giving ritual—the doleful Arlequin having been welcomed into the cellar to form a *ménage-à-trois*—as the ogrish threesome munch on a hot, freshly-baked Colombine loaf.

The return of Arlequin is predicated on the universally-recognised nursery rhyme, 'Au clair de la lune', the encrypted text on which, it is claimed, the narrator bases his story, a story which will in its turn help elucidate the meaning of the original nursery rhyme. Arlequin returns because he needs shelter and warmth and, more importantly, because he has recognised the power of the scribe. However, the identification of 'Au clair de la lune' as a typical Tournier *hypotexte*, though already a clever device in that it fixes the narrative within both a child context and a collective and therefore truly popular adult consciousness, does not explain the pronounced eroticism of the final scene. The answer lies in the fact that the nursery rhyme lyric reprinted in almost every collection of nursery rhymes, and helpfully cited by Tournier's narrator, is only the first of four verses. Tournier has inverted the narrative of the nursery rhyme, in which Arlequin is the successful suitor and Pierrot merely his informant. However, the concluding (usually absent) verse introduces a note of coquettishness that seems rather incongruous in the context of a nursery rhyme but complements the erotic suggestivenes of Tournier's *dénouement* rather nicely:

> Au clair de la lune
> On n'y voit que peu;
> On chercha la plume
> On chercha le feu.
> Cherchant de la sorte
> Ne sais c'qu'on trouva;
> Mais je sais qu'la porte
> Sur eux se ferma.

Such a typically Tournierian disclosure should not obscure the magical qualities of 'Pierrot' in which the simplicity of the language is distilled in an immaculate structure of complementary terms. Even the apparently unheralded eroticism of the final scene may be read in ironic counterpoint to the narrator's earlier rejection of voyeurism when he refuses to describe what the heart-broken Pierrot sees having scaled the scaffolding and peeped into Colombine's bedroom. 'Pierrot' is a masterpiece of form which is ultimately motivated by a concern for education. From the beginning key terms and images (night-time, work, birds, flowers, etc.) are repeated, once or several times. The reader or listener is encouraged to perceive that each term has its complement. In the first instance this exists as a different word or concept of equal importance which generates its own sub-set of words, or what Lakoff and Johnson term 'entailments'. However, each concept is also liable to split into complementary halves and ultimately to form a constellation of related words. In *Pierrot* the narrator chooses to exploit the semantic possibilities inherent in the sub-category 'birds' because, whilst it allows him to differentiate imagistically between Arlequin and Pierrot, he can also establish important links between the key concepts of nature, wisdom and art. 'Flowers' should contain a similar abundance of conceptual potential and possibilities of metaphorical characterisation, but this particular sub-category is left unexplored. The metaphorical pattern overlays a dialectical narrative structure. The night–day equilibrium of Pierrot and Colombine is shattered by the arrival of Arlequin; the Arlequin and Colombine idyll is then progressively undermined by the seasonal anti-thesis driven by Pierrot, before synthesis is finally achieved with Arlequin's initiation into the baker's 'fournil'.

Tournier's spectacular achievement with 'Pierrot', given its covert patterns of reference to his own fictional work and its intricate formalistic design, is that it works as an educational, or rather educative text. In grammatical terms it is an exercise in denomination. All the key words are nouns. This helps children to name things, but it also suggests that language has or should regain an ontological force that philosophers believe existed in the pre-Socratic age when the distinction between word and object either was elided, or had yet to be recognised. It is a story which celebrates the evocative power of language through the reconciliation of the oral and written traditions. It presents an heuristic model of learning in which the process of discovering the world is equated with the organic evolution of a particular language. Learning is about making associations and connections which have already been enshrined in language. Hence, our use of language fuses with the way in which we interact with the world. The conceptual basis to this experience is, of course, what Lakoff and Johnson define as metaphorical.

NEW BEGINNINGS

I have often doubted the validity of my own approach to Tournier's work. It is based on a theory and theories tend to wither on the vine. However, in his recently published essay 'Real Presences', George Steiner seems to reaffirm my partly intuitive notion that fictions exist in relation to the real world as extended metaphors. Steiner declares that 'We must read as if'.[58] These five words are given the status of an entire paragraph in his text. For Steiner we must never abandon the belief that literature dispenses meaning. As he says, 'Only in trivial or opportunistic texts is the sum of significance that of the parts'.[59] Metaphor—Steiner's 'as if'—governs 'our leap into sense'.[60] Without it, he says, 'literacy becomes transient Narcissism',[61] an excuse to show off. Nowhere is this metaphorical 'leap into sense' enacted in more spectacular fashion than through a mini-fable, in which, appropriately, Tournier outlines the writer's role in a contemporary western society.

In his work the writer should be polemical. He should reject all connivence with any political ideology or religious orthodoxy and must at all costs refuse to be brow-beaten. He, personally, may accept honours bestowed upon him by the State, provided that through his work he remains fundamentally *irrécuperable*. This is the gospel according to Tournier's first-person narrator of 'Écrire debout', a short, three-page story from *Le Médianoche*. The story is related to a factual incident. Tournier was once sent a lectern à la Balzac, but not by a group of admiring inmates at a prison he had visited who had taken up carpentry to pass the time spent inside, but by a group of young mentally-handicapped people holed up in their own institutional prison. Given his evangelical desire to communicate with all sections of society—he frequently expresses his pleasure at the number of his books which have been converted into braille text—Tournier's decison to change the identity of the donators in such a fundamental way is curious. There is, however, a possible explanation. Having visited the institution and spoken about the absolute and necessary freedom of the writer, that one should always write 'debout', he must have wondered with the arrival of the marvellous gift whether his mentally handicapped audience had understood what he was trying to tell them. Their handicap in this instance would have translated into an inability to understand words in any other than their most literal senses. Tournier's assumption must therefore have been that the general public do understand literature as metaphor, and that this is an intuitive reaction to literary text, whatever the style, genre, or foundation to the narrative, shared by all other than those who are simply unable to read.

As this study was nearing completion, Tournier published a new work of fiction, his first for more than seven years. *Éléazar ou La source et le buisson* is a short novel, which aspires to be a modern parable. In theme and style it equates to his ideal of the 'universal story', a narrative which should stretch across generations and cultural divides. Appearing on *Bouillon de Culture*[62] the author reiterated his commitment to a young readership. Children of eleven should feel comfortable with a style which he describes as 'sec'. Hard-nosed, punchy narration—the action is rendered for the most part in the past historic tense—is leavened with concise explanations as to the allegorical significance of places and events featuring in the story. This latter tendency is a prerequisite, if Tournier is to make good his promise to a younger readership, for this novel marks the return of the 'big idea'. Éléazar embodies a didactic tradition of teaching and learning which is rooted from a Christian perspective in the Old Testament, and from a Judaic perspective in the Torah. The Moses narrative is invested with an authority which is dissipated in the interpretive diversity of the Gospels. This authority is expressed through a rhetoric which draws on natural forces far greater than the power of Man, in particular the elemental coupling of fire and water that orders the material and spiritual lives of the protagonists in the story. Thus, Tournier's description of his own novel is apt. The narrator is spare with his words, but those he uses tell a story which is fire-blown. Dryness is equated with the Sinai desert and the Sierra Nevada; material poverty, the power of the mind, the adventure of the spirit, and an absolute lucidity that can be obtained only on recognition of God's omnipotence. The example of Moses. With wetness comes material well-being, squabbling churches, and the rotting away of moral standards, symbolised by the legend in which it is said that Saint Patrick rid Ireland of all troublesome serpents, thus inadvertently removing the principle of divine deterrence.[63] With *Éléazar*, Tournier has turned proselytiser; the pedagogic novelist has pulled on his hair-shirt and set off, in pursuit of an aesthetic of the ascetic.

The appeal to a young readership, which is now customarily flagged whenever Tournier publishes a new work of fiction, barely disguises a strong parentage of texts. A chain of coincidences forges a distinctive union between Tournier's version of the 'western' and the biblical exodus of the Jews. Effectively Tournier transposes Moses' story to the nineteenth century when a new world again beckoned to the disadvantaged, persecuted peoples of the Old Continent. The unifying principle of the novel is focused through the main protagonist. Éléazar is driven by a sense of his vocation, as priest, shepherd and minister. His biblical forerunner is mentioned on numerous occasions, in Numbers and Deuteronomy, as Éléazar the priest, a disciple of Moses who inherited the mantle of the priesthood from his father Aaron. A discordant note is introduced into the allegorical parallelism with some (albeit distant) referencing to the Proper Name. Tournier *aficionados* will not be surprised to learn that there are no fewer than three Eleazars in the Jerusalem Old Testament, including one who, at the age of ninety, refused to eat the pig-meat forced upon him by pagans and was martyred (II Maccabees, 6: 18–31). On disembarcation, the first destination for Tournier's Éléazar and his family is Cincinatti, a settlement which in the nineteenth century thrived on intensive pig-farming![64] However, like his dominant biblical namesake Éléazar takes Moses as his example. The *rapprochement* is apparent to the reader from the early details of Éléazar's life. He kills the bullying henchman of a local landowner with his boa-headed staff. Then, rather than awaiting the possible consequences of his insurrection, and with the Irish Potato Famine looming, he decides to leave and take his family across the wasteland, represented here by the Atlantic Ocean.

Éléazar finds comfort in what he takes to be the essence of Ireland, 'humide et verte ... pour moi la plus belle et la plus vivante des églises' (E, 42). The beauty and charm of the land is expressed through his wife, Esther, and her playing of the Celtic harp. Yet, even prior to the migration, he finds himself ever more drawn, as if already embarked on a spiritual quest, to the 'haute et imposante figure de Moïse qui l'habitait et sur lequel il s'interrogeait passionnément' (E, 43). As the O'Braid family trek across the American Plains, this inward meditation is transmuted into an outward initiation into the realm of full consciousness, and, pointedly in the case of Éléazar, into a meaningful consciousness of the self. The process of his identification with Moses culminates on a hillside overlooking the citrus groves of California, where he finally surrenders the charge of his people to his annointed successor, having opted for the Bush in deference to the Spring, for Yahweh before the Hebrew people, for the Sacred instead of the Profane.

Tournier takes issue with the usual theological explanation for Yahweh's refusal to allow Moses to go forth into the Promised Land, namely, that he was provoked by a lack of trust on Moses' part signified by the latter's striking of the tablet not once but twice in order to bring forth the spring waters. According to Tournier, this interpretation is the result of 'un immense malentendu' (E, 110). The Hebrew people were simply panic-stricken at the prospect of having to settle in the desert. Thus, the story of the Golden Calf becomes 'le triomphe du profane, la recherche instinctive et puérile par les Hébreux du lait et de la vache nourricière' (ibid.). God's anger is therefore directed not at Moses but at 'ce peuple, cette foule geignarde, ces femmes chargées d'enfants braillards et pisseux avec leurs troupeaux stupides' (E, 111). Moses prevails on Yahweh to give his people one last chance, but he Moses will live out his own destiny inscribed in the etymology of his name—Moïse, 'sauvé des eaux'—and thus stay next to Yahweh, 'au pays du Buisson ardent' (ibid.). The mortally-wounded Éléazar can go no further. It is left to Joshua, in the guise of warm-hearted, itinerant Mexican bandit José, to guide his flock safely down to the spring of life.

Éléazar, however, seems to represent more than merely a Wild West double of Moses. He bears the mark of Cain.[65] Thus, his forced emigration is contrasted with the naturally nomadic life-style of the Native Americans. Interestingly, instead of blinding him to such contrasts, Éléazar's ever-closer union with the figure of Moses and consequently his ever-firmer sense of purpose appears to enhance both his perceptiveness and his intellectual curiosity. As we know, Tournier adheres to the Socratic principle according to which the teacher must be prepared to learn from his students. Éléazar, with his thirst for knowledge and self-scrutiny, is the radical embodiment of this view. By the time of his congress with the Indian chief, Serpent d'Airain, it is established that Éléazar and his fellow pioneers are motivated less by a colonising spirit and more by a desire for knowledge. 'Enseigne-moi ta sagesse' (E, 101), he improbably asks of the chief.

Learning demands a certain humility, but more importantly it initiates a process of communication. Hence the action in the novel is saturated with various kinds of dialogue. Éléazar persistently reviews the current situation of his own faith and spiritual well-being. On occasions passages from the scriptures are recited communally, and, tellingly, there are at least two lengthy conversations recorded in the text. These talk sequences are both strong and weak points in the novel: weak in the sense that they interrupt the diegesis and effectively immobilise a narrative which is supposed to be lean and without frippery; strong in the sense that they animate the intellectual flame that burns through it. The first of these dialogues involves Éléazar and Esther, who is soon to be the pastor's wife. Their courtship masquerades, bizarrely, as a theological conversation on the subject of angels. Naturally the movement is from a New Testament perspective which stresses the rapport between the innocence of children and the

angel's asexuality to a more earthy Old Testament critique of forni-
cating angels provoking the wrath of Yahweh. Éléazar is impressed
with Esther's elegant formulation of the angel's special characteristics:

> Ce qui fait la force de l'ange ... c'est qu'il possède à la fois des bras et des
> ailes. C'est un privilège exorbitant, car les simples vivants doivent
> obligatoirement choisir entre bras et ailes. L'oiseau, parce qu'il a des ailes,
> n'a pas de bras. L'homme a des bras, mais point d'ailes. Ce n'est pas une
> mince alternative. Elle signifie qu'il faut choisir entre agir et planer, se
> compromettre dans la vie quotidienne ou survoler les choses et les êtres. (E,
> 35–36)

The figure of the angel reconciles the classic dichotomy between
transcendence and engagement; the flight of the mind, or dirty hands.
According to Esther's logic, wingless humans are deemed incapable of
spiritual or mental transcendence. We are reminded of Tournier's ideas
on narrative, and especially his view of the *conte* as mythical and
timeless, in contrast to the bruising reality of the *nouvelle*. Still, the
angels are a pleasant diversion. Éléazar's other long conversation, this
time with Serpent d'Airain, adds a new verse to a favourite Tournier
refrain on the myth of the Creation. The encounter constitutes the
intellectual centre of the novel. The outcome goes right to the heart of
Tournier's fictional project.

The novel is framed by death. Having fulfilled his destiny, Éléazar's
death at the end of the book crowns a meaningful life. It also imparts a
cyclical structure to the narrative, in that it returns us to the beginning
of the text where he is pictured as a child listening to the funereal
tolling of nearby church bells. He wonders vaguely who has died. The
answer is not supplied; the identity of the dead person is unimportant,
for this is the routine business of death. The young Éléazar observes
Sam Palfrey passing beneath his window, 'debout sur son éternelle
charrette' (E, 12). The owner of four horses, two white and two black,
Sam doubles as wedding usher and undertaker. Now, the life–death
cycle normally engenders an impulsive return to the question of our
origins, or roots. Christian theology, likewise, is rooted in the myth of
the Creation. As we know, Tournier is fascinated by the Genesis story.
He has provided conflicting, partial versions on numerous occasions, in
both fictional and non-fictional contexts, accounts which are, nonetheless, always based on some astute fine-tuning of textual indicators.
Thus, it is appropriate that the same reverse movement informs the
narrative structure of his most overtly theological novel to date. As
Éléazar disappears behind a thicket to die, the image of Ireland is

uppermost in his mind: 'Il en caressa les feuilles et crut reconnaître des sycomores, dernier tendre et discret sourire de sa patrie irlandaise' (E, 140). Encouraged by the pattern of the narrative, the reader is led indirectly to (re)consider the issue of the Creation, which is fore-grounded in Éléazar's discussion with Serpent d'Airain. Only here, Éléazar's inquisition diverges from Old Testament creed. As the Chief speaks his wisdom, Tournier's story of a nineteenth-century Moses becomes a pretext for a typically audacious attempt to rescue the snake from the dustbin of Christian aetiology.

For the duration of the trek across the Sierra Nevada, the O'Braid family comes under the aegis of the snake, which is perceived as a totem, or as a symbol of the desert. Éléazar's son, Benjamin, is bitten by a rattlesnake, though he is later cured of his affliction by the balms offered by the Indian tribe. The snake is shown to be emblematic of Éléazar's search for wisdom; the intuitive, prescient kind that he perceives in his own daughter, Coralie. It is Coralie who instigates his discussion with Serpent d'Airain. Her action in preventing the disposal of the arrow which had mysteriously penetrated one of the wagons overnight, ensures a friendly reception from the Native Americans. The family learn later that, according to the custom of the tribe, should an arrow fired at night towards the moon mother, 'notre mère la lune' (E, 99), be returned, then great honour is due to the retriever. Before then, we are told, it is Coralie who notices first the sparser grass coverage, a sure sign of the imminence of the desert, and, on their first dangerous encounter with the rattlesnake, she alone perceives the deep affinity between the desert and its 'incarnation animale' (E, 93). However, Coralie's principal function is that of an agent, who brokers the discussion between Éléazar and Serpent d'Airain.

As the Indian chief examines the stricken Benjamin, Éléazar is drawn to his eyes, 'Des yeux qui ne clignent pas ... des yeux sans paupières, des yeux de serpent' (E, 100). The Chief, who is presented throughout as a benefactor, as the representative of a people who live in harmony with their environment, personifies a creature which has very different resonances in Éléazar's belief system. Initially, the Chief's words strike some reassuring chords. Snakes fall broadly into two categories, according to the Chief: the venomous snake that kills with a kiss, and the constrictor that kills with an embrace, the point being that each involves a fatal attraction, 'c'est toujours par un geste d'amour qu'il tue' (E, 101). The symbolic significance of the Chief's words is immediately clear to his interlocutor. Éléazar evokes Lucifer, 'le plus beau des anges', who was stripped of his appendages by God's soldiers—'ils en ont fait une colonne de cuir terminée par un masque, le serpent' (E, 102)—and cast down into the Garden of Eden. However, instead of confirming the moral message of Éléazar's interjection with a fable taken from his own culture, the Chief seizes on the notion of the mask. The desert, he argues, represents the face of God *as a landscape*, and the serpent, with its retractable head, is his/its 'symbole animal' (ibid.). Moreover, the snake is the only reptile without eyelids. Again, Éléazar mistakes the Chief's intention. He interjects in order to reaffirm the opposition between desert aridity and Irish humidity through a metaphorical comparison of the snake's unblinking stare with the moistness of his own lidded eyes, 'l'organe meme de ma patrie, la douce et pluvieuse Irlande' (E, 103), whereas, for the Chief, the snake is a metaphor for lucidity, for the sort of clairvoyant wisdom that distinguishes Coralie and raises her to a higher level of consciousness. The snake's skin, which is shed annually, could be regarded as one giant eyelid, the proof being that what appear to be the eye sockets of a snake are in fact transparent layers of skin. Thus, the serpent 'n'est qu'un visage, qu'un regard' (E, 104). Serpent d'Airain chides Éléazar. The latter is wrapped in furs to protect him from the cold night air, though his face is bare, it doesn't fear the cold. The Chief is naked from head to foot, still he doesn't feel the cold—'c'est que je suis visage partout!' (ibid.). The personification of the snake is complete.

In the Garden of Eden the serpent tempts Eve with the apple, using the following words: 'For God doth know that in the day ye eat thereof, then your eyes shall be opened, and ye shall be as gods, knowing good and evil' (Genesis 3: 5). Adam and Eve eat the fruit and 'the eyes of them both were opened, and they knew that they were naked' (Genesis 3: 7) The emphasis on the eyes and their connection with the serpent is unmistakable. However, the epistemological shift into full consciousness recorded in Genesis has accrued a more limited interpretation in the Christian world where it is typically understood as the inception of (illicit) desire. Through the dialogue between Éléazar (his Moses interloper) and an Indian Chief, Tournier restores the full impact of the serpent's intervention in the Garden of Eden. Seeing, cognition and consciousness are rendered through the biblical totem of the snake; figure of dread, figure of the Fall, but also figure of knowledge and perception. Thus, our preoccupation with origins is brought back to the present day. As Michael Worton writes at the close of his essay on Tournier's rewriting of Genesis, 'Tournier's speculations proclaim—

essentially!—that origin is always-forever to be created (anew)'.[66] In *Éléazar*, Tournier the educator is once again assembling a coherent model of the world, engaged, as always, in a work of reconstruction in the wake of the vicissitudes of human history.

Conclusion

The vituperative turn against naturalism and the nineteenth-century novel spearheaded by Alain Robbe-Grillet and other proponents of the *nouveau roman* has contributed towards an insular vision of what constitutes the modern French novel. We can identify two main camps: the Flaubertians and the Sartreans. The former incorporate the *nouveaux romanciers* as well as ancillary figures such as Queneau, Duras and Perec, writers who in their vastly different ways strive for what a television pundit once described as the 'heaven of pure style'. Existentialists, polemicists, women writers and many contemporary francophone writers rally to a different flag, which represents what may broadly be termed a 'literature of ideas'. Other groups, notably the Surrealists, have practised a very French form of *alternance*. Proust and Céline stand together alone.

It is worth reflecting on to what extent this description of a national culture, crass and simplistic though it may be, determines the reception of its literature, both new and old. Consider a view from the outside, in this instance supplied by the American novelist John Updike:

> The trouble with the French love of pure thought is that thought must operate on *something*—the world as it impurely exists, an apparently ill-thought-out congeries of contradictory indications and arbitrary facts. The novelist must be thoughtless, to some degree, in submitting to the world's facts: he must be naïve enough, as it were, to let the facts flow through him and unreflectingly quicken recognition and emotion in his readers. And this the French find difficult to do.[1]

Updike elaborates on what many would regard as a stereotypical view of French culture. His remarks conclude an essay on the early fiction of Michel Tournier, and they adumbrate the reasons for Tournier's failure to catch on in the anglo-saxon world. The surprise is not that Updike misreads Tournier—he doesn't, the essay is astute and perceptive—but that the stereotype of the national culture is so strong that it can be used to sum up an iconoclast like Tournier, who has been described by others variously as a 'bankrupt traditionalist' and a 'postmodern writer', and by himself as a 'un naturaliste mystique' (PP, 245).

There is no doubt that Tournier produces a 'literature of ideas'. A superficial reading of *Éléazar* confirms that his fiction is, in a radically evident way, palimpsestuous, and thus it is interesting to see what his reading of the 'big question' is, whether that question concerns the Genesis story, or the pre-eminence of anthropology over psychology, or the importance of initiation in the education of the child. However, to do this at the expense of any discussion of narrative suspense, verisimilitude, characterisation, humour, or any other aspects of his writing which may excite the reader's passion as well as his or her intellect, seems to defeat the purpose of a project in which the whole is palpably more than the sum of the parts. Tournier imparts an imaginary vision of real worlds and any reading of his fiction is beholden to that vision. My interest in his work originates in a fascination with the dynamic and evolving interaction between the fictional world of the book and the real world on which it is predicated, a relationship which Tournier explores more deeply, more assiduously, and with more subtlety than any other modern writer. This is also the reason for my interest in metaphor, for, as we have seen, discussions of metaphor in linguistic, literary and especially philosophical arenas tend to circle around the possibilities of non-literal realities and non-literal truths. My research has led me away from the French national culture on the trail of Paul Ricoeur, whose work combines the theoretical rigour of formalist linguistics with the more speculative reasoning of modern American philosophy. Lakoff and Johnsons' bold dissolution of the body/mind dialectic has proved especially useful in that their theory highlights the performative aspects of language (thus by extension the oral roots of literature) and the iconic value of written text. Also, to the extent that their theory follows an evolutionary pattern, it provides a base from which it is possible to approach the difficult area of Tournier's child-centred view on his own work.

In *A la recherche du temps perdu* Proust puts a value on what it is to be a human being, tormented by the need to make sense of past experience whilst driving forward into uncertain futures, in thrall to a desperate desire, ultimately fulfilled, for recognition, for the solid, certain knowing of what one's place is in the world, in relation to others. The unattainable future is narrative suspense; the past which, Proust believed, could be reached via analogy, is metaphor. This glorious fusion of narrative and metaphoric possibilities in the *Recherche* is predicated on the build-up of an ever-increasing degree of identification between the narrator and his reader, and in itself this process presupposes some initial commonality of experience. Proust manages this reciprocity of experience so skilfully that in, for example,

La Prisonnière the narrator's erratic behaviour fits perfectly with an overpowering state of mind that many readers will recognise all too readily from their own pasts; *La Prisonnière* thus reads as an elegant, truthful account of jealousy in all its aspects. Now the dominant critical discourse of the postmodern age with its pithy, catch-all categories seems utterly inadequate as a means to help elucidate the momentous efforts of Proust and his translators, or for that matter the work of Camus, Beckett, Malraux, Sarraute, and a host of other major twentieth-century figures. One brief example should suffice to illustrate the poverty of the modern critical idiom. Poststructuralist discourse has coined the term 'l'illusion mimétique'; readers or spectators should be aware that art can never represent reality, that any apparent attempt to convey reality through art is either artifice or simply one among many possible codes of representation. Clearly, the notion of the mimetic illusion is more suited to the visual arts. In respect of prose narrative it can only describe those works in which there is a purposeful attempt conducted through the formal composition of the text to subvert the basic conditions on which we base our understanding of reality. In the context of Proust, Updike, Tournier, and any number of major figures this century, the idea of non-reality or the mimetic illusion is as absurd as it would seem to the vast majority of the reading public.

If French literature has been under the spell of self-referentiality and a postmodern ludism for a considerable time—and there is nothing essentially wrong with a good dose of either or both these things—then the last decade or so has seen a welcome rush of new talented writers from different backgrounds, employing diverse approaches, who are breaking the mould. The rapid-fire narration, limitless invention, attention to character detail, gallows' humour, and linguistic verve of Daniel Pennac are qualities which have already afforded him superstar status. Pennac's optimism is countered by the questing narratives tinged with a tired resignation bordering on desperation of fellow-traveller Jean Echenoz, who also explores a range of popular genres through his fiction. The broad visionary qualities of Pennac and Echenoz contrast with the microscopic gaze of Jean Rouaud, whose quest for his own identity in the roots of his family and upbringing in the lower reaches of the Loire valley is characterised by writing of a rare formal beauty, and with the extraordinary mix of the confessional and the absurd in *Truismes*, the first novel which in 1996 shot Marie Darrieussecq to fame and fortune. More generally, the Éditions de Minuit publishing house boasts a raft of exciting new novelists, of whom Eric Chevillard,

François Bon, Marie NDiaye and Jean-Philippe Toussaint have all achieved international recognition, and a number of writers associated with the *roman noir*, notably Sébastien Japrisot, Didier Daeninckx, Jean-Bernard Puoy, and Jean-François Vilar have begun to command wider critical attention. Although linguistic diversity, a sense of exploring the imagination through metaphor, an emphasis on narrative and the role of the narrator, and some limited textual experimentation are all recognisable features of this latest body of French fiction, the most conspicuous element involves a resurgence of the principle of literary reference and consequently a restatement of the novelist's freedom to evaluate and possibly change the society in which he or she lives through the unique qualities of his or her literary expression. Zola has effectively come of age. In years to come Tournier, along with Patrick Modiano and J.M.G. Le Clézio, whom countless authors of 'end-of-the-millennium' compendiums of French literature have recently struggled to squeeze into the 'postmodern' category, may be seen as pioneers of a new, and decidedly un-nineteenth-century literary realism.

Notes to Preface

pp. ix–xi

1 M. Hester, 'Metaphor and Aspect Seeing', *Journal of Aesthetics and Art Criticism*, vol. 25 (1966), pp. 205–21.

2 In an important essay, Tournier metaphorises the reception of his work, imagining his texts as vampires feasting on the blood of his readers. In spite of its innate aggressiveness, the sense of the metaphor is reassuring; Tournier seeks to establish an intimate bond with his readership, without which, he believes, his literary career would soon fade. See M. Tournier, *Le Vol du Vampire: Notes de Lecture*, Paris, Mercure de France, 1981, pp. 9–24.

3 Mireille Rosello, one of Tournier's most astute critics, constantly refers in her analyses of his work to her own position and personal experience as a Tournier reader. See M. Rosello, *L'In-différence chez Michel Tournier*, Paris, Librairie José Corti, 1990, 'Vers une nouvelle grammaire amoureuse (micro-lecture d'un texte de *Des clefs et des serrures*)', *Images et Signes de Michel Tournier: Actes du Colloque du Centre Culturel International de Cérisy-la-Salle*, ed. A. Bouloumié and M. de Gandallic, Paris, Gallimard, 1990, pp. 255–75, and 'Art and Impertinence in *The Midnight Love Feast*', *Michel Tournier*, ed. M. Worton, London, Longman, 1995, pp. 174–88.

4 In *The Real Thing* the character Henry pontificates on the job of the writer: 'What we're trying to do is to write cricket bats, so that when we throw up an idea and give it a little knock, it might ... travel' (T. Stoppard, *The Real Thing*, London, Faber, 1982, Act 2, Scene V, p. 53). Later, he describes words as 'innocent, neutral, precise, standing for this, describing that, meaning the other, so if you look after them you can build bridges across incomprehension and chaos' (p. 55).

5 M. Tournier, 'L'Espace canadien', *La Nouvelle Critique*, no. 105 (1977), p. 52: '...je crois en la profondeur voilée d'ironie du calembour. Sahara-Canada. Ces deux mots de six lettres dont trois *a* placés aux mêmes points sont d'une saisissante analogie.'

6 G. Steiner, *No Passion Spent: Essays 1978-1996*, London, Faber, 1996, p. 35.

7 Ibid., p. 31.

8 Ibid., p. 35.

9 *L'Imagerie de Michel Tournier*, Paris, Paris-Musées, 1987.

Notes to Chapter One

pp. 1–40

1 G. Steen, *Understanding Metaphor in Literature: An Empirical Approach*, London, Longman, 1994, p. 55.

2 Ibid., p. 3.

3 Though Proustian studies is naturally saturated with reflections on the scope of literary metaphor, the discussion has for the most part remained germane to the *Recherche*. The notable exception is Paul Ricoeur, who, in the course of his mammoth opus *Temps et Récit, Vols 1–3* (Paris, Seuil, 1983–85) analyses the critical role of metaphor, and especially Proust's theory of metaphor, in the contingent processes of memory and recognition.

4 See S. Haugom Olsen, *The End of Literary Theory*, Cambridge, Cambridge University Press, 1987.

5 Ibid., pp. 163–64.

6 F. de Saussure, *Cours de linguistique générale*, Paris, Payot, 1973, pp. 171–72.

7 M. Tournier, 'Je suis comme la pie voleuse', in J-L. de Rambures, *Comment travaillent les écrivains*, Paris, Flammarion, 1978, pp. 163–67.

8 G. Genette, *Palimpsestes: la littérature au second degré*, Paris, Seuil, 1982, p. 425.

9 *Michel Tournier*, ed. M. Worton, London, Longman, 1995 p. 192, 'I have never written anything more serious or more profound than these two tales'.

10 'Tournier face aux lycéens' (interview with schoolchildren from the Lycée Montaigne), *Magazine littéraire*, no. 226 (1986), pp. 20–25. On a television programme ('Droit de réponse', TF1, 22 February 1986) representatives of his target audience confessed that they had found it rather hard-going.

11 *Images et Signes de Michel Tournier: Actes du Colloque du Centre Culturel International de Cérisy-la-Salle*, ed. A.Bouloumié and M. de Gandillac, Paris, Gallimard, 1990, p. 319.

12 X. Delcourt, 'En déjeunant avec Michel Tournier', *La Quinzaine Littéraire* (March 1977), p. 25.

13 *Comment travaillent les écrivains*, p. 163.

14 Mireille Rosello investigates this theme in her study of *Le Médianoche amoureux*, in *Michel Tournier*, ed. Worton, pp. 174–88.

15 M. Roberts, *Michel Tournier: Bricolage and Cultural Mythology*, Saratoga, Stanford University/ANMA Libri, 1994, p. 135.

16 Aristotle, *Complete Works*, ed. W. D. Ross (12 vols.), Oxford, Clarendon Press, 1908–52.

17 J. Lacan, 'L'Instance de la lettre dans l'inconscient', *Ecrits I*, Paris, Seuil, 1966, p. 507.

18 I shall be referring to two of these papers, 'Aphasia as a Linguistic Topic' and 'Two Aspects of Language and Two Types of Aphasic Disturbances', in R. Jakobson,

Selected Writings II, The Hague/Paris, Word and Language, Mouton, 1971, pp. 229–38 and 239–59 respectively.

19 'Aphasia as a Linguistic Topic', p. 232.

20 'Two Aspects of Language and Two Types of Aphasic Disturbances', p. 254.

21 S. Ullmann, *Language and Style*, Oxford, Blackwell, 1964, p. 63: 'metonymies are interesting ... only when they resemble metaphors.'

22 D. Cooper, *Metaphor*, Oxford, Blackwell, 1986. Cooper criticises the practical application of Jakobson's theories, demonstrating convincingly that they have at best a limited value with respect to our 'abilities to produce metaphors and metonymies *as usually understood*' (p. 37) (italics my own). However, Cooper misreads Jakobson to the extent that he assumes that the latter is concerned with a language conceived in its most sophisticated, grammatical form. Rather, the language to which Jakobson refers exists in a grammatically embryonic state. It is a language in which the principal grammatical players are nouns, verbs and adjectives, articulated by speakers for whom a grammar is, at most, a sub-conscious phenomenon. Therefore, Jakobson would see no contradiction in talking about the syntagmatic relationship of words as the juxtaposition of verbal units according to the law of metonymy, provided of course that the scope of the equation is confined to, or rather refined in, the semantic progression of (a) discourse. Whereas Jakobson attempts to provide some criteria for the functioning of metaphor in discourse, and thereby contributes to the sticky debate on the nature of metaphorical meaning, Cooper merely comments on pre-set, conventional ideas on metaphor, with reference to stock examples of metaphorical language. On the other hand, the latter does have the merit of questioning whether Saussurean linguistics is adequate to the task of providing a foundation for a satisfactory theory of metaphor.

23 'L'Instance de la lettre dans l'inconscient', p. 507.

24 Inspired by Lacan's reading of the Freudian Unconscious, structured like the conscious mind by language, Kristeva demonstrates how the Freudian dream mechanisms of *condensation* and *displacement* find their natural homes in the metaphoric and metonymic principles underlying the processes by which we talk. (Kristeva prefers to use the more neutral terms of the linguist, pairing symbol and syntax and, of course, signified and signifier, but the same dialectic holds sway.) The science of linguistics provides us with the tools, therefore, to access the psyche. Reciprocally, the practice of psychoanalysis, by separating out the component parts, by 'leafing through' language, enables the subject firstly to perceive the ways in which the world is interpreted for him or her through language, and then to re-evaluate his or her sense of being in that world. See J. Kristeva, 'Psychoanalysis and Language', in *Language, The Unknown*, trans. Anne M. Menke, Brighton, Harvester Press, 1989, pp. 265–77.

25 S. Freud, *The Interpretation of Dreams*, ed. and trans James Strachey, London, Allen and Unwin, 1954. 'On Dreams' is included in *The Essentials of Psychoanalysis*, ed. Anna Freud, Harmondsworth, Penguin, 1986, pp. 81–125.

26 D. Macey, *Lacan in Contexts*, London, Verso, 1988, p. 157.

27 Ibid., p. 159.

28 T. Todorov, *Théories du symbole*, Paris, Seuil, 1977, p. 59.

29 Ibid., p. 62: 'La démocratie est la condition indispensable à l'épanouissement de l'éloquence; réciproquement, l'éloquence est la qualité supérieure de l'individu appartenant à une démocratie: aucune des deux ne peut se passer de l'autre. L'éloquence est "nécessaire": voici son trait dominant, et en même temps l'explication de son succès.'

30 P. Ricoeur, *La Métaphore vive*, Paris, Seuil, 1975, p. 18.

31 C. Perelman, 'Rhétorique, dialectique, et philosophie', in *Rhetoric Revalued*, ed. B. Vickers, New York, Medieval and Renaissance Texts and Studies 19, 1982, pp. 277–81, (p. 280). Perelman's work on rhetoric is heavily influenced by Thomistic thought, which gives rise to an elaborate theory of metaphor. In brief, metaphor is seen as a condensed analogy, the fusion of an element of the *phoros* (the two terms of a four term analogy which supports the theme or topic) and one from the theme. The analogy 'A is to B as C to D' permits the construction of the formula 'C's B' to designate 'D'. For a detailed account of Perelman's methodology, see C. Perelman and L. Olbrechts-Tyteca, *Traité de l'argumentation*, Paris, PUF, 1958.

32 *Cours de linguistique générale*, p. 98.

33 On the basis of some intriguing research concerning a young woman who, having entered a trance-like state, was apparently able to speak in tongues of which she had no conscious knowledge at all, Todorov chronicles Saussure's apparent refusal to countenance the possibility of a referential or symbolic function of language. See *Théories du symbole*, pp. 321–38.

34 *Metaphor*, p. 36.

35 *Cours de linguistique générale*, p. 171.

36 See L. Wittgenstein, *Philosophical Investigations*, trans. G. Anscombe, Oxford, Oxford University Press, 1953, p. 194.

37 I. Richards, *The Philosophy of Rhetoric*, Oxford, Oxford University Press, 1971, p. 96.

38 Cited in M. Black, *Models and Metaphors*, Ithaca, Cornell University Press, 1962, p. 225.

39 Ibid., p. 227.

40 Ibid., p. 229.

41 Ibid., p. 231.

42 E. Kittay, *Metaphor*, Oxford, Oxford University Press, 1987, p. 316.

43 Ibid., p. 318.

44 Ibid., p. 320.

45 P. Ricoeur, 'The Metaphorical Process as Cognition, Imagination and Feeling', *Critical Inquiry*, no. 5 (1978), p. 143. This article is re-published in *Philosophical Perspectives on Metaphor*, ed. M. Johnson, Minneapolis, University of Minnesota Press, 1981, pp. 228–47. Future page references will be taken from the latter edition. This important paper, written in English, complements and embellishes many of the ideas contained in *La Métaphore vive*, which was published during the previous year. Wherever possible the two should be read in conjunction.

46 *Philosophical Perspectives on Metaphor*, ed. Johnson, p. 232.

47 Ibid., p. 241.

48 In another essay contained in the Johnson compilation, Max Black argues strongly that we should accept metaphors as 'cognitive instruments' that enable us to see aspects of reality that the metaphor's production helps to constitute. Consequently, Black says, it is no longer surprising if one believes that 'the world is necessarily a world *under a certain description*—or a world seen from a certain perspective. Some metaphors can create such a perspective.' See M. Black, 'More about Metaphor', in ibid., p. 454.

49 See R. Jakobson, 'Closing Statements: Linguistics and Poetics', in *Style in Language*, ed. T. A. Sebeok, New York, John Wiley., 1960, pp. 350–77.

50 'Closing Statements', p. 356.

51 Ibid., p. 371.

52 *La Métaphore vive*, p. 289.

53 *Philosophical Perspectives on Metaphor*, ed. Johnson, p. 242.

54 J. Ricardou, *Les Lieux-dits: Petit guide d'un voyage dans le livre*, Paris, Gallimard, 1969, p. 29.

55 Ibid., p. 30.

56 Ibid., p. 33.

57 See E. Benveniste, *Problèmes de linguistique générale*, Paris, Gallimard, 1966, pp. 289–307.

58 *Les Lieux-dits*, pp. 137–39.

59 Ibid., p. 41.

60 Ibid., p. 55.

61 Ibid., p. 108.

62 Ibid., p. 160.

63 The reference to La Fontaine's famous verse is made explicit in the text. See *Les Lieux-dits*, p. 107.

64 Ibid., p. 133.

65 Ibid., p. 134.

66 Ibid., p. 136

67 See Robbe-Grillet's exposé of Camus' anthropomorphism in A. Robbe-Grillet, *Pour un nouveau roman*, Paris, Editions de Minuit, 1963, pp. 70–72.

68 'Or, non loin, penché sur la source du Damier, Albert Crucis remarque:—Tout cela, une fois de plus, aujourd'hui, est une métaphore.' *Les Lieux-dits*, p. 160.

69 See G. Lakoff and M. Johnson, *Metaphors We Live By*, Chicago, University of Chicago Press, 1980. Many of the examples of metaphoric usage given in the book gain more succinct expression along with a slightly embellished argument in G. Lakoff and M. Johnson, 'Conceptual Metaphor in Everyday Language', *Journal of Philosophy*, no. 77 (1980), pp. 453–86. Although there is much common ground, I shall refer to both texts.

70 'Conceptual Metaphor in Everyday Language', p. 456.

71 *Metaphors We Live By*, p. 12.

72 'Conceptual Metaphor in Everyday Language', p. 469.

73 *Metaphors We Live By*, p. 230.

74 M. Heidegger, 'On the Essence of Truth', *Basic Writings*, trans. and ed. D. F. Krell, London, Routledge and Kegan Paul, 1978, pp. 124–25.

75 *Metaphors We Live By*, p. 142.

76 The term 'verbomotor', or rather 'verbo-moteur', was originally coined by Marcel Jousse, the Jesuit scholar and priest, who spent his adult life in the first decades of this century in the Middle East, soaking up its oral culture. 'Verbo-moteur' is a label he invented to cover the general phenomenon of oral cultures, and the personality structures they produce. See M. Jousse, *Le Style oral, rythmique et mnémotechnique chez les verbo-moteurs*, Paris, G. Beauchesne, 1925.

Notes to Chapter Two

pp. 41–82

1 In the introduction to one study of Defoe's fiction, Pat Rogers reports that by 1900 there were at least 200 English editions of *Robinson Crusoe*, 110 translations, 115 revisions and adaptations, and 277 imitations. See P. Rogers, *Robinson Crusoe*, London, Allen and Unwin, 1979.

2 In *Le Vent Paraclet* Tournier refers to Saint-John Perse's *Images à Crusoé* and Giraudoux's *Suzanne et le Pacifique* as direct textual antecedents, and to the influence of the Crusoe predicament on the protagonists in Jules Verne's *L'Île mystérieuse* (VP, 213).

3 See *Le Vent Paraclet*, pp. 213–17.

4 J. Ricardou, *Problèmes du nouveau roman*, Paris, Seuil, 1967, pp. 134–36. The view that *Robinson Crusoe* excites a deep-seated, semi-conscious desire for the exotic, often termed 'escapism', should not be too readily dismissed. Commenting on Ian Watt's opinion of Defoe's Robinson as a profiteering businessman, J. Sutherland maintains that it is 'primarily as an adventure story that it—Defoe's novel—still lives'. See J. Sutherland, *D. Defoe: A Critical Study*, Massachussetts, Harvard University Press, 1971, p. 28. And, in a rigorous analysis of the philosophical implications of *Vendredi*, Gilles Deleuze describes how Tournier's project embraces both the spirit of the exotic and the literary heritage of Defoe's novel. He defines it punningly as 'un étonnant roman d'aventures comique, et un roman cosmique d'avatars'. See G. Deleuze, 'Michel Tournier et le monde sans autrui,' originally published in *Logique du sens*, Paris, Editions de Minuit, 1968, appearing later as a postface to the Folio edition of *Vendredi*, pp. 257–83.

5 G. Genette, *Palimpsestes, la littérature au second degré*, Paris, Seuil, 1978, p. 11.

6 This term is used by Lynn Salkin Sbiroli in her exegesis of *Vendredi*. See L. Salkin Sbiroli, *Michel Tournier: La Séduction du jeu*, Geneva/Paris, Editions Slatkine, 1987.

7 Myth has it that Robinson Crusoe constructed an edifice of civilisation from nothing; however, Defoe's Crusoe, in common with Tournier's antecedent, counted amongst his possessions salvaged from the wreck a fair amount of ironware and a supply of gunpowder. Octavio Paz points out that Neolithic Man (probably Woman) invented the arts and crafts which are the foundation of all civilised life—ceramics, weaving, agriculture, and the domestication of animals—and that the Neolithic era existed thousands of years before the invention of writing, metallurgy and the birth of urban civilisation. See O. Paz, *Claude Lévi-Strauss*: An Introduction, London, Jonathan Cape, 1970, pp. 73–74. Robinson's achievements should not, therefore, be over-estimated.

8 *Michel Tournier: La Séduction du jeu*, p. 32.

9 M. Roberts, *Michel Tournier. Bricolage and Cultural Mythology*, Saratoga, Stanford University/ANMA Libri, 1994, p. 27.

10 *La Séduction du jeu*, p. 36.

11 D. Defoe, *Robinson Crusoe*, Oxford, Oxford University Press, 1972, pp. 124, 128.

12 See *Palimpsestes*, pp. 418–25.

13 Ibid., p. 422.

14 M. Tournier, 'Lévi-Strauss, mon maître', *Le Figaro Littéraire* (26 May 1973), p. 18.

15 Lévi-Strauss's seminal analyses of myth structures are principally contained in the four volumes of his *Mythologiques: Le Cru et le cuit*, Paris, Seuil, 1964; *Du Miel aux cendres* and *L'Origine des manières de table*, Paris, Seuil, 1967; and *L'Homme nu*, Paris, Seuil, 1971. The collective title of the series indicates that Lévi-Strauss was not interested in the classification of 'mythologies' as such, but rather in the 'logics of myth', the *Mythologiques*, in their relation to other logics. The genesis of these investigations is to be found in another essay in which Lévi-Strauss elaborates the first version of the Culinary Triangle. See C. Lévi-Strauss, 'L'analyse structurale en linguistique et en anthropologie', *Word: Journal of the Linguistic Circle of New York* (1945), pp. 1–21.

16 For a cogent example of this similarity, see Jakobson's commentary on Baudelaire's 'Spleen' in R. Jakobson, 'Qu'est-ce que la poésie?', *Questions de poétique*, Paris, Seuil, 1973, pp. 113–26.

17 C. Lévi-Strauss, *Tristes tropiques*, Paris, Plon, 1955, p. 421.

18 *Palimpsestes*, p. 424.

19 See R. Barthes, *Mythologies*, Paris, Seuil, 1957, p. 201, '...naïf ou pas, je vois bien ce qu'elle me signifie: que la France est un grand Empire, que tous ses fils, sans distinction de couleur, servent fidèlement sous son drapeau, et qu'il n'est de meilleure réponse aux détracteurs d'un colonialisme prétendu, que le zèle de ce noir à servir ses prétendus oppresseurs'.

20 In spite of its origins in antiquity, the Tarot has been used elsewhere as a metaphor for modernism. It is the subject of Italo Calvino's *Castle of Crossed Destinies*, and, more recently, Lindsay Clarke's *The Chymical Wedding* includes a starred Tarot reading.

21 *La Séduction du jeu*, p. 85.

22 Ibid., p. 125. Her analysis goes some way towards explaining why some Tournier critics, like Deleuze, see *Vendredi* as a process leading towards a culmination—'la rencontre de la libido avec les éléments libres' ('Michel Tournier ou le monde sans autrui', p. 259)—whereas others, like Colin Davis, argue that it is a novel of beginnings (see C. Davis, 'Michel Tournier's *Vendredi ou Les limbes du Pacifique*: A Novel of Beginnings', *Neophilologus*, vol. 73 [1989], pp. 373–82). The answer, according to Salkin Sbiroli, lies in the parallelogism of the two founding narratives, each of which reveals a different aspect of myth. Defoe's *Robinson Crusoe* constitutes the origin in fiction of the predetermined, universal story which we now receive in the form of myth. However, the Tarot reading recalls the earliest manifestation of myth as a message to the people from the Greek gods, which was transmitted in the form of an oracle. Tournier is attracted to the myth of the oracle, the effect of which he likens to radio broadcasting by comparing the verbal actions of gods to the diction of the anonymous disc-jockey, whose voice nonetheless captivates the masses. (See *Le Vent Paraclet*, p. 173, and the short story from *Le Coq de bruyère*, entitled 'Tristan Vox', which is discussed in Chapter 4.)

23 T. Todorov, *Le Poétique de la prose*, Paris, Seuil, 1971, p. 77.

24 Ingmar Bergman achieves just such an effect at the start of his film, *Fanny and Alexander*. For fifteen minutes, the single camera adopts the perspective of one of the participants in a game of hide and seek. The duration of the game is precisely fifteen minutes.

25 M. Foucault, *Les Mots et les choses*, Paris, Editions de Minuit, 1965, p. 26.

26 Ibid., p. 27.

27 M. Quilligan, *The Language of Allegory*, Ithaca, Cornell University Press, 1979.

28 George Steiner appropriately emphasises the almost carnivalesque sexuality of the Song of Songs or Song of Solomon which he describes as 'this cantata of love and desire'. Goethe apparently regarded it as 'the finest of its kind in world literature', and Rabbi Akiva, 'the wiset of the wise', declared that 'the whole world is not worth the day on which the Song was given'. Interestingly, Steiner argues that given the overwhelming intensity of the sexual rapture conveyed through the poem, it would be foolish to read it allegorically: 'Exercises in officious allegory are largely fatuous'. See his *No Passion Spent: Essays 1978–1996*, London, Faber, 1976, p. 75. Robinson's performance of the song effectively brings to an end his own biblical allegorising in *Vendredi*.

29 The text of an essay on 'The Song of Songs' by Francis Landy is thick with detailed references to various poetic effects in the original Hebrew verses which have been lost in translation. See R. Alter and F. Kermode (eds), *The Literary Guide to the Bible*, London, Fontana, 1989, pp. 305–19. Writing in the same edition and from a similar perspective, Luis Alonso Schökel unravels the poetic intricacies buried in the Hebrew text of the Book of Isaiah. Moreover, Schökel emphasises that the Book of Isaiah is generally believed to be a collaborative work. See *The Literary Guide to the Bible*, pp. 165–83.

30 *The Language of Allegory*, p. 67.

31 Ibid., p. 226.

32 For a typical response see S. Koster, *Images et Signes*, p. 302: 'L'enfantin public cher à Rousseau n'entre en possession, inévitablement, que du modèle réduit de l'univers tourniéren'.

33 *Les Mots et les choses*, p. 317.

34 J. Derrida, *De la grammatologie*, Paris, Editions de Minuit, 1970, p. 141.

35 For an excellent discussion of Robinson's writing materials and the symbolic importance of *écriture* in the context of Tournier's rewriting of the Crusoe myth, see Roberts, *Michel Tournier: Bricolage and Cultural Mythology*, p. 26.

36 For an analysis of the symbolic implications of Robinson's baking see E. Wilson, 'Cannibal Crusoe: The Desire to Devour in Tournier's *Vendredi ou les limbes du Pacifique*', *French Studies Bulletin* (Winter 1989–90), pp. 14–16.

37 C. Davis, *Michel Tournier: Philosophy and Fiction*, Oxford, Oxford University Press, 1988, pp. 9–33.

38 'Michel Tournier et le monde sans autrui', p. 269.

39 J-J. Rousseau, *Essai sur l'origine des langues*, Bordeaux, Ducros, 1968, p. 45.

40 C. Lévi-Strauss, *Le Totémisme aujourd'hui*, Paris, Plon, 1962.

41 Cited in T. Todorov, *Théories du symbole*, Paris, Seuil, 1997, p. 249.

42 *Les Mots et les choses*, p. 302.

43 *De la grammatologie*, p. 343.

44 See L. Wittgenstein, *Philosophical Investigations*, trans. G. Anscombe, Oxford, Oxford University Press, 1953, pp. 193–213.

45 P. Henle (ed.), *Language, Thought, and Culture*, Ann Arbor, University of Michigan Press, 1958, pp. 173–95.

46 Aristotle, *Rhetoric 3*: 10. 1410 b 10–15.

47 Davis, p. 17.

48 J. Derrida, 'La Mythologie blanche: la métaphore dans le texte philosophique', *Marges de la philosophie*, Paris, Editions de Minuit, 1972, p. 290.

49 *Marges de la philosophie*, p. 289.

50 G. Hegel, Introduction to *Lectures on the Philosophy of History*, J. Sibree trans., New York, The Colonial Press, 1900, pp. 109–10.

51 *Marges de la philosophie*, Paris, Editions de Minuit, 1972, p. 291.

52 Ibid.

53 The cavern or grotto figures 'l'en deçà et l'au-delà de la vie' (V, 112), Robinson's symbolic return to the womb and his final resting-place.

54 See Davis, *Michel Tournier: Philosophy and Fiction*, pp. 31–32. For a mythological interpretation of Vendredi's departure see Wilson, 'Cannibal Crusoe', p. 15.

55 *La Séduction du jeu*, p. 47.

56 *Vendredi ou La vie sauvage*, p. 10.

57 *Les Mots et les choses*, p. 187.

58 Ibid., p. 202.

59 Ibid, p. 237.

Notes to Chapter Three

pp. 83–130

1 See for example J. Améry, 'Asthetizismus der Barbarei: Uber Michel Tourniers Roman *Der Erlkönig*', *Merkur*, vol. 297 (1973), pp. 73–79. Tournier later replied by confirming Améry's insight into the aesthetic nature of his portrayal of Nazism, adding that it is only under its aesthetic aspect that the horrifying reality of Nazism may be properly perceived:

> I quote from Léon Blum: 'Communism is a technique, socialism is a moral code, fascism is an aesthetic.' Whether we're talking about Hitler or Mussolini, fascism is inseparable from a certain Wagnerian splendour, with parades, music and nocturnal feasts. If you abstract this aspect of Nazism you denature it. Nazism was a midnight feast, a murderous festival ... not ridiculous, but terrifying. In order to give a complete picture of Nazism, you must see it as a shop window, seductively filled with splendour and violence; in the back room are the concentration camps and the murders. These two aspects are inseparable. (Cited by Bouloumié in *Michel Tournier*, ed. M. Worton, London, Longman, 1995, pp. 142–43.)

2 Of the flush of Tournier monographs which appeared in the years 1986–88, only Colin Davis in his *Michel Tournier: Philosophy and Fiction* provides a sustained analysis of Nazism in *Le Roi des aulnes*. Winifred Woodhull gives an interesting psychoanalytic perspective on the same theme in her article 'Fascist bonding and euphoria in Michel Tournier's *The Ogre*', *New German Critique*, vol. 42 (1987), pp. 79–112.

3 See *Le Vent Paraclet*, pp. 188–89.

4 See A. Finkielkraut, *La Défaite de la pensée*, Paris, Folio, 1987, pp. 52–59.

5 See *Le Vent Paraclet*, p. 86.

6 As we can see from this section of *Le Vent Paraclet*, Tournier chose his symbol with care: 'Assez vite le mythe de l'Ogre s'imposa comme le thème central ... Je m'etais trouvé en Allemagne au moment de la montée et de l'épanouissement du nazisme à un âge—celui du Petit Poucet—qui intéresse au premier chef les Ogres, et j'avais nettement senti combien le nouveau régime allemand était axé sur moi et mes semblables' (VP, 102). Tiffauges is drawn to the young for whom he represents danger and tenderness.

7 This descriptive phrase is in point of fact absent from the earlier Gallimard edition. The editorial inclusion in the Folio text gives the impression that Tournier wished to reinforce further the importance of the discovery of this 'new writing'.

8 See *Le Roi des Aulnes*, pp. 554–61. The Napola (nationalpolitische Erziehungsanstalte) mirrors effectively the fanaticism inspired by the Nazi state, of which the concentration camp is the equally condensed biproduct.

9 *Michel Tournier: Philosophy and Fiction*, p. 55.

10 We should note the importance of proper names to Frege's philosophy of language, in which the notion of a first level predicate, and consequently of every other linguistic category, is explained in terms of the notion of the proper name. Frege points to the proper name as simple proof of the fact that the existence of language derives from the capacity of human beings to form concepts; therefore it follows that any linguistic communication is predicated upon a shared system of reference. See the chapter on Frege's treatment of proper names in M. Dummett, *Frege: Philosophy of Language*, London, Duckworth, 1973.

11 If anyone is in doubt, they should consult H. Ott, *Martin Heidegger: Eléments pour une biographie*, trans. J-M. Beloeil, Paris, Payot, 1990.

12 The English language version, from which this quotation was taken, was published bi-lingually. See *What is Philosophy?* trans. W. Kluback and J. Wilde, New York, 1958.

13 Translated as *Being and Time* by Macquarrie and Robinson, Oxford, Blackwell, 1967.

14 See G. Steiner, *Heidegger*, London, Fontana, 1978, especially pp. 108–09.

15 Quoted in Steiner, *Heidegger*, p. 114.

16 Paul Ricoeur describes how this fundamental principle of metaphor achieves a unique coherence in the language of literature. See *La Métaphore vive*, Paris, Seuil, 1975, p. 313:

> Dire 'cela est', tel est le moment de la *croyance*, *l'ontological commitment* qui donne sa force 'illocutionnaire' à l'affirmation. Nulle part cette véhémence d'affirmation est mieux attestée que dans l'expérience poétique. Selon une de ses dimensions, au moins, cette expérience exprime le moment *extatique* du langage—le langage hors de soi; elle semble ainsi attester que c'est le désir du discours de s'effacer, de mourir aux confins de l'être-dit.

17 See J. Derrida, *De l'esprit, Heidegger et la question*, Paris, Galilée, 1987. I am indebted to Christopher Norris for his commentary on *De l'esprit*, contained in the postscript to C. Norris, *Paul de Man*, London, Routledge, 1988.

18 The echoes of Roquentiń perusing the portraits of the *bons bourgeois* of Bouville in *La Nausée* are unmistakable. As a young philosophy student, Tournier deplored Sartre's post-war, humanistic swerve, a deviation all the more depressing since the author of *L'Etre et le Néant* had exerted an unparalleled influence over Tournier and his fellow students. See *Le Vent Paraclet*, pp. 155–58.

19 *Le Vent Paraclet*, pp. 109–10.

20 See *Le Roi des aulnes*, pp. 185–91.

21 Brasillach is described as both 'écrivain médiocre et traître majeur', the charge against him as 'une sinistre cacologie vomie par un ramassis de métèques mal débar-bouillés', in *Le Vent Paraclet*, p. 86.

22 Shown as part of the *Grands Entretiens* series on Antenne 2 (24 October 1990).

23 The implied self-referentiality of this final scene recalls Tiffauges' earlier meditation on the Prussian landscape: 'Un pays noir et blanc, pensa Tiffauges. Peu de gris, peu de couleurs, une page blanche couverte de signes noirs' (RA, 180).

24 *Michel Tournier: Bricolage and Cultural Mythology*, Saratoga, Stanford University, ANMA Libri, 1994, p. 54.

25 Ibid., p. 58.

26 P. de Man, *The Resistance to Theory*, Minneapolis, University of Minnesota Press, 1986, p. 64.

27 See W. Redfern, 'Approximating Man: Tournier and Play in Language', *Modern Language Review*, vol. 80 (1985), p. 312.

28 Ibid., p. 307.

29 As he is sometimes wont to do, Tournier uses his central protagonist as a temporary mouth-piece in order to 'signpost' the pun. See *Le Roi des aulnes*, p. 27.

30 This habit of Tournier's is not confined to *Le Roi des aulnes*. Many of his characters rejoice in highly symbolic names; the family name 'Surin' in *Les Météores* foretells Alexandre's fate ('surin' is Parisian slang for 'knife'), the third king in *Gaspard, Melchior et Balthazar* commutes his name to Taor's feasting on the hill above Bethlehem, and the advertising agent in *La Goutte d'or*, M. Achille Mage, is brought down from his director's pedestal by his 'point faible', a passion for the adolescent boys in the pinball hall.

31 'Approximating Man', p. 306: 'The matter of wordplay is intimately bound up with the whole relationship between the author and his readers'.

32 Ibid., p. 308: 'Punning permeates the literalisation of the metaphorical in which prefigurations come true'.

33 Ibid., pp. 306 and 312.

34 As Tournier himself confirms, 'Toute immixtion de l'auteur ne pourrait qu'affaiblir la puissance communicative de la vision de Tiffauges' (VP, 113).

35 C. MacCabe, 'On Discourse', *Theoretical Essays: Film, Linguistics and Literature*, Manchester, Manchester University Press, 1985, p. 93.

36 *Essai sur l'origine des langues*, Bordeux, Ducros, 1968, p. 47.

37 Both Françoise Merllié (*Michel Tournier*, Paris, Belfond, 1990, Chapter 1), and Colin Davis (*Michel Tournier: Philosophy and Fiction*, pp. 187–88) discuss the significance of non-linguistic sound in Tournier's fiction.

38 *Philosophical Perspectives on Metaphor*, p. 245.

39 Ibid., p. 243.

40 See *Le Roi des aulnes*, pp. 542–45.

41 As evinced by Colin Davis, who describes the metaphoric representation of Arnim's death as an 'ecstatic and intensely disturbing litany of death'. See *Michel Tournier: Philosophy and Fiction*, p. 56.

42 *Problèmes du nouveau roman*, Paris, Seuil, 1967, p. 137.

43 See M. Tournier, 'Kant et la critique littéraire', *Le Vol du vampire*, pp. 52–65: 'Il serait bien surprenant ... qu'aucune lumière ne tombât de l'imposant édifice kantien sur les multiples taupinières soulevées ça et là par les critiques littéraires.'

44 'Empirical verification' has indeed shown that quantum mechanics and the Theory of Relativity are not consistent with each other—'they cannot both be correct': see S. Hawking, *A Brief History of Time*, London, Bantam Press, 1988, p. 12.

45 I. Kant, *Critique of Judgement*, trans., J. H. Bernard, New York, Hafner, 1951, p. 150.

46 Tournier gives examples of each paradox in a rather ponderous section of his discussion (VV, 56–60).

47 See Kant, *Critique of Judgement*, p. 108, where he describes the Sublime as 'an object (of nature) the representation of which determines the mind to think the unattainability of nature regarded as a presentation of ideas'.

48 F. Nietzsche, 'On Truth and Falsity in their Ultramoral Sense', *The Complete Works of Friedrich Nietzsche*, ed. O. Levy and trans. M. Magge, New York, Gordon Press, 1974, p. 180.

49 Quoted in J. Stern, *Nietzsche*, London, Fontana, 1978, pp. 127–28.

50 'Idea' or 'form' comes from the Latin root *video*, so the mental image is directly linked with the visual impression, and the diffusion of light.

51 See *Les Météores*, pp. 222–26.

52 Ibid., pp. 190–93.

53 G. Steiner, *Extraterritorial: Papers on Literature and the Language Revolution*, London, Faber, 1972, p. 63.

54 See D. Diderot, *Oeuvres Complètes*, ed. J. Assezat and M. Tourneux, Paris, Garnier Frères, Libraries-éditeurs, (20 vols), 1875–77, Vol. 11, p. 11, '... arrêter sous vos yeux et recopier servilement, à moins que vous ne veuilliez vous faire portraitiste. Convenez donc que quand vous faîtes beau, vous ne faîtes rien de ce qui est, rien même de ce qui peut être.'

55 P. de Man, *The Rhetoric of Romanticism*, New York, Columbia University Press, 1984, p. 120.

56 See *Le Vent Paraclet*, p. 150: '... et plus d'un lecteur n'a vu dans le roman que l'histoire d'Alexandre et a été deçue par sa mort ... Balzac et Proust n'avaient certainement pas prévu la place exorbitante que prendraient respectivement Vautrin dans *La Comédie humaine* et Charlus dans *A la recherche du temps perdu*.'

Notes to Chapter Four
pp. 131–160

1 Some critics prefer to emphasise the 'impossibility' of Tournier's enterprise, though not necessarily in a negative sense. Colin Davis speaks of the 'frustrated promise of intelligibility' (*Michel Tournier: Philosophy and Fiction*, Oxford, Oxford University Press,1988 p. 93) and David Gascoigne, in a book which further underlines the extent to which Tournier's fiction rewards the efforts of the genuine scholar, suggests that the 'fascination of Tournier's oeuvre may derive precisely from the sense in which it seems at once to promise and withold a unitary pattern of meaning...'. See D. Gascoigne, *Michel Tournier*, Oxford, Berg, 1996, p. 204.

2 See K. Fergusson, 'Metaphysical Desires and Ironist Devices in the Works of Michel Tournier', *Michel Tournier*, ed. M. Worton, London, Longman, 1995, pp. 89–100.

3 *Michel Tournier: Bricolage and Cultural Mythology*, Saratoga, Stanford University/ANMA Libri, 1994, p. 160: 'Through the reconciliation of Pierrot and Arlequin, then, *Pierrot* enacts an imaginary solution to an aesthetic conflict which underpins Tournier's fiction, between a Platonic aesthetic which continues to privilege the model over the copy, and a postmodernist one which affirms the reverse.' These remarks conclude Roberts' discussion of Tournier's exemplary short story, 'Pierrot ou Les secrets de la nuit'. My own reading of 'Pierrot' is elaborated in Chapter 5.

4 See M. Worton, 'Intertextuality: to inter textuality or to resurrect it?', in *Cross References: Modern French Theory and the Practice of Criticism*, ed. D. Kelly and I. Llasera, Leeds, The Society for French Studies, 1986, pp. 14–23.

5 See C. Davis, 'Authorship and Authority in *The Wind Spirit*', in *Michel Tournier*, ed. Worton, pp. 159–73. Gascoigne hints that there may be a single unifying factor in Tournier's work, namely the 'apotheosis of the author himself' (*Michel Tournier*, p. 212).

6 *Michel Tournier: Bricolage and Cultural Mythology*, pp. 91–95.

7 References to the Creation myth and to the Cain and Abel schism abound throughout Tournier's fiction and have attracted much critical attention. His most provocatively playful treatment of the Genesis story is La Famille Adam, from the *Le Coq de bruyère* collection of short stories. See Roberts' discussion of La Famille Adam in *Michel Tournier: Bricolage and Cultural Mythology*, pp. 87–91, and also Michael Worton's comprehensive treatment of Tournier's engagement with the Genesis story in *Michel Tournier*, pp. 68–88.

8 Tournier has frequently proclaimed his own lack of originality. When he famously compared himself to Gide, it was precisely in order to explain this facet of his writing rather than a means of claiming equal status with an illustrious forbear:

> André Gide a dit qu'il n'écrivait pas pour être lu mais pour être relu. Il voulait dire par là qu'il entendait être lu au moins deux fois. J'écris moi aussi pour

être relu, mais, moins exigeant que Gide, je ne demande qu'une seule lecture. Mes livres doivent être reconnus—relus—dès la première lecture. (VP, 184)

9 M. Worton, *Tournier: La Goutte d'or*, Glasgow, University of Glasgow French and German Publications, 1992, p. 38.

10 Ibid.

11 Ibid., p. 68.

12 Another somewhat paradoxical drawback involved in the unpicking of textual fabric *à la* Worton is that the reader may come to place more stress on leads supplied by the author and increasingly less on pathways suggested in the primary text. Colin Davis warns elegantly against such an approach in a recent article on *Le Vent Paraclet*. Even the tonsillotomy Tournier endured as a child, which many critics, including Worton, regard as a highly significant formative event, is disparaged by Davis as 'disconcertingly similar to an event described in Michel Leiris's *L'Age d'homme*'. See *Michel Tournier*, ed. Worton, p. 163.

13 Worton, 'Intertextuality: to inter textuality or to resurrect it?', p. 15.

14 Walter Ong imagines that Plato thought of writing as an external, alien technology, as many people today think of the computer. Writing, especially alphabetic writing, still is a technology, calling for the use of tools and other equipment: styli or brushes or pens, carefully prepared surfaces such as animal skins, strips of wood, paper, as well as ink, pens, etc. ... Ong describes writing as the most 'drastic' of the three technologies. He asserts: 'It initiated what print and computers only continue, the reduction of dynamic sound to quiescent space, the separation of the word from the living present, where alone spoken words can exist'. See W. J. Ong, *Orality and Literacy: The Technologising of the Word*, London, Methuen, 1982, p. 82.

15 Taor is a product of myth, a legend told in the Russian Orthodox church, rather than of the author's immediate imagination. Moreover, it appears that Tournier borrowed a number of ideas from two twentieth-century texts which feature a fourth king, especially E. Schaper's *Der Vierte König* (Cologne, Hegner, 1961). For a detailed discussion of the specific episodes in these source texts which Tournier imported into *Gaspard*, see Roberts, *Michel Tournier: Bricolage and Cultural Mythology*, pp. 113–15.

16 For an extended discussion of this point which stresses Tournier's faith in the precise use of language, see Worton in *Michel Tournier*, pp. 74–75.

17 The 'état originel' refers both to the theory that the prelapsarian Adam was connoted by his blackness and to the evolutionary notion more recently popularised by Black pressure groups in the USA that the human race originated in Africa.

18 See G. Steiner, *Extraterritorial: Papers on Literature and the Language Revolution*, London, Faber, 1972, p. 96. Lexicographers estimate that the English tongue, which is less impoverished than its European neighbours, contains in excess of 600,000 words. In the 1970 study it is revealed that less than 100 words account for 75 per cent of all messages transmitted by telephone in the USA.

19 In a masterly essay novelist Daniel Pennac shows how the pleasure of reading experienced by all young children fades not in competition with the glitzy allure of televison and computer games but on account of the pain inflicted on schoolchildren in the name of 'literature' and 'literary study' by the demands of an ossified education system. See D. Pennac, *Comme un roman*, Paris, Folio, 1992.

20 See E. Havelock, *Preface to Plato*, Massachussetts, Harvard University Press, 1963.

21 In a later work, *Origins of Western Literacy*, Toronto, Ontario Institute for Studies in Education, 1976.

22 *Orality and Literacy: The Technologising of the Word*, p. 7.

23 See A. Parry (ed.), *The Making of Homeric Verse: The Collected Papers of Milman Parry*, Oxford, Clarendon Press, 1971, p. 20.

24 *Orality and Literacy*, p. 22.

25 Cited in *Orality and Literacy*, p. 142.

26 Ibid., p. 146. R. Scholes and R. Kellog (*The Nature of Narrative*, Oxford, Oxford University Press, 1966) have shown, in more detail, some of the ways in which the western narrative has developed from its ancient oral origins into present-day forms.

27 *Orality and Literacy*, p. 137.

28 E. Said, *Orientalism*, London, Routledge and Kegan Paul, 1978, p. 16.

29 Ibid., p. 42.

30 Said chides Massignon, an apparent liberal, for failing to represent any of the 'eccentricities' of the Orient, that is, those aspects which are not readily comprehended by the western mind.

31 The making of the commercial and its post-suite occupy pages 147–59 of the narrative.

32 L. Salkin-Sbiroli, 'Learning and Unlearning: Tournier, Defoe, Voltaire', in *Michel Tournier*, ed. Worton, p. 117.

33 *Tournier: La Goutte d'or*, p. 19.

34 *Michel Tournier: Bricolage and Cultural Mythology*, p. 145.

35 Ibid.

36 See M. Tournier, *Le Pied de la lettre: Trois cents mots propres*, Paris, Mercure de France, 1994. Both these qualities—linguistic play and the precise use of language—contribute to the objectives and structure of this mini-dictionary, in which Tournier expands on definitions of known words, gives tighter definitions of new ones, and confirms the meanings of those he has invented.

37 See *La Goutte d'or*, p. 219.

38 See *Le Médianoche amoureux*, p. 303.

39 See *Le Médianoche*, pp. 35–36.

40 Tournier puts great store by Perrault's classification of the short narrative into three types: *conte, nouvelle* and *fable*: 'Nous voici donc placés en face de trois types d'histoires courtes; le conte et son "instruction cachée", la nouvelle qui se recommande par sa vraisemblance, et la fable avec sa morale. On peut dire que trois siècles de littérature européenne n'ont fait que confirmer, en la radicalisant, l'analyse de Perrault' (VV, 35).

Notes to Chapter Five

pp. 161–210

1 D. Gascoigne, *Michel Tournier*, Oxford, Berg, 1996, p. 147.

2 Ibid., p. 150.

3 Tournier has frequently asserted to general bemusement that Flaubert's *Salambô* is the greatest novel ever written, and his description of abortionists as 'the sons and grandsons of the monsters of Auschwitz' in a *Newsweek* interview (November 1989) created a mild stir.

4 Tournier provides an extended analysis of what he understands by initiation in the field of education in *Le Vent Paraclet*, pp. 47–63.

5 B. Potter, *The Tale of Peter Rabbit*, London, Warne, 1902, pp. 56–59.

6 D. Hately (adaptor), *The Tale of Peter Rabbit*, Loughborough, Ladybird, 1987, unpaginated.

7 Gascoigne, *Michel Tournier*, p. 148.

8 See O. Rank, *The Double*, ed. Harry Tucker, Jr., Chapel Hill, University of North Carolina, 1971.

9 The twins in *Les Météores*, whose relationship is explicitly sexual, refer by name to the German Romantic writer Jean Paul, whose work is characterised by the figure of the Doppelgänger.

10 One of the themes discussed in the dialogue which functions as a sort of introduction to the story is Goethe's dissatisfaction with Isaac Newton's theory of colours. The narrator argues that, although Newton's theory of the seven colours of the spectrum was accepted into modern physics, the visual arts are intuitively predicated on a conception of colour formation that Goethe favoured: '... il serait facile de montrer que toute l'histoire de la peinture a pris le parti de Goethe et de son ombre polychrome' (MA, 149).

11 Tournier is fascinated by the whole issue of tactile perception. He speaks of the paradox of the braille text, which communicates in spite of being deprived of the umbilical cord that links the printed word to the vast array of mental images stored in the human mind. See M. Tournier, 'Quand les mains savent lire', in *Petites Proses*, pp. 221–24.

12 S. Freud, 'Three Essays on Sexuality (I)', *The Essentials of Psychoanalysis*, ed. A. Freud, Harmondsworth, Penguin, 1986, p. 300.

13 Gascoigne, *Michel Tournier*, p. 163.

14 Ibid., p. 162.

15 Ibid., p. 163.

16 Ibid.

17 *Michel Tournier*, ed. M. Worton, London, Longman, 1995, p. 114.

18 Ibid., pp. 120–21.

19 P. Hunt, *Criticism, Theory, and Children's Literature*, Oxford, Basil Blackwell, 1991, p. 100.

20 Ibid., p. 65.

21 Ibid., p. 76.

22 For example, children's literature produced during the Occupation and thereafter the Liberation fell prey to the crudest propaganda, disseminated by both sides. For an informative discussion of these aspects, see J. Proud, 'Plus ça change...? Propaganda Fiction for Children, 1940–1945', *The Liberation of France: Image and Event*, ed. H. Kedward and N. Woods, Oxford, Berg, 1995, pp. 57–74.

23 Quoted in *Criticism, Theory, and Children's Literature*, p. 45.

24 Ibid., p. 63.

25 M. Halliday, *Spoken and Written Language*, Oxford, Oxford University Press, 1989, p. 101.

26 See *Spoken and Written Language*, especially Chapter 6, 'Spoken language: grammatical intricacy', pp. 76–91.

27 Tournier's determination to master the various sub-genres of prose fiction—novella, short story, *conte*, children's stories, etc.—would indicate that, in the exercise of his craft, he does not rest easy.

28 G. Summerfield, *Topics in Education for the Secondary School*, London, Batsford, 1965, pp. 16–17.

29 Worton reminds us that Tournier's 'invention' of a Fourth King justifies itself on account of the lacunary nature of the Gospels' account of the Wise Men episode, given in Matthew 2: 1–13. Thus, he argues that the suppression of different narrative perspectives in *Les Rois Mages* constitutes a return to a more authentic, evangelistic narration which respects the dually enigmatic and analogical qualities of the biblical parable. The result is a more allusive text that solicits a more active intervention on the part of the reader: 'Au lecteur donc d'interpréter ou plutôt de spéculer, de s'efforcer de combler les lacunes' (M. Worton, 'Écrire et ré-écrire: le projet de Tournier', *Sud*, vol. 61, 1986, pp. 52–69). This emphasis on the 'speculative' nature of *Les Rois Mages* recalls Jill Paton Walsh's description of the poetic qualities found in 'good' children's literature (cited above).

30 Tournier argues that the overweening pleasure afforded to the child through recognition of repetitive patterns nullifies his or her appreciation of narrative suspense, which is consequently a pleasure reserved for adults: 'L'enfant obéit à une esthétique de l'antisuspense dont on trouve le modèle chez les conteurs ruraux professionnels qui résument d'abord en quelques mots l'histoire qu'ils s'apprêtent à raconter, comme pour tuer la curiosité intempestive de leur auditoire...' (VP, 32). In this instance, Tournier's impeccable binarist logic should give way to child-rearing experience. Whilst it is true to say that the child typically demands exact repeated renditions of a given story within a brief time frame, once the child considers that he or she has fully mastered the story, he will waste no time in signalling that it is time to move on. On the other hand, present a new, often more challenging story to an audience of children, preferably one featuring dangerous snakes, witches, crocodiles, or wizards, and a vulnerable child protagonist, and the sound of the proverbial dropping pin will echo around the room.

31 *Michel Tournier*, ed. Worton, p. 99.

32 Tournier does not seem to have taken much of a detour via Jean Giono's 1936 novel which also borrows its title from Bach's cantata. Giono's visionary faun Bobi

bestows an idealistic vision on a rural society; Tournier's young pianist learns that he lives in a world which has lost its ideals.

33 A. Bouloumié, 'Germanic Variations on the Theme of Phoria in *The Erl-King*', *Michel Tournier*, ed. Worton, p. 140.

34 The small herd is located in the Domaine de Ménez-Meur, Finistère. I should like to express my gratitude to Margaret Atack who showed me some photographs of surviving aurochs.

35 See *Tournier: La Goutte d'or*, Glasgow, University of Glasgow French and German Publications, 1992, p. 57.

36 Tournier plays cleverly on the easy rhythmic association between 'tigresse' and 'ogresse'. Hector, the model, always wears a Bengali talisman around his neck to protect him from the unwelcome attentions of 'tigresses'. With his 'disappearance' at the end of the story the narrator notices the talisman dangling from the neck of Véronique.

37 M. Proust, *Le Temps retrouvé*, Paris, Bibliothèque de la Pléiade, Gallimard, 1989, p. 394.

38 See Roberts, *Michel Tournier: Bricolage and Cultural Mythology*, Saratoga, Stanford University/ANMA Libri, 1994 p. 98.

39 Roberts points out that, in this instance, Tournier's source is not 'textual but iconic'. The legend of Veronica is primarily associated with the cult of the Turin Shroud. See *Michel Tournier: Bricolage and Cultural Mythology*, pp. 96–97.

40 For a discussion of the controversy surrounding Vesalius' later life, see J. Saunders and C. O'Malley, *The Illustrations from the Works of Andreas Vesalius of Brussels*, New York, The World Publishing Co., 1950, pp. 39–40, and *The Epitome of Andreas Vesalius*, trans. L. Lind, New York, Macmillan, 1949, 'Translator's Introduction', pp. xviii-xix.

41 *Le Médianoche amoureux*, pp. 182–85.

42 H. de Balzac, *Le Curé de Tours*, Paris, Folio, 1976, p. 69.

43 Ibid., p. 71.

44 This expresion is adapted from the title of an article on Claude Simon. See A. Cheal Pugh, 'Facing the matter of history: Les Géorgiques', in *Claude Simon: New Directions*, ed. A. Duncan, Edinburgh, Scottish Academic Press, 1985.

45 P. Ricoeur, *La Narrativité*, Paris, Centre Nationale de la Recherche Scientifique, 1980, p. 28.

46 See G. Frege, 'On Sense and Reference', *Translations from the Philosophical Writings of Frege*, ed. and trans. P. Geach and M. Black, Oxford, Blackwell, 1952, pp. 57–78.

47 G. Genette, *Figures I*, Paris, Seuil, 1966, p. 108.

48 F. Kermode, *The Sense of an Ending: Studies in the Theory of Fiction*, Oxford, Oxford University Press, 1966, p. 45.

49 M. Ignatieff, 'Europe's fairytale casts its spell', *The Observer*, 29 July 1990, p. 17.

50 S. Hawking, *A Brief History of Time*, London, Bantam Press, 1988, p. 25.

51 N. Lewis (ed. and trans.), *Hans Andersen's Fairy Tales*, Harmondsworth, Penguin, 1981, p. 142. For a splendid commentary on 'The Snow Queen', see W. Lederer, *The Kiss of the Snow Queen: Hans Christian Andersen and Man's Redemption by Woman*, Berkeley, University of California Press, 1986.

52 *Comme un roman*, Paris, Folio, 1992, p. 17.

53 He refers to his story as, 'ces trente pages … pour lesquelles je donnerais tout le reste de mon oeuvre', M. Tournier, 'Faut-il écrire pour les enfants?', *Courrier de l'UNESCO*, June 1982, pp. 33–34.

54 *Michel Tournier: Bricolage and Cultural Mythology*, p. 160.

55 It is precisely the lack of a third dimension, obliterated in a blanket of snowy foundation, which Barthes perceived as endowing the face of Greta Garbo with a mythical quality. See R. Barthes, 'Le visage de Garbo', *Mythologies*, Paris, Seuil, 1957, pp. 70–71.

56 Tournier draws frequently on this personality binarism, citing with obvious relish historical pairings of the 'primary' and the 'secondary'. Thus Voltaire, a man of the moment whose thinking reached out to the concerns of the day, contrasts with Rousseau, whose morose, nostalgic introspection led him to the dawn of mankind. Their relationship, their very existences—they died within weeks of each other—depended on a love–hate, admiration–scorn reciprocity. Tournier notes that a similar state of affairs existed between the great diplomat Talleyrand, whose outlook was anchored to his experience of the Ancien Régime, and the military genius of Bonaparte who had no such well-defined hinterland. For the most developed yet tapered account of the *primaire/secondaire* distinction see M. Tournier, *Le Miroir des idées*, Paris, Mercure de France, 1994, pp. 179–83.

57 L. Salkin-Sbiroli, *Michel Tournier*, ed. Worton, p. 117.

58 *No Passion Spent*: *Essays 1978–1996*, London, Faber, 1996, p. 34.

59 Ibid.

60 Ibid., p. 35.

61 Ibid.

62 *FR 2* (20 September 1996).

63 Tournier's field of reference naturally extends beyond the Old Testament and into the Hebrew Bible. However, it is unclear as to whether he is rewriting the Moses story from within the Christian or the Judaic tradition. The contrapuntal referencing to the Gospels woven into the narrative and expressed through the wetness/dryness figuration suggests the former; on the other hand, Éléazar's intense identification with the figure of Moses would imply the latter. In the Hebrew Bible sacredness attaches to the Torah or book of Moses. It is possible that Tournier wanted to consolidate the parallelism between the two traditions. Typically, he 'delays' the natural departure of his New World seekers by some two centuries; it was the Pilgrim Fathers, rather than the Irish émigrés, who notably took their inspiration from Moses and the exodus of the Jews.

64 Play with proper names reaches the ludicrous extremes of *La Goutte d'or*. There are two references to the wisdom of mystic Angelus Choiselus, no doubt the Roman founder of Tournier's home village of Choisel, the second of which is supported by a Choiselus maxim: 'Entreprends sans peur et le coeur léger le voyage aventureux de la vie, de l'amour et de la mort. Et rassure-toi: si tu trébuches, tu ne tomberas jamais plus bas que la main de Dieu!' (E, 125–26).

65 See *Éléazar*, p. 17.

66 *Michel Tournier*, ed. Worton, p. 86.

Note to Conclusion
pp. 211–214

1 J. Updike, *Odd Jobs: Essays and Criticism*, New York, Alfred A. Knopf, 1991, p. 404.

Bibliography

A: Tournier

1: Fiction (Gallimard Folio)

Vendredi ou Les limbes du Pacifique, 1967.
Le Roi des aulnes, 1970.
Vendredi ou La vie sauvage, 1971.
Les Météores, 1975.
Le Coq de bruyère, 1978.
Pierrot ou Les secrets de la nuit, 1979.
Gaspard, Melchior et Balthazar, 1980.
Gilles et Jeanne, 1983.
Les Rois mages, 1983.
La Goutte d'or, 1985.
Le Médianoche amoureux, 1990.
Éléazar ou La source et le buisson, 1996 (Gallimard).

2: Non-fiction

Le Vent Paraclet, Paris, Gallimard, 1977.
Canada. Journal de voyage, Ottawa, Editions de la Presse, 1977. Photographs by Edouard Boubat. Also published as *Journal de voyage au Canada*, Paris, Robert Laffont, 1984.
Des Clefs et des serrures: images et proses, Paris, Chêne/Hachette, 1979.
Le Vol du vampire: notes de lecture, Paris, Mercure de France, 1981.
Vues de dos, Paris, Gallimard, 1981. Photographs by Edouard Boubat.
François Miterrand, Paris, Flammarion, 1983. Photographs by Konrad R. Müller.
Le Vagabond immobile, Paris, Gallimard, 1984. Drawings by Jean-Max Toubeau.
Petites Proses, Paris, Folio, 1986.
L'Imagerie de Michel Tournier, Paris, Paris-Musées, 1987.
Le Tabor et le Sinaï. Essais sur l'art contemporain, Paris, Belfond, 1988.
Le Crépuscule des masques, Paris, Hoëbeke, 1992.
Le Miroir des idées, Paris, Mercure de France, 1994.
Le Pied de la lettre: trois cents mots propres, Paris, Mercure de France, 1994.

3: Articles/Interviews

'Variations sur la solitude', *Les Nouvelles littéraires* (23 November 1967), p. 1.
'La dimension mythologique', *La Nouvelle Revue Française*, no. 238 (1972), pp. 124–29.
'Lévi-Strauss, mon maître', *Le Figaro littéraire* (26 May 1973), pp. 15–18, also in *Le Vol du vampire*, Paris, Mercure de France, 1981, pp. 384–87.

'En déjeunant avec Michel Tournier', Xavier Delcourt in *La Quinzaine littéraire* (1 March 1977), p. 25.

'L'Espace canadien', *La Nouvelle Critique*, vol. 105 (1977), pp. 51–52.

'Je suis comme la pie voleuse', in J-L. de Rambures, *Comment travaillent les écrivains*, Paris, Flammarion, 1978, pp. 163–67.

'Dix-huit questions à Michel Tournier', with J-J. Brochier, *Magazine littéraire*, no. 138 (June 1978), pp. 11–13.

'An interview with Michel Tournier', with Penny Hueston, *Meanjin*, no. 38 (1979), pp. 400–05.

'Entretien avec Michel Tournier', with Daniel Bougnoux and André Clavel, *Silex*, no. 14 (1979), pp. 12–16.

'Une conversation avec Michel Tournier', with Alison Browning, *Cadmos*, no. 11 (1980), pp. 5–15.

'La logosphère et les taciturnes', *Sud*, 'Hors Série' (1980), pp. 167–77.

'Faut-il écrire pour les enfants?' *Courrier de l'UNESCO* (June 1982), pp. 33–34.

'Gustave et Marguerite', *Sud*, no. 55 (1984), pp. 68–77 (on Flaubert's *Salammbô* and Marguerite Yourcenar's *Mémoires d'Hadrien*).

'Les Mots sous les mots', *Le Débat*, no. 33 (1985), pp. 195–109.

'Tournier face aux lycéens', *Magazine littéraire*, no. 226 (January 1986), pp. 20–25.

'Vers la concision et la limpidité', with Jean-Marie Magnan, *La Quinzaine littéraire* (1 February 1986), p. 16.

'Quand Raymond Queneau "lisait" Tournier', *Sud* no. 61 (1986), pp. 7–11.

'Interview with Tournier', *Newsweek* (November 1989), p. 60.

'Quelqu'un est là qui nous dépasse', *La Croix* (16 December 1996), pp. 12–13.

B: Books and Articles on Tournier

J. Amery, 'Asthetizismus der Barbarei: Uber Michel Tourniers Roman *Der Erlkönig*', *Merkur*, vol. 27 (1973), pp. 73–79.

D. Bevan, *Michel Tournier*, Amsterdam, Rodopi, 1986.

D. Bougnoux, 'Des métaphores à la phorie', *Critique*, vol. 301 (1972), pp. 527–43.

A. Bouloumié, *Le Roman mythologique*, Paris, Librairie José Corti, 1988.

—— '*Vendredi ou Les limbes du Pacifique*' *de Michel Tournier*, Paris, Gallimard/ Foliothèque, 1991.

A. Bouloumié and M. de Gandillac (eds), *Images et Signes de Michel Tournier: Actes du Colloque du Centre Culturel International de Cérisy-la-Salle*, Paris, Gallimard, 1990.

W. Cloonan, *Michel Tournier*, Boston, Twayne's World Author Series, 1985.

C. Davis, *Michel Tournier: Philosophy and Fiction*, Oxford, Oxford University Press, 1988.

—— 'Art and the Refusal of Mourning: The Aesthetics of Michel Tournier', *Paragraph*, vol. 10 (1987), pp. 29–44.

—— 'Michel Tournier: Between Synthesis and Scarcity', *French Studies* 42 (1988), pp. 320–31.

—— 'Michel Tournier's *Vendredi ou Les limbes du Pacifique*: A Novel of Beginnings', *Neophilologus*, vol. 73 (1989), pp. 373–82.

G. Deleuze, 'Michel Tournier et le monde sans autrui', originally published in *Logique du sens* (Paris, Editions de Minuit, 1969), appearing later as a postface to the Folio edition of *Vendredi ou les limbes du Pacifique*, pp. 257–83.

D. Gascoigne, *Michel Tournier*, Oxford, Berg, 1996.

M-A. Hutton, *Tournier: Vendredi ou Les limbes du Pacifique*, Glasgow, University of Glasgow French and German Publications, 1992.

S. Jay, *Idriss, Michel Tournier et les autres*, Paris, Editions de la différence, 1986.

S. Koster, *Michel Tournier*, Paris, Henri Veyrier, 1986.

J. Krell, *Tournier élémentaire*, West Lafayette, Indiana, Purdue University Press, 1994.

E. Lehtovuori, *Les voies de Narcisse ou le problème du miroir chez Michel Tournier*, Helsinki, Annales Academiae Scientiarum Fennicae Dissertationes Humanarum Litterarum 75, 1995.

F. Merllié, *Michel Tournier*, Paris, Belfond, 1990.

L. Milne, *L'Évangile selon Michel: la Trinité initiatique dans l'oeuvre de Tournier*, Amsterdam, Rodopi, 1994.

C. Nettlebeck, 'The Return of the Ogre: Michel Tournier's *Gilles et Jeanne*', *Scripsi*, vol. 2/4 (1984), pp. 43–50.

S. Petit, *Michel Tournier's Metaphysical Fictions*, Amsterdam/Philadelphia, Purdue University Monographs in Romance Languages, John Benjamins Publishing, 1991.

—— 'The Bible as Inspiration in Tournier's *Vendredi ou Les limbes du Pacifique*', *French Forum*, vol. 9 (1984), pp. 343–54.

D. Platten, 'Terms of Reference: Michel Tournier's *Le Roi des aulnes*', *Journal of European Studies*, vol. 21 (1991), pp. 281–302.

—— 'The *Geist* in the Machine: Nazism in *Le Roi des aulnes*', *Romanic Review*, vol. 84 (1993), pp. 181–94.

—— 'Narrative Secrets: Tournier's Exemplary Tale, "Pyrotechnie ou La commémoration"', *The French Review*, vol. 69 (1995), pp. 229–45.

A. Purdy, '*Les Météores* de Michel Tournier: une perspective hétérologique', *Littérature*, vol. 40 (1980), pp. 34–43.

W. Redfern, 'Approximating Man: Tournier and Play in Language', *Modern Language Review*, vol. 80 (1985), pp. 304–19.

M. Roberts, *Michel Tournier: Bricolage and Cultural Mythology*, Saratoga, Stanford University/ANMA Libri, 1994.

M. Rosello, *L'in-différence chez Michel Tournier*, Paris, Librairie José Corti, 1990.

—— 'Du bon usage des stéréotypes orientalisants: vol et recel de préjugés anti-maghrébins dans les années 1990', *L'Esprit Créateur*, vol. 34 (Summer 1994), pp. 42–57.

R. Sale, 'Enemies, Foreigners and Friends—*Project for a revolution in New York* by Robbe-Grillet and *The Ogre* by Tournier', *The Hudson Review*, vol. 25 (1972), pp. 17–26.

L. Salkin-Sbiroli, *Michel Tournier: La Séduction du jeu*, Paris/Geneva, Editions Slatkine, 1987.

M. Sankey, 'Meaning through Intertextuality: Isomorphism of Defoe's *Robinson Crusoe* and Tournier's *Vendredi ou Les limbes du Pacifique*', *Australian Journal of French Studies*, vol. 18 (1981), pp. 77–88.

R. Shattuck, 'Michel Tournier: Why Not the Best?', *New York Review of Books* (April 1983), pp. 8–15.

F. **Stirn**, 'Vendredi ou Les limbes du Pacifique'—Tournier, Paris, Hatier-Profil Littérature, 1983.

G. **Strickland**, 'The Latest Tournier: *Gaspard, Melchior et Balthazar*', *The Cambridge Quarterly*, vol. 10 (1982), pp. 238–41.

M. **Taat**, 'Et si le roi était nu?—Michel Tournier, romancier mythologue', *Rapports*, vol. 52 (1982), pp. 49–58.

J. **White**, 'Signs of Disturbance: The Semiological Import of Some Recent Fiction by Michel Tournier and Peter Handke', *Journal of European Studies*, vol. 4 (1974), pp. 233–54.

E. **Wilson**, 'Cannibal Crusoe: The Desire to Devour in Tournier's *Vendredi ou Les limbes du Pacifique*', *French Studies Bulletin* (Winter 1989–90), pp. 14–16.

W. **Woodhull**, *Transfigurations of the Maghreb: Feminism, Decolonisation and Literatures*, Minneapolis, University of Minnesota Press, 1993.

—— 'Fascist Bonding and Euphoria in Michel Tournier's *The Ogre*', *New German Critique*, vol. 42 (1987), pp. 79–112.

M. **Worton** (ed.), *Michel Tournier*, London, Longman, 1995.

—— *Tournier: La Goutte d'or*, Glasgow, University of Glasgow French and German Publications, 1992.

—— 'Myth-reference in *Le Roi des aulnes*', *Stanford French Review*, vol. 6 (1982), pp. 299–310.

—— 'Ecrire et ré-écrire: le projet de Tournier', *Sud*, vol. 61 (1986), pp. 52–69.

—— 'Intertextuality: to inter textuality or to resurrect it?', in *Cross References: Modern French Theory and the Practice of Criticism*, ed. D. Kelley and I. Llasera, Leeds, The Society for French Studies, 1986, pp. 14–23.

—— 'Use and abuse of metaphor in Tournier's "Le Vol du vampire"', *Paragraph*, vol. 10 (1987), pp. 12–28.

F. **Yaiche**, 'Vendredi ou La vie sauvage' de Michel Tournier, Paris, Pédagogie Moderne—Bordas, 1981.

R. **York**, 'Thematic Construction in *Le Roi des aulnes*', *Orbis litterarum*, vol. 36 (1981), pp. 76–91.

C: General

R. **Alter** and F. **Kermode** (eds.), *The Literary Guide to the Bible*, London, Fontana, 1989.

Aristotle, *Complete Works*, ed. W. Ross, 12 vols., Oxford, Clarendon Press, 1908–52.

R. **Barthes**, *Mythologies*, Paris, Seuil, 1957.

—— *Essais Critiques*, Paris, Seuil, 1964.

—— *S/Z*, Paris, Seuil, 1970.

G. **Bataille**, *Le Procès de Gilles de Rais*, Paris, Le Club français du livre, 1959.

M. **Beardsley**, *Aesthetics*, New York, Harcourt, Brace and World, 1958.

E. **Benveniste**, *Problèmes de linguistique générale*, Paris, Gallimard, 1966.

M. **Black**, *Models and Metaphors*, Ithaca, Cornell University Press, 1962.

—— 'More about Metaphor', *Dialectica*, vol. 31 (1977), pp. 431–57.

D. **Cooper**, *Metaphor*, Oxford, Blackwell, 1986.

J. **Culler**, *The Pursuit of Signs*, London, Routledge and Kegan Paul, 1981.

D. **Davidson**, 'What Metaphors Mean', *Critical Inquiry*, vol. 5 (1978), pp. 31–47.

—— 'On the Very Idea of a Conceptual Scheme', *Proceedings and Addresses of the American Philosophical Association*: vol. 47 (1974), pp. 5–20.

—— 'A Nice Derangement of Epitaphs', *Philosophical Grounds of Rationality: Intentions, Categories, Ends*, ed. R. Grandy and R. Warner, Oxford, Clarendon Press, 1986, pp. 157–75.

P. De Man, *Blindness and Insight: Essays in the Rhetoric of Contemporary Criticism*, London, Methuen Second Edition, 1983.

—— *The Rhetoric of Romanticism*, New York, Columbia University Press, 1984.

—— *The Resistance to Theory*, Minneapolis, University of Minnesota Press, 1986.

D. Defoe, *Robinson Crusoe*, Oxford, Oxford University Press, 1972.

J. Derrida, *De la grammatologie*, Paris, Editions de Minuit, 1970.

—— *Marges de la philosophie*, Paris, Editions de Minuit, 1972.

—— *De l'esprit, Heidegger et la question*, Paris, Galilée, 1987.

R. Descartes, *Oeuvres philosophiques et morales*, Paris, Bibliothèque des Lettres, 1950.

D. Diderot, *Oeuvres Complètes*, ed. J. Assezat and M. Tourneux, 20 vols, Paris, Garnier Frères, Libraires-éditeurs, 1875–77.

M. Dummett, *Frege: Philosophy of Language*, London, Duckworth, 1973.

A. Duncan (ed.), *Claude Simon: New Directions*, Edinburgh, Scottish Academic Press, 1985.

U. Eco, *The Role of the Reader*, Bloomington, Indiana University Press, 1979.

A. Finkielkraut, *La Défaite de la pensée*, Paris, Folio, 1987.

M. Foucault, *Les Mots et les choses*, Paris, Editions de Minuit, 1965.

—— *Histoire de la sexualité* (Vol. 1). *La Volonté de savoir*, Paris, Gallimard, 1976.

A. Freud (ed.), *The Essentials of Psychoanalysis*, Harmondsworth, Penguin, 1986.

S. Freud, *The Interpretation of Dreams,* ed. and trans. J. Strachey, London, Allen and Unwin, 1954.

P. Geach and M. Black (ed.) and trans, *Translations from the Philosophical Writings of Gottlob Frege*, Oxford, Blackwell, 1952.

G. Genette, *Figures I*, Paris, Seuil, 1966.

—— *Figures III*, Paris, Seuil, 1972.

—— *Palimpsestes, la littérature au second degré*, Paris, Seuil, 1978.

N. Goodman, *Languages of Art: An Approach to a Theory of Symbols*, Indianapolis, Bobbs-Merrill, 1968.

M. Halliday, *Spoken and Written Language*, Oxford, Oxford University Press, 1989.

D. Hately (adaptor), *The Tale of Peter Rabbit*, Loughborough, Ladybird, 1987.

S. Haugom Olsen, *The End of Literary Theory*, Cambridge, Cambridge University Press, 1987.

E. Havelock, *Preface to Plato*, Massachusetts, Harvard University Press, 1963.

—— *Origins of Western Literacy*, Toronto, Ontario Institute for Studies in Education, 1976.

S. Hawking, *A Brief History of Time*, London, Bantam Press, 1988.

G. Hegel, *Lectures on the Philosophy of History*, trans. J. Sibree, New York, The Colonial Press, 1900.

M. Heidegger, *What is Philosophy?*, trans. W. Kluback and J. Wilde, New Haven, College Press, 1958.

—— *Sein und Zeit*, translated as *Being and Time* by Macquarrie and Robinson, Oxford, Blackwell, 1967.

—— *Basic Writings*, trans. and ed. D. Krell, London, Routledge and Kegan Paul, 1978.

P. **Henle** (ed.), *Language, Thought, and Culture*, Ann Arbor, University of Michigan Press, 1958.

M. **Hester**, 'Metaphor and Aspect Seeing', *Journal of Aesthetics and Art Criticism*, vol. 25 (1966), pp. 205–12.

P. **Hunt**, *Criticism, Theory, and Children's Literature*, Oxford, Basil Blackwell, 1991.

M. **Ignatieff**, 'Europe's Fairytale Casts its Spell', *The Observer* (29 July 1990), p. 17.

R. **Jakobson**, 'Closing Statements: Linguistics and Poetics', ed. T. Sebeok, *Style in Language*, New York, John Wiley, 1960, pp. 350–77.

—— *Selected Writings II*, The Hague/Paris, Word and Language, 1971.

—— *Questions de poétique*, Paris, Seuil, 1973.

M. **Johnson** (ed.), *Philosophical Perspectives on Metaphor*, Minneapolis, University of Minnesota Press, 1981.

M. **Jousse**, *Le Style oral, rythmique et mnémotechnique chez les Verbo-moteurs*, Paris, G. Beauchesne, 1925.

I. **Kant**, *Critique of Judgment*, trans. J. Bernard, New York, Hafner, 1951.

—— *Critique of Pure Reason*, trans. H. Palmer, Cardiff, University College Press, 1983.

C. **Kappler**, *Monstres, démons et merveilles à la fin du Moyen Age*, Paris, Payot, 1980.

H. **Kedward** and N. **Wood** (eds)., *The Liberation of France: Image and Event*, Oxford, Berg, 1995.

F. **Kermode**, *The Sense of an Ending: Studies in the Theory of Fiction*, Oxford, Oxford University Press, 1967.

E. **Kittay**, *Metaphor*, Oxford, Oxford University Press, 1987.

J. **Kristeva**, *Language: The Unknown*, trans A. Menke, Brighton, Harvester Press, 1989.

J. **Lacan**, *Ecrits I*, Paris, Seuil, 1966.

G. **Lakoff** and M. **Johnson**, *Metaphors We Live By*, Chicago, University of Chicago Press, 1980.

—— 'Conceptual Metaphor in Everyday Language', *Journal of Philosophy*, vol. 77 (1980), pp. 453–86.

W. **Lederer**, *The Kiss of the Snow Queen: Hans Christian Andersen and Man's Redemption by Woman*, Berkeley, University of California Press, 1986.

C. **Lévi-Strauss**, 'L'analyse structurale en linguistique et en anthropologie', *Word: Journal of the Linguistic Circle of New York* (1945), pp. 1–21.

—— *Tristes Tropiques*, Paris, Plon, 1955.

—— *Le Totémisme aujourd'hui*, Paris, Plon, 1962.

—— *La Pensée sauvage*, Paris, Plon,1962.

—— *Mythologiques*, published in four volumes as *Le Cru et le cuit* (Paris, Seuil, 1964); *Du Miel aux cendres* and *L'origine des manières de table* (Paris, Seuil, 1967); and *L'homme nu* (Paris, Seuil, 1971).

N. **Lewis** (ed. and trans.), *Hans Andersen's Fairy Tales*, Harmondsworth, Penguin, 1981.

C. **MacCabe**, *Theoretical Essays: Film, Linguistics and Literature*, Manchester, Manchester University Press, 1985.

D. **Macey**, *Lacan in Contexts*, London/New York, Verso, 1988.

F. **Nietzsche**, *The Twilight of the Idols, or How to Philosophize with a Hammer*, trans. A. Ludovici, New York, Russell and Russell, 1964.

—— *The Complete Works of Friedrich Nietzsche*, ed. O. Levy and trans. M. Magge, New York, Gordon Press, 1974.

C. Norris, *Paul de Man*, London, Routledge, 1988.

W. Ong, *Orality and Literacy: The Technologising of the Word*, London, Methuen, 1982.

A. Ortony, 'Beyond Literal Similarity', *Psychological Review*, vol. 86 (1979), pp. 161–80.

H. Ott, *Martin Heidegger: Éléments pour une biographie*, trans. J-M. Beloeil, Paris, Payot, 1990.

M. Parry, *The Making of Homeric Verse: The Collected Papers of Milman Parry*, ed. A. Parry, Oxford, Clarendon Press, 1971.

O. Paz, *Claude Lévi-Strauss: An Introduction*, London, Jonathan Cape, 1970.

D. Pennac, *Comme un roman*, Paris, Folio, 1992.

C. Perelman and L. Olbrechts-Tyteca, *Traité de l'argumentation*, Paris, PUF, 1958.

B. Potter, *The Tale of Peter Rabbit*, London, Warne, 1902.

M. Proust, *Le Temps retrouvé*, Paris, Bibliothèque de la Pléiade, Gallimard, 1989.

M. Quilligan, *The Language of Allegory*, Ithaca, Cornell University Press, 1979.

O. Rank, *The Double*, trans. and ed. H. Tucker Jr, Chapel Hill, University of North Carolina, 1971.

J. Ricardou, *Problèmes du nouveau roman*, Paris, Seuil, 1967.

—— *Les lieux-dits: Petit guide d'un voyage dans le livre*, Paris, Gallimard, 1969.

I. Richards, *The Philosophy of Rhetoric*, Oxford, Oxford University Press, 1971.

P. Ricoeur, *La Métaphore vive*, Paris, Seuil, 1975.

—— 'The Metaphorical Process as Cognition, Imagination and Feeling', *Critical Inquiry*, vol. 5 (1978), pp. 143–59.

—— *La Narrativité*, Paris, Centre National de la Recherche Scientifique, 1980.

—— *Temps et Récit*, 3 vols, Paris, Seuil, 1983–85.

A. Robbe-Grillet, *Pour un nouveau roman*, Paris, Editions de Minuit, 1963.

P. Rogers, *Robinson Crusoe*, London, Allen and Unwin, 1979.

J-J. Rousseau, *Essai sur l'origine des langues*, Bordeaux, Ducros, 1968.

E. Said, *Orientalism*, London, Routledge and Kegan Paul, 1978.

J. Saunders and C. O'Malley, *The Illustrations from the Works of Andreas Vesalius of Brussels*, New York, The World Publishing Co., 1950.

F. de Saussure, *Cours de linguistique générale*, Paris, Payot, 1973.

R. Scholes and R. Kellog, *The Nature of Narrative*, Oxford, Oxford University Press, 1966.

G. Steen, *Understanding Metaphor in Literature: An Empirical Approach*, London, Longman, 1994.

G. Steiner, *In Bluebeard's Castle: Some Notes towards the Re-definition of Culture*, London, Faber, 1971.

—— *Extraterritorial: Papers on Literature and the Language Revolution*, London, Faber, 1972.

—— *Heidegger*, London, Fontana, 1978.

—— *No Passion Spent: Essays 1978–1996*, London, Faber, 1996.

J. Stern, *Nietzsche*, London, Fontana, 1978.

T. Stoppard, *The Real Thing*, London, Faber, 1982.

G. Summerfield, *Topics in Education for the Secondary School*, London, Batsford, 1965.

J. Sutherland, *D. Defoe: A Critical Study*, Massachussetts, Harvard University Press, 1971.

T. Todorov, *Le Poétique de la prose*, Paris, Seuil, 1971.

—— *Théories du symbole*, Paris, Seuil, 1977.

S. Ullmann, *Language and Style*, Oxford, Blackwell, 1964.

J. Updike, *Odd Jobs: Essays and Criticism*, New York, Alfred A. Knopf, 1991.

B. Vickers (ed.), *Rhetoric Revalued*, New York, Medieval and Renaissance Texts and Studies (vol. 19), 1982.

—— *In Defence of Rhetoric*, Oxford, Clarendon Press, 1988.

I. Watt, *The Rise of the Novel: Studies in Defoe, Richardson and Fielding*, Glasgow, Fourth Impression, 1963.

L. Wittgenstein, *Philosophical Investigations*, trans. G. Anscombe, Oxford, Oxford University Press, 1953.

R. Zazzo, *Les Jumeaux: Le Couple et la personne*, Paris, PUF, 1960.

Index